Creative Nonfiction
G. Douglas Atkins, *Series Editor*

THE LONELY OTHER

T H E   L O N E L Y

UNIVERSITY OF ILLINOIS PRESS   Urbana and Chicago

O T H E R

A Woman Watching America

Diana Hume George

The photos for parts 1, 4, and 5 are by Michael Richardson. The
photo for part 2 is in the author's collection. The photo for part 3 is
by Malcolm Nelson.

© 1996 by the Board of Trustees of the University of Illinois
Manufactured in the United States of America
P 5 4 3 2 1
This book is printed on acid-free paper.
Library of Congress Cataloging-in-Publication Data
George, Diana Hume, 1948-
The lonely other : a woman watching America / Diana Hume George.
p.   cm. — (Creative nonfiction)
ISBN 0-252-06534-4 (pbk. : alk. paper)
1. United States—Description and travel. 2. Women—United States.
I. Title. II. Series: Creative nonfiction (Urbana, Ill.)
E169.04G47   1996
917.304'92—dc20   95-32488
CIP

For family: Bernie, Mary Ellen,
Sequoia, Kris, Ayron, and Richard
and in memory of
Nancy Espersen Luce
1948–95

When everything else has gone from my brain—
the President's name, the state capitals, the
neighborhoods where I lived, and then my own
name and what it was on earth I sought, and
then at length the faces of my friends, and finally
the faces of my family—when all this has
dissolved, what will be left, I believe, is topology:
the dreaming memory of land as it lay this way
and that.
—Annie Dillard, *An American Childhood*

I release you, my beautiful and terrible
fear. I release you. You were my beloved
and hated twin, but now, I don't know you
as myself. I release you with all the
pain I would know at the death of
my daughters.

You are not my blood anymore.
.   .   .   .
I take myself back, fear.
You are not my shadow any longer.
I won't hold you in my hands.
You can't live in my eyes, my ears, my voice
my belly, or in my heart my heart

But come here, fear
I am alive and you are so afraid
                                of dying.
—Joy Harjo, "I Give You Back"

CONTENTS

ACKNOWLEDGMENTS

Essays in this collection have been previously published, sometimes in other versions, in *Ontario Review, Missouri Review, Ms. Magazine, Georgia Review, Best American Essays, Kaleidoscope, Creative Nonfiction, Original Essays on the Poetry of Anne Sexton,* and *Laurel Review.*

Grateful acknowledgment is made for permission to quote from the following works: "The Road Not Taken" from *The Poetry of Robert Frost,* edited by Edward Connery Lathem (New York: Henry Holt, 1979). "I Give You Back" from the book *She Had Some Horses* by Joy Harjo. Copyright © 1983 by Joy Harjo. Used by permission of the publishers, Thunder's Mouth Press. Excerpt from "The Rendezvous" by Maxine Kumin, from *Looking for Luck,* is reprinted with the permission of W. W. Norton & Company, Inc. © 1992 by Maxine Kumin. Originally appeared in the *New Yorker.* The lines from "Turning" are reprinted from *Time's Power: Poems 1985–1988* by Adrienne Rich, by permission of the author and W. W. Norton & Company, Inc. Copyright © 1989 by Adrienne Rich. The lines from "Storm Warnings" are reprinted from *Collected Early Poems: 1950–1970* by Adrienne Rich, by permission of the author and W. W. Norton & Company, Inc. Copyright © 1993 by Adrienne Rich. Copyright © 1967, 1963, 1962, 1961, 1960, 1959, 1958, 1957, 1956, 1955, 1954, 1953, 1952, 1951 by Adrienne Rich. Copyright © 1984, 1975, 1971, 1969, 1966 by W. W. Norton & Company, Inc. "The Consecrating Mother," "Funnel," "Grandfather, Your Wound," "Kind Sir: These Woods," and "The Rowing Endeth" are from *The Complete Poems* by Anne Sexton. Reprinted by permission of Sterling Lord Literistic, Inc. Copyright © 1981 by Estate of Anne Sexton. "Don't You Think Too Much" by Greg Brown. "Sheep Production: 101" by Jesse Loren.

I thank the New York Foundation on the Arts for a writing fellowship and the Pennsylvania State University, the Behrend College, for a sabbatical and funding support for this project. Roberta Salper and John Lilley have enabled my work in crucial ways. I appreciate the support of journal and magazine editors who were helpful with various pieces here, including Barbara Findlen at *Ms.*, Stephen Corey at the *Georgia Review*, Darshan Perusek at *Kaleidoscope*, and Lee Gutkind at *Creative Nonfiction*. Douglas Carlson read versions of the manuscript and offered critical feedback during the early stages. I thank Joyce Carol Oates for supporting my writing in more ways than she knows. Alicia Ostriker is responsible for making sure I included some of my writing on Anne Sexton, and I appreciate that nudge, and all the others she has given me over the past decade. Ann Lowry at the University of Illinois Press was, as always, patient with me, and I am grateful for her consistent excellence as an editor through three of my books. Becky Standard was a real find as a copyeditor; her attention to detail has been invaluable. Diane Freedman's suggestions as an outside reader made this a far stronger book. Doug Atkins, series editor, has my lasting appreciation for initiating this series and wanting my book to be part of it. Conversations with writer friends have enriched every word I write, every step I take: Richard Lehnert, Tony Trigilio, Lucia Getsi, Constance Coiner, Tom and Marilyn Bridwell, Judy Emerson, Diane Wood Middlebrook, Luciana Bohne, Natalia Rachel Singer, I thank you. Dan Sargent transcribed tapes, and Susan Lavrey brought her sharp editorial eye to early drafts of several essays. As always, my friend Norma Hartner has my deepest thanks for her dedicated professionalism in preparing this manuscript with me over a period of years. Michael Richardson's suggestions sharpened the clarity and accuracy of my descriptions of the natural world. To other friends whose support has sustained me in unnameable, sometimes even unspeakable ways during the writing of this book, sometimes on travels years ago, sometimes now, I offer gratitude and affection: Karen Courts, Chris Sorgen, Chip Susol, Linda Kelsey, Glenn Strand, Molly and Anil Asher, Sue Daley, Donna Douglas, Claire DeSantis, Christelle Decrease, Karl Steiner, Cecilia Velasquez, Jan Hurlbert, Shelly Hubman, Jim McEnery, David Bennett. To Deanna Ferraino, Pat Lee, and Sandra Barnard, I owe what fellow travelers owe their mentors, teachers, and healers, the ones they sometimes do not recognize for years among their friends.

INTRODUCTION

The Lonely Other is related to two kinds of lively American writing: the revisionist mythmaking feminists are engaged in, especially but not exclusively in poetry, practiced by Susan Griffin, Alicia Ostriker, Sharon Olds, Maxine Kumin, Terry Tempest Williams, Sandra Gilbert, and many others; and also the kind of meditative thinking about the human relationship to landscape and to other forms of life embodied in the works of American writers about land and travel. Here I have in mind Annie Dillard, Edward Abbey, John McPhee, William Least Heat Moon.

Despite the lack of a wide reading public for travel writing by women in English until recently, the genre can be traced back centuries in epistolary, journal, and diary form. Victorian women travelers hitched up their skirts and journeyed to the far reaches of the globe. American women involved in settling the frontier wrote accounts of their experiences, restored from obscurity by the work of critics such as Annette Kolodny in *The Land before Her: Fantasy and Experience of the American Frontiers, 1630–1860* (Chapel Hill: University of North Carolina Press, 1984). In the last few years, anthologies of environmental and nature writing such as *Words from the Land,* edited by Stephen Trimble (Salt Lake City: Peregrine Smith, 1988), and *Reading the Environment,* edited by Melissa Walker (New York: Norton, 1994), include essays by women. Literary quarterlies publishing creative nonfiction have joined *Sierra,* the magazine of the Sierra Club, in dedicating space to nature and travel writing, such as the spring 1993 *Georgia Review* edited by Douglas Carlson, author of *At the Edge* (Fredonia, N.Y.: White Pine Press, 1989). *Creative Nonfiction,* edited by Lee Gutkind

at the University of Pittsburgh, the only American quarterly solely devoted
to the personal essay, publishes women's writing. *Another Wilderness: New
Outdoor Writing by Women,* edited by Susan Fox Rogers (New York:
Norton, 1994), marks the creation of a larger public for anthologies, joining books published since Dillard's groundbreaking *Pilgrim at Tinker Creek*
that have enriched my own thinking: Maxine Kumin's *Women, Animals,
Vegetables;* Terry Tempest Williams's *Refuge: An Unnatural History of Family
and Place;* Deborah Tall's *From Where We Stand;* Kathleen Norris's *Dakota: A Spiritual Geography.* Natalia Rachel Singer's essays on female desire
and landscape have also been central to discovering my own desire to
represent my shifting relationship to place.

Women's visions of American places can help to make a clearer, more
whole sense of who we are and what this geography of ours means to us.
Our symbolic meanings for geography are matters of gender because of
the deep urge humans always feel to anthropomorphize the environment,
to make it human, to interpret it as a body. This urge is both inevitable
and dangerous. The body of nature viewed as female engenders patterns
of conquest, possession, cultural imperialism. Feminist strategies interrupt the way such psychic emblems inscribe themselves on our American lives, even though ecofeminists continue to contribute to the anthro-
pomorphic urge, albeit in a register of difference. This quotation—I will
call it seminal, that gendered word denoting originary significance—is
from Natalia Rachel Singer's "Whiteout: Editing our Metaphors for the
Land," published in the *AWP Chronicle* in 1994:

> The earth is alive, we know that much. . . . But should we, in the
> 1990s, view land as a manifestation of only the feminine, as think-
> ers from Plato to Starhawk, the well known ecofeminist, have con-
> tinued to do? Doesn't this distinction still make both women and the
> earth, as Simone de Beauvoir has charged, the Other? Does this met-
> aphor continue to place women outside of civilization and culture
> in a way that is ultimately repressive to women? . . .
>
> . . . But who says this planet of ours has to be a girl? For a long
> time I have thought the earth should be not our mother or some man's
> lover, but an altar. A living one, that breathes. . . .
>
> . . . Let us kneel before it and learn how to live. But let's not kneel
> for too long or too hard. Sometimes the best religion is the least or-
> ganized, unwilling or unready to impose its icons everywhere it looks.
> Let's not impose doctrines upon the landscape, or impose the meta-

phors of the body. Sometimes it's better to leave the earth un-incorporated. Sometimes we love best by letting go, letting our loves just be themselves, unpossessed.

With Singer, I realize how deeply my ways of perceiving place are inflected by gender—by which I mean that I gaze with an eye constructed by being a female in a patriarchy; for all I know, I may also gaze with an eye that is more essentially feminine, in a biological sense. I don't know about that, nor do I know of anyone who does know. That does not mean all of these essays are consciously feminist, although some are; it does mean that I acknowledge my ways of seeing, of processing, of ruminating upon what I see, as deeply connected to my other ways of knowing, ones that are feminist. I don't always manage to leave unpossessed the places my eye colonizes, but I try to remain aware of my own agenda.

My career as literary critic, poet, teacher of English and women's studies, and essayist has been both highly focused and diverse. At the core of it is what appear to be a series of paradoxes or polarities. My unifying principle is an enduring interest in eros and thanatos—or, to be more down to earth about it, sexuality and death. I'm interested in beginnings and endings and how the two are related to each other. Sex and death are among our greatest cultural taboos as well as our greatest obsessions. The primary vehicle for my exploration of opposites has always been gender—itself a potential site of opposition or duality—and the way of knowing that I have found most useful in my literary criticism as a method of mediating is psychoanalytic theory, founded on yet another seeming duality, the split between conscious and unconscious psychic structures.

So I have been for years both a Freudian and a feminist, a practitioner of the kind of criticism called psychoanalytic feminism. The union of these two ways of knowing (and they are also, importantly and dangerously, ideologies) is not comfortable or easy, but I find the illumination that results from their interpenetration worth the difficulty of maintaining the contradictions. Their productive dialogue helps my continuing effort to make my thinking become more honest and to prevent the complacencies of single vision, or of political simplicities. These essays are not psychoanalytic, but that stance informs them.

I still believe in the tenets of William Blake that fueled my first book, *Blake and Freud.* Speaking of life's intricate "contraries"—male and female, good and evil, reason and feeling, body and soul—he said that their vigorous, painful interaction is the basis of human progression. Freud echoed him a century later with the idea that "opposition" constitutes true friendship. If feminism and psychoanalysis seem opposites, I remember that they both rest on the enduring conviction that to make our way toward truths that may heal us, we need to look beneath the glimmering, urgently maintained, and misleading surfaces of our individual psyches and our cultural institutions, straight into the core where wish and fear are so indefinably entwined. Although they are not in any way theoretical, I try to look into the heart of my own darkness in these essays.

When I write about gender—which I am always doing, whether my ostensible subject is William Blake or Anne Sexton and Maxine Kumin or Freud or suicide or Wounded Knee or cervical cancer—I hope always to be thinking it through in ways that help to heal the wounds between men and women, whose interdependent, symbiotic struggles are so often waged in terms of battle, war, conflict, but who probably most want to live without hurting or being hurt too much, and who also want, at our best, to find ways to help the world's life endure.

At a certain juncture in both my personal and professional life, I began to compose this book of essays that are neither scholarly nor political in the usual ways. The relationship I wish to explore between my mind and the land, my mind and the other minds I meet on the roads and trails, the enclosures and open fields of America, is one that tries to minimize boundaries and divisions, even as it also tries to acknowledge the private separation of one living being from another.

My framing metaphor, and my title, come from a visit to the home monastery of Thomas Merton at Gethsemani, which is recorded in the center of this book. Merton writes in a letter collected in *The Monastic Journey,* edited by Patrick Hart (Mission, Kans.: Sheed, Andrews, and McMeel, 1977):

> The contemplative has nothing to tell you except to reassure you that if you dare to penetrate your own silence and dare to advance without fear into the solitude of your own heart, and risk the sharing of that solitude with the lonely other who seeks God through you and with you, then you will truly recover the light and the capacity to understand what is beyond words because it is too close to be explained: it is the intimate union in the depths of your own heart, of God's spirit and your own secret inmost self, so that you and He are in all truth one Spirit. (173)

I implicitly set myself against as well as with Merton, in the spirit of friendship. I try to use words to express what he says is unavailable to language. I employ not the contemplative's way of life, but the busy traveler's. And I am traveling toward, or with, not a god I can call He, nor one I would call She, not toward a god at all, but toward some form of transcendence of the ordinary that I believe is available *to* the human spirit, *through* the human spirit. I ask myself, during this journey, Who is the "lonely other?" Is it within the individual heart, the secret sharer with whom each of us lives? Or is the lonely other the brother or sister penitent and celebrant? Is some healing expression of spirit and heart available to us? Can I learn to travel alone as a woman, without fear? And without my other, or another? I seek to know my possibilities with women and men I meet, and with whatever spirit of our national life is available in the spaces we have collectively named sacred: national parks, forests, mountains, caves, and also the kind of site sacralized because it gives a local habitation and a name to our damaged body politic. Here I mean, most especially, Wounded Knee.

I have been preparing to write this book for years, by traveling, keeping journals, writing poems, and sending letters home from the road. When I began to keep a trip journal in 1987, I had at first no other purpose than to record my perceptions of new places I saw in my American travels. Before I began the journal, I'd lost too many precise memories. Although I'd traveled west from New York State extensively in the American National Park System for fifteen years, camping in many parks and driving both main highways and backroads with my then-partner, Mac Nelson, and had gone to many New England locations annually as part of research on early American gravestones, I had not recorded the places I'd been or the ways they'd made my mind move.

The notes for these essays were written between 1987 and 1994, but in a sense they cover my travels from as early as 1970. Some of the places I write about here, such as Yellowstone, I returned to several times. Others of my earlier destinations, and the locations of some of my finest American moments, were lost to me because I didn't revisit them after I began to take notes—thus Arches, Canyonlands, Mesa Verde, the Grand Canyon, are not here. They'll wait for another book. I'll always regret not having recorded what I felt when I first encountered the American West, when desert stretches sanded their way into my cells, literally, I believe, changing the shape of my thought for the rest of my life.

I feel a similar loss in not having written essays as I made my way through the graveyards of New England, writing another kind of book,

Epitaph and Icon: A Field Guide to the Old Burying Grounds of Cape Cod, Martha's Vineyard, and Nantucket (co-authored with Mac Nelson). I was indeed taking notes, but they were about epitaphs, icons, carving schools, motif development, town histories. This fragile early American sculpture, displayed in the outdoor museums of burying grounds, endures in a landscape equally fragile in the case of the cape and islands, and I know that my sense of connection with them was full of discoveries about mortality and gender. Those moments of personal discovery are gone; only their scholarly counterparts appear in that book. What's left of these losses is my knowledge that I'll never travel paperless again.

I've found that I can only write about place, with any sense of immediacy or worth, by beginning on the spot; thus my notes expanded into drafts of essays while I was still in Yellowstone, for instance, or Carlsbad Caverns or Yosemite. When I write in the present tense, as I often do here, it's authentic rather than reconstructed after the fact. I build on my rough drafts and notes, written at campsites or gas stations, even in windstorms. In recent years I've also traveled with a tape recorder, speaking into it when I'm driving or backpacking, which removes complete dependency on recollecting my experiences in tranquility—which I also do, in any case. My taped transcriptions form the barest draft, but they are invaluable. I do not think that my backpacking trip and climbing accident in the White Mountains could have been rendered with clarity after the fact, at least not the kind achieved by recording my way through it and then meditating on its meanings for me.

I have constructed this book thematically rather than chronologically. Part 1, "Wounded Chevy at Wounded Knee," takes place entirely at Wounded Knee, Yellowstone, and Devil Canyon. These essays are linked in the ways that they connect place and psyche, in the intersections they afford me between my personal history and our country's policies about its indigenous and displaced peoples and animals. Native Americans live on reservations; so do bears and wild horses. Part 2 is the home of my most consciously feminist essays—about pornography, power and powerlessness, female fear, control of the body, abortion marches, women traveling alone on roads and in life.

Part 3 is a partial record of road notes constructed from a journal kept through a single summer traveling America. I have, I hope, no single-minded vision, but an open eye, as I travel through the South and the West, seeking a sense of places and people. Part 4, "Blowing in the Wind," hearkens back to "Wounded Chevy at Wounded Knee" in a personal rather than political sense—or in the sense that the personal is the political. I planned this journey as one woman's victory over her own fear through backpacking and mountain hiking. I blew it, or it blew me.

Part 5 comes to terms with my struggle toward more mindful, contemplative ways of walking in the world, specifically disjunctive with Western modes of what passes for "thought." I believe that this "struggle toward" informs most of the essays in the book, culminating in the White Mountains; part 5 records a movement toward *giving up* a personal paradigm based on struggle, on wrestling and wrangling with an issue, a person, a situation, a cultural custom. It is here that I return to Thomas Merton, developing a textual relationship that I had left implicit.

Because the collection is more thematically than chronologically arranged, a few clarifications regarding my life, and especially the people and partners that appear here, may help to prevent confusion. At seventeen, I married John (not his real name), a Native American of the Iroquois Nation, Seneca tribe. My son, Bernie, was born when I was eighteen. At twenty-two I began to live with Mac, the male partner most frequently referred to here. We became the second parents of Krissy, my oldest friend Nancy's daughter; I refer to Krissy as my daughter here, and her daughter, Ayron, as my granddaughter. I shared them as family with Nancy, as well as with Mac, until Nancy's unexpected death in October 1995.

My son's wife is Mary Ellen, and their daughter is Sequoia. An early essay takes place after my granddaughter Sequoia was born, whereas the letter to my son that ends this book was written before her birth. Mac and I parted company in 1989. Most of part 2 occurred after Mac and I separated, but all of part 3 took place when Mac and I traveled together. In 1990 I began to live with Dirk (not his real name), the partner of part 4; one essay in part 2 records our temporary separation. We went our separate ways permanently in late 1993, shortly after the climbing accident.

Recording this chronology, and acknowledging its violations in the narrative, is a vaguely comic activity. Had I been a woman of another time, the likelihood is that one partner would have endured with me, I with him, through the sequence of my narrative. But then, my story would probably not have been about gender tensions—nor would a singly partnered woman have been likely to lead the life that occasions the textures of this book. I intend these essays above all to be readable. They are not literary, except in the sense that poetry infuses my writing in what I hope are unobtrusive ways. They are not theoretical, except in the sense that anyone trying to comprehend structural dynamics engages in theory. They are not even political, except in the sense that anyone thinking about gender is thinking about power.

My friend Glenn Strand once said that everything falls into one of four categories: epistemology, how we know what we know; ontology, the study of being; eschatology, the study of the ends of things; and drainage. And of these, the most important is drainage. He said that fifteen years ago, and I've found that he's right. I'm amazed at how many of my life's events, and those of the people I know and love, end up in the drainage category—the flowing and emptying of rivers and bodies and loves and hearts.

PART I

WOUNDED CHEVY AT

WOUNDED KNEE

LOVE LOST ON THE ROAD

I believe that it's a sin
to try to make things last forever.
Everything that exists in time
runs out of time some day.
—Bruce Cockburn, "Mighty Trucks of Midnight"

The only thing that amazes me more than the slowness of the human heart to heal from the wounds of love and loss is the fact that it heals at all. When a partnership of love has been long and painful, its end is inflected with ambivalence. The dread of its demise is balanced by the wish for it. It's been that way with me twice, in my first marriage of five years, over when I was twenty-two, and once again just as I was finishing the body of this book.

The body of this book; my own body; a woman's body; the body of the land; experiencing the body of the land through the body traversing it; (back to) my own body. I have titled this book *The Lonely Other,* not an allusion to a woman writer, not even a woman. The words are those of a man, a mystic, a visionary, a Christian, a celibate, Trappist monk Thomas Merton. I am not a mystic nor a celibate, despite the occasional wish to become what a friend calls a born-again virgin. I have experienced my life firmly and fundamentally in the body, sometimes comfortably and sometimes not. And in the body of this book, where I strive to unite spirit and flesh however I can through the yearning representations that writers call words, I am a body inscribing herself on paper. I am also sometimes a body alone, often content to be there, other times searching for the antidote to lonely, that equally lonely other person. But I like to talk about that part in terms that are asexual.

For the past few years, my oldest and dearest male friend and I have carried on a mutually exhausted, determined dialogue about our relationships with lovers. We have dissected our personal histories, littered with disasters for ourselves and our beloveds. Richard Lehnert is a poet and the music editor of *Stereophile* magazine in Santa Fe. We have vowed to ourselves, to each other, that we're done with the search for ideal partnership, indeed for permanent partnership at all. It is, we both believe, the desperate hope for that relationship, a hope that turns into expectation every time, that blights all possibility of it in most people's lives, certainly in both of our own thus far. We've seen each other through love's labors lost for a quarter of a century. We know that one reason we've remained so close is that we've never been lovers, and we never will be. No *When Harry Met Sally* for us. We intend to be friends to the end of our lives. We're monitoring each other's conduct in relationships. We're on the wagon. Sometimes we fall off.

While some of my travels take place on my own—and make much of that coveted, sought after, finally achieved aloneness—others of my trips are undertaken with male companions. Some early readers have been confused by my alternating stance of woman-on-her-own and woman-grafted-at-the-hip-to-a-man. My frequent defensiveness on this point stems from a conviction that although my traveling companions are important people in my life, they are seldom essential to the event, nor to my relationship with the places I encounter in these pages, nor to the kinds of questing in which I see myself engaged. Thus I have dismissed reasonable questions: Why did you leave Mac, the man with you in so many of your travels? What happened to Dirk? Why this withholding reticence about romance in writing otherwise so personal?

Perhaps it's natural to wonder about people who suddenly disappear from a writer's pages after they have become characters in a narrative thread. I remember that frustration when I read Nancy Mairs's *Plaintext.* Her husband, clearly a central presence in her life, appeared and disappeared throughout that ostensibly plain text. Perhaps she thought that when she was writing about being crippled (her word) or about fish tanks, her most intimate daily companion was beside the point. Using her refusal to elaborate, I have said little here about my dearest ones. I stand by that decision to a degree, because, oh Christ, what could be more predictable than a woman writing about her lost loves? I can explain my avoidance of the deepest human wounds here by poking at an old one I will refer to in "Wounded Chevy at Wounded Knee."

I still loved my first husband when I left him, not madly (at the start it *was* a form of normal insanity), but genuinely. Yet I'd known for at least the two final years that the marriage must end, so I had time to prepare myself for the inevitable. Still, it took all my strength, though it hurts my pride to recall this. I'd rather shake my head that I could ever have taken that fever of misshapen, mistaken identity for love. But it was love, unless you define love by an ideal so stringent, so healthy, so balanced, that I have seldom known it lived for long in anyone's life. My own evidence that I continued to love the father of my child in recesses unavailable even to myself came years after the marriage had ended, years after I'd ceased to think of him except on the occasional holiday when family intricacies brought him to my irritated attention. When my son was twelve, his father was arrested, tried, and imprisoned for a serious crime. I took my son to see his father in the holding center. We huddled into the confessional-sized booth where his father was brought to gaze at us, and we at him, through yellowed and thick glass.

Seeing his father there, shamed and incarcerated, my son threw his own young body into the wall, remaining adhered to it with his eyes glazed in terror. By later that night the whites of his eyes were blazing red, the result of broken capillaries from trying not to cry out. My long-ex husband spoke my name desperately, asking me to get him out of there, proclaiming his innocence, choking out beseeching words. I handled it calmly, assuring him that he'd get good legal counsel. All the way home I comforted my heartbroken boy, who had worshipped his father in absence, creating of him a father hero who never existed, as I had years before created a mythic husband who had never existed. I felt sorrow for my son, helplessness as a parent unable to save him from this inexorable and unwanted truth. And I felt something vague—compassion, I supposed—for this man to whom I had been married long ago, in another life, possibly on another planet.

So the screaming that seized my entire body hours later took me by complete surprise. I had not cried at all during my adult life, a fact I regarded by turns as healthy and pathological—but on balance, I thought it was a good thing. I never had to worry that I'd weep at politically inopportune moments, for instance. I'd experienced my share of normal human sorrows for a woman in her early thirties, but no tears for them, even when I was deeply affected. I thought it was just how I was constructed, and I'd analyzed the roots of it in my childhood. Yet here I was in my bathroom, fully dressed and splay-legged on the toilet, yelling myself hoarse, appalled, my screams melding into sobs, then throwing up, then sobbing again, my body nearly in convulsions. It went on for several *hours*. I'd think this possession by an alien invader was over, start to wash my face, bewildered at the panting creature with the swollen eyes, and then it would begin all over again. I lost my voice completely for two days.

My son and I made quite a pair, he with his eyes from *The Omen*, me like a widow from a particularly expressive culture, rending her garments and wailing—wailing, it became clear, for her lost first lover after all those years. In some of these pages you'll find his shadow. I learned from that experience how we carry old loves and wounds through the years, those clearly detailed, perfectly recorded fossil remains in the geology of the psyche. A better legacy of that night is that from then on I could sometimes weep.

The second time I lost a love that I had known must eventually fail is also referred to here, my relationship with a man named Dirk, with whom I lived for three years. By the time I was with him, I no longer believed in far futures, certainly not in permanence. Perhaps it seems less important to explain what happened to me and Dirk because the story is coded here in symbolic form in part 4. But if I sound breezy about the end of us— that section is titled "Blowing in the Wind," and it's about one's best laid plans going astray—I hope for an understanding that it wasn't easy. I assume everyone knows that these things never are, between people who care for each other. He disappears from the trail, and the book, and my life, in ways that now seem to me predetermined.

But the story of my first love-gone-wrong and my last love-gone-wrong are comparatively the forethought and afterthought to the primary lover whose presence haunts my pages, now here, now past, then back again, then gone. I was with Mac for almost twenty years, and some of the travels in this book happened because of him. I owe him a debt for having inspired me to hit the road, the ground, the parks, the trails. For the better part of two decades he got me out there, on planes and trains and in endless gridlocked, vapor-locked vehicles, tiny Rabbits and old couchlike vans, leaking tents and ratty sleeping bags and campsites that might as well have been on the moon.

It was his vision to some day visit not only every national park but every national monument about to be upgraded, and each one lost to downgrading. May he be able to do it. As his new wife, Elizabeth, says, he must have been a tire in a previous life. In this life, we went as far as we could go together. I began this narrative about lovers and partners by saying that it's hard enough to leave each other when you've always known the end was in sight, or ought to be. That's not what was supposed to happen with me and Mac. We both believed in forever together, and felt, to the very core of our beings, that nothing could ever destroy our partnership in life. We were wrong. But I'm not willing, even at the remove of six years, to patronize those two people who believed, to call us naive or misled, or to nod sagely with the wisdom of hindsight or of cynicism. Some few people do stay passionately in love throughout their adult lives, and we thought that was us.

Maybe I should have explored the wound of that parting more closely here, in the book that had some of its genesis with him. I know why I didn't, and couldn't. For years after we parted, I was still in daily sorrow about the failure of my relationship with Mac, and I know that he was, too. Addressing my exasperation with how long it was taking me to feel better, film critic and friend Luciana Bohne said to me, "How long has it been? Three years? That's not long enough. You'll start to *really* heal in five years, minimum." Another writer told me that her husband stood in their kitchen eight years after his first marriage ended and wept on the day of his former wife's remarriage. As I said, amazing that we recover at all. It takes me years to write with honesty or integrity about the relationships that have shaped my life most deeply. I was out of my first marriage for close to twenty years before I began to touch it in writing, in "Wounded Chevy at Wounded Knee." I've written a few naked paragraphs about Mac in this book and I'll leave it at that. We didn't make it, and that's all I can say, except to thank Mac for the traveling bug and for my half of our camping equipment.

I have lost one more love on the road, just as this book goes to press. About this one I also remain silent here, because I didn't know this death was going to happen, and the grief is too much now. Nancy Espersen Luce and I met in gym class when we were thirteen, both sitting on the bleachers, excused from the dread rope-climbing ordeal by pretending to have our periods. For the next thirty-five years, we often really had those menstrual periods at the same time, as women living together do. We shared everything two humans can—we raised kids and mourned dead parents and loved the same men and women. For the past decade, she has lived far from me. We were estranged for a while, but in recent years we found our way back to each other. Krissy and Ayron and Nancy were living together in three-generation harmony when Nancy died of cancer in October 1995. With Nancy's fine partner, Tom, Krissy did one of the most difficult things a grown child can do: she nursed her own mother to her death.

At Thanksgiving they brought her ashes north to my kitchen, and then we buried Nancy near her mother in the small town where she and I grew up, in the very cemetery where we used to meet boys, including the ones we later married. This book was written while we lived far apart, and the only sign of her here is the pornography adventure. It figures. My mom always said we were a bad influence on each other, and we certainly got into most of our big life troubles together. Nancy was never half as scared as I was of who we were together or of what we knew or how we came to know it. We were writing a book together years ago about the kinds of knowledge we felt we shared. Now that she is buried, I will resurrect her in my writing heart, and it will evolve into a book about her. In the meantime, I dedicate this one to her memory.

I f you break down on that reservation, your car belongs to the Indians. They don't like white people out there." This was our amiable motel proprietor in Custer, South Dakota, who asked where we were headed and then propped a conspiratorial white elbow on the counter and said we'd better make sure our vehicle was in good shape. To get to Wounded Knee, site of the last cavalry massacre of the Lakota in 1890 and of more recent confrontations between the FBI and the American Indian Movement, you take a road out of Pine Ridge on the Lakota Reservation and go about eight miles. If you weren't watching for it, you could miss it because nothing is there but a hill, a painted board explaining what happened, a tiny church, and a cemetery.

The motel man told us stories about his trucking times, when by day his gas stops were friendly, but by night groups of Indian men who'd been drinking used to circle his truck looking for something to steal—or so he assumed. He began carrying a .357 Magnum with him "just in case." Once he took his wife out to Pine Ridge. "She broke out in hives before we even got there." And when they were stopped on the roadside and a reservation policeman asked if they needed help, she was sure he was going to order her out of the car, steal it, and, I suppose, rape and scalp her while he was at it. As he told us these contradictory stories, he seemed to have no awareness of the irony involved in warning us that the Indians would steal our car if they got a chance and following it with a story about an Indian who tried to help them just in case they might be having trouble.

He did make a distinction between the reservation toughs and the police. He wasn't a racist creep, but rather a basically decent fellow whose view of the world was narrowly white. I briefly entertained the notion of staying a while, pouring another cup of coffee, and asking him a few questions that would make him address the assumptions behind his little sermon, but I really wanted to get on my way, and I knew he wasn't going to change his mind about Indians here in the middle of his life in the middle of the Black Hills. I always feel vaguely irresponsible when I don't take on that sort of thing, but it never helps when I do.

Mac and I exchanged a few rueful remarks about it while we drove. But we both knew that the real resistance to dealing with Indian culture on these trips that have taken us through both Pueblo and Plains Indian territories hasn't come from outside of our car or our minds, but rather from within them. More specifically, from within me. For years Mac has read about the Plains Indians with real attentiveness and with an openness to learning what he can about the indigenous peoples of North America. He reads histories, biographies, novels, essays, thinks carefully about the issues involved, remembers what he has read, informs himself with curiosity and respect about tribes that have occupied the areas we visit. For a couple of years he urged me toward these materials, many of which have been visible around our home for years: *Black Elk Speaks, In a Sacred Manner We Live, Bury My Heart at Wounded Knee,* studies of Indian spiritual and cultural life. While we were in Lakota country this time, he was reading Mari Sandoz's biography of Crazy Horse. But he has long since given up on getting me to pay sustained attention to these rich materials, because my resistance has been firm and long standing. I am probably better informed about Indian life than most Americans ever thought of being, but not informed enough for a thoughtful reader and writer. My resistance has taken the form of a mixture of pride and contempt: pride that says I already know more than these books can tell me and contempt for the white liberal-intellectuals' romance with all things Indian. But my position has been very strange perhaps, given that I was married to a Native American for five years, lived on a reservation, and am the mother of a half-Indian son.

I've been mostly wrong in my attitudes, but it's taken me years to understand that. Wounded Knee is where I came to terms with my confusion, rejection, and ambivalence, and it happened in a direct confrontation with past events that are now twenty years old. My resistance broke down because of an encounter with a young Lakota named Mark, who is just about my own son's age.

I grew up in the 1950s and 1960s in a small white community on the edge of the Cattaraugus Seneca Indian Reservation in western New York State. Relations between Indians and whites in my world were bitter and in many respects replicated the dynamics between whites and blacks in the South, with many exceptions for the very different functions and circumstances of these two groups of people of color in white America. The school system had recently been integrated after the closing of the Thomas Indian School on the reservation. The middle-class whites wanted nothing to do with the Indians, whom they saw as drunkards and degenerates, in many cases subhuman. When I rebelled against my restrained white upbringing, the medium for asserting myself against my parents and my world was ready-made, and I grabbed it.

I began hanging out on the reserve with young Native Americans, shifted my social and sexual arena entirely to the Indian world, fell in love with an idea of noble darkness in the form of a carnival worker, got pregnant by him, married him, left the white world completely, and moved into his. Despite the fact that this was the sixties, my actions weren't politically motivated; or, rather, my politics were entirely personal at that point. While my more aware counterparts might have done some of the same things as conscious political and spiritual statements, I was fifteen when I started my romance with Indians, and I only knew that I was in love with life outside the constricting white mainstream and with all the energy that vibrates on the outer reaches of cultural stability. My heart and what would later become my politics were definitely in the right place, and I have never regretted where I went or what I came to know. But that knowledge spoiled me for twenty years for another kind of knowing.

Whatever my romantic notions were about the ideal forms of American Indian wisdom—closeness to land, respect for other living creatures, a sense of harmony with natural cycles, a way of walking lightly in the world, a manner of living that could make the ordinary and profane into the sacred—I learned that I was inhabiting a world on the reservation that was the contrary of all these values. American Indian culture at the end of the road has virtually none of these qualities. White America has destroyed them. Any culture in its death throes is a grim spectacle, and there can be no grimmer living reality than that endured by people on their way to annihilation, genocide completed by suicide. I did not live among the scattered wise people or political activists of the Seneca Nation. I did not marry a nominal American Indian from a middle-class family. I married an illiterate man who dropped out of school in the seventh grade and was only sporadically in school before that. He traveled around the East with carnivals running a ferris wheel during the summer months and logged wood on the reservation during the winter when he could get work. Home base was an old trailer without plumbing in the woods where his mother lived. He drank sporadically but heavily, and his weekends, often his weekdays, were full of pool tables, bar brawls, the endlessness of hanging out with little to do. He didn't talk much. How I built this dismal life into a romanticized myth about still waters running deep gives me an enduring respect for and belief in the mythopoetic, self-deluding power of desire, wish, will.

When I was married to him, my world was a blur of old cars driven by drunk men in the middle of the night, honky-tonk bars, country music, late night fights with furniture flying, food stamps and welfare lines, stories of injury and death. The smell of beer still sickens me slightly. I was sober as a saint through all of this, so I didn't have the insulation of liquor, only of love. I lived the contrary of every white myth about Indian life, both the myths of the small-town white racists and those of the smitten hippies. When I finally left that life behind, extricating myself and my child from it in the certain knowledge that to stay would mean something very like death for him and for me, I removed myself in every respect. I knew how stupid white prejudice against Indians was, understood the real story about why they drank and wasted their lives, felt the complexities so keenly that I couldn't even try to explain them to anyone white. But similarly, I knew how bird-brained the love-child generation's romance with Indian culture was.

My son pulled me back toward Native America with his own love for his father, and I still kept in touch with my husband's mother on the reservation, sometimes helping her to handle white bureaucracy, but that's all. I heard at a remove of miles, of eons, about the early deaths of young men I'd known well, death by diabetes after lost limbs or by car at high speed, and I felt something, but I didn't have to deal with it. When I tried to think about that past life in order to put it into some kind of perspective, no whole picture could emerge. When I tried to write about it, no words would come. And when I tried to be open to learning something new about Indians in America on my trips, my heart closed down tight, and with it my mind. When I went to Wounded Knee, the wounds of these other Indians half a continent and half a lifetime away were a part of the landscape.

✳

We pull off the side of the road to read the billboard that tells what happened here. "MASSACRE OF WOUNDED KNEE" is the header, but upon close inspection you see that *Massacre* is a new addition, painted over something else. *Battle,* perhaps? What did it used to say, I wonder, and hope I'll run into a local who can tell me. While I'm puzzling over this, an old Chevy sputters into the pull-off and shakes to a stop. It's loaded with dark faces, a young man and an older woman with many small children. The man gets out and walks slowly to the front of the car, rolling up his T-shirt over his stomach to get air on his skin. As he raises the hood, a Comanche truck pulls in beside him with one woman inside. It's very hot, and I weave a little in the glare of sun. An old tape runs through my eye, superimposing the past on this hot moment. I've seen this before again and again, cars full of little Indian kids in the heat of summer on the sides of roads. I glance again, see the woman in the front seat, know that she's their mother or their aunt. She looks weary and resigned, not really sad. She expects this.

And then in another blink it's not only that I have seen this woman; I have been this woman, my old car or someone else's packed with little kids who are almost preternaturally quiet, big eyed and dark skinned and already knowing that this is a big part of what life is about, sitting in boiling backseats, your arms jammed against the arms of your brother, your sister, your cousin. There is no use asking when we'll get there, wherever there is. It will happen when it happens, when the adults as helpless as you figure out what to do. In the meantime you sweat and stare. But I am not this woman anymore, not responsible for these children, some of whose intelligent faces will blank into a permanent sheen of resignation before they're five. I am a tourist in a new Plymouth Voyager, my luggage rack packed with fine camping equipment, my Minolta in my hand to snap pictures of the places I can afford to go.

When Mac suggests that we offer to help them, I am not surprised at my flat negative feeling. He doesn't know what that means, I surmise, and I don't have any way to tell him. Help them? Do you want to get anywhere today, do you have the whole afternoon? The young man's shoulders bend over the motor. He is fit and beautiful, his good torso moves knowingly but powerlessly over the heat rising from beneath the hood. I recognize him as well as the woman. He has no job. He talks about getting off the reservation, finding work, living the dreams he still has. He'll talk this way for a few more years, then give up entirely. He drinks too much. He has nothing to do. Drinking is the only thing that makes him really laugh and his only way to release rage. I also know that the car is out of gas, whatever else is wrong with it, and that these people have no money. Okay, sure, I say to Mac, standing to one side while he asks how we can help. Close now to the car, I see that the woman is the young man's mother. These kids are his brothers and sisters.

The car is out of gas and it needs a jump. The battery is bad. The woman in the other car is the young man's aunt, who can give him a jump but has no money to give him for gas, or so she says. I know her, too. She is more prosperous than her relatives and has learned the hard way never to give them any money, because she needs it herself and if she gives it to them she'll never see it again. She made her policy on this years ago and makes it stick no matter what. She has to. Well, then, we'll take them to the nearest gas station. Do they have a gas can? No, just a plastic washer fluid jug with no top. Okay, that will have to do. How far is the nearest pump? Just up the road a couple of miles. But they don't have any money because they were on their way to cash his mother's unemployment check when they ran out of gas, and the town where they can do that is many miles away. So can we loan them some money for gas? We can. He gets in the front seat. I get in the back, and as we pull away from the windy parking area, I look at the woman and the kids who will be sitting in the car waiting until we return. She knows she can't figure on how soon that will be. She stares straight ahead. I don't want to catch her eye, nor she mine.

Right here up this road. Mark is in his early twenties. Mac asks him questions. He is careful and restrained in his answers at first, then begins to open up. No, there's no work around here. Sometimes he does a little horse-breaking or fence-mending for the ranchers. All the ranches here are run by whites who had the money to make the grim land yield a living. They lease it from the Lakota. Mark went away to a Job Corps camp last year, but he had to come back because his twenty-one-year-old brother died last winter, leaving his mother alone with the little ones. He froze to death. He was drinking at a party and went outside to take a leak. Mark said they figured he must have just stopped for a minute to rest, and then he fell asleep. They found him frozen in the morning. So Mark had to come back home to bury his brother and help his mother with the kids.

As we bounce over the dirt road, I stare at the back of Mark's head and at his good Indian profile when he turns toward Mac to speak. He is so familiar to me that I could almost reach out to touch his black straight hair, his brown shoulder. He is my husband, he is my son. I want to give him hope. He speaks about getting out of here, going to "Rapid"—Lakota shorthand for Rapid City—and making a life. He is sick of having nothing to do, he wants work, wants an apartment. But he can't leave yet, he has to stay to help his mother. But things are going to be okay, because he has just won a hundred thousand dollars and is waiting for them to send the check.

What?

"You know the Baja Sweepstakes?" He pronounces it Bay-jah. "Well, I won it, I think I won it, I got a letter. My little brother sent in the entry form we got with my CD club and he put my name on it, and it came back saying that I'm one of a select few chosen people who've won a hundred thousand dollars. That's what it said, it said that, and I had to scratch out the letters and if three of them matched it means I win, and they matched, and so I sent it back in and now I'm just waiting for my money. It should come pretty soon and then everything will be okay." He repeats it over and over again in the next few minutes: he's one of a select few chosen people.

As he speaks of this, his flat voice becomes animated. Slowly I begin to believe that he believes this. Whatever part of him knows better is firmly shelved for now. This hope, this belief that hundreds of thousands of dollars are on the way is what keeps him going, what keeps him from walking out into the sky—or to the outhouse in the winter to take a leak and a nap in the snow. What will you do with the money, I ask. Well, first he is going to buy his mother and the kids a house.

The first gas stop is a little shack that's closed when we finally get there. Sandy wind and no sign of life. Miles on down the road is a small Lakota grocery store with only a few items on the shelves and a sign that reads "stealing is not the Lakota way." Mac hands Mark a five-dollar bill. You can kiss that five bucks good-bye, I say to Mac. I know, he nods. When Mark comes back out he has the gas, and also a big cup of Seven-Up and a bag of Nachos. You want some, he asks me? He hands Mac a buck fifty in change. On the way back I hold the gas can in the backseat, placing my hand over the opening. Despite the open windows, the van fills with fumes. My head begins to ache. I am riding in a dream of flatness, ranch fences, Mark's dark head in front of me wishing away his life, waiting for the break that takes him to Rapid. Later I learn that we are in Manderson, and this is the road where Black Elk lived.

Mark is talking about white people now. Yes, they get along okay. For

"yes" he has an expression of affirmation that sounds sort of like "huh."
Mari Sandoz spells it "hou" in her books on the Lakota. The Lakota are
infiltrated in every way by whites, according to Mark. Lots of people in
charge are white, the ranchers are white. And there's a place in Rapid called
Lakota Hills, fancy houses meant for Lakotas, but whites live in them.
Later it occurs to us that this is probably a development named Lakota
Hills that has nothing at all to do with the Indians, but it has their name
and so Mark thinks it belongs to them—which, in a sense, it does. I am
angry for him that we borrow their name this way and paste it on our air-
conditioned prosperity. I don't have anything to say to him. I lean back
and close my eyes. It would be easy to be one of them again. I remember
now how it's done. You just let everything flatten inside.

And when we return to Wounded Knee, the pull-off is empty. Mother,
children, car, aunt, all are gone. There's nothing but wind and dust. This
doesn't surprise me. Mark's mother knows better than to wait for her son's
return if other help comes along. Mark means well, but maybe she has
learned that sometimes it's hours before he gets back with gas, hours and
a couple of six-packs if he has the chance. Now we face the prospect of
driving Mark around the reservation until we can find them. I have just
resigned myself to this when his aunt pulls back in and says they're broke
down again a couple of miles up. So we can leave now. Mark thanks us,
smiles, and shyly allows us the liberty of having his aunt take a picture of
all three of us. I am feeling a strange kind of shame, as though I had seen
him naked, because he told us his secret and I knew it was a lie.

✳

Unemployment, high rates of suicide and infant mortality, fetal alcohol
syndrome, death by accident and drinking-related diseases such as diabetes, these are now the ways that American Indians are approaching their
collective demise. Over a century ago, American whites began this destruction by displacing and killing the *pte,* the Indian name for the buffalo the
Plains Indians depended upon. We herded the Native Americans together in far crueler ways than they had herded the bison, whose sacredness
the Indians respected even as they killed them for food and shelter. The
history of our genocide is available in many historical and imaginative
sources. What is still elusive, still amazingly misunderstood, is how and
why the Indians seem to have participated in their own destruction by
their failure to adapt to changed circumstances.

Whites can point to the phenomenal adjustments of other nonwhite groups in America, most recently the Asians, who were badly mistreated and who have nevertheless not only adapted but excelled. Indians even come off badly in comparison to the group in some respects most parallel to them, American blacks, whose slowness in adapting seems at first glance to have more justification. Blacks were, after all, our slaves, brought here against their will, without close cultural ties to keep them bound together in a tradition of strength; and on the whole blacks are doing better than Indians. However slowly, a black middle class is emerging in America. What's the matter with Indians? Why haven't they adjusted better as a group?

The American Indian Movement is of course strong in some areas, and Indians have articulate, tough leaders and savvy representatives of their cause who are fighting hard against the tide of despair gripping the heart of their people. But they're still losing, and they know it. Estimates of unemployment on the Pine Ridge and Rosebud Reservations run as high as 85 percent. Health officials at Pine Ridge estimate that as many as 25 percent of babies born on the reservation now have fetal alcohol syndrome. This culturally lethal condition cannot be overemphasized, since it means that the next generation of Lakota are genetically as well as socioeconomically crippled: one of the birth defects associated with fetal alcohol syndrome is mental retardation. The consequences are phenomenally depressing for Lakota leaders, whose traditional values are associated with mental acuity and imaginative wisdom. Mark is vastly ignorant and gullible, but he is intelligent. Many of his younger brothers and sisters, in the cultural if not the literal sense, are not only underprivileged and without educational advantages but also—let the word be spoken—stupid. When the light of inquiry, curiosity, mental energy dies out in the eyes of young Indians early in their stunted lives because they have nowhere to go and nothing to do, it is one kind of tragedy. When it is never present to die out in the first place, the magnitude of the waste and devastation is exponentially increased. Indian leaders who are now concentrating on anti-alcohol campaigns among their people are doing so for good reasons.

Indian leaders disagree about culpability at this point. Essentially the arguments become theories of genocide or suicide. On one end of the spectrum of blame is the theory that this is all the fault of white America. The evidence that can be marshaled for this point of view is massive: broken treaties, complete destruction of the Indian ways of life, welfare dependency established as the cheapest and easiest form of guilt payment, continued undermining of Indian autonomy and rights. The problem with this perspective, say others, is that it perpetuates Indian desperation and permits the easy way out—you spend your life complaining that white America put you here and drink yourself into the oblivion of martyrdom instead of taking responsibility for your own life. Therefore some Indians say they've heard enough about white America's culpability and prefer to transfer responsibility—not blame, but responsibility—to the shoulders of their own people. "White people aren't doing this to us—we're doing it to ourselves," said one Pine Ridge health official on National Public Radio's "Morning Edition." She sees the victim stance as the lethal enemy now.

The situation is as nearly hopeless as it is possible to be. Assimilation failed the first time and would fail if tried concertedly again, because it is definitive of Indian culture that it is rural and tribal and tied to open land, not urban airlessness. The Indian model is the encampment or village—the latter more recently and under duress—and not the city. Even the more stationary pueblo model is by definition not urban. The only real hope for Indian prosperity would be connected to vast tracts of land—not wasteland, but rich land. Nor are most Indians farmers by tradition at all, in the sense that white America defines the farm. Even if they might be and have been successful farmers under pressure, this too is not their milieu. Supposing that many tribes could adapt to the farming model over hunting and gathering, they would need large tracts of fine land to farm—and there is none left to grant them.

When the American government gave the Lakota 160 acres apiece and said, "Farm this," they misunderstood the Indians completely; and even if Indians had been able to adapt readily—a change approximately as difficult as asking an urban yuppie to become a nomad moving from encampment to encampment—the land they were given was inadequate to the purpose. Grubbing a living out of the land we have given them—in what John Wesley Powell called "the arid region" west of the one hundredth meridian—takes a kind of know-how developed and perfected by white Americans, and it also takes capital. It is no coincidence that the large ranches on Pine Ridge are almost entirely leased by whites who had the initial wherewithal to make the land yield.

The Sioux were a people whose lives were shaped by a sense of seeking and of vision that white America could barely understand, even if we were to try—and we do not try. The life of a Sioux of a century and a half ago was framed by the Vision Quest, a search for goals, identity, purpose. One primary means of fulfillment was self-sacrifice. Now, as Royal Hassrick has written, "No longer is there anything which they can deny themselves, and so they have sacrificed themselves in pity." Whereas they were once people whose idea of being human was bound to creative self-expression, their faces now reflect what Hassrick calls "apathy and psychic emaciation." They have become a people without a vision, collectively and individually.

Why do they drink themselves into this obliteration and erasure? Why not? When white America approaches the problem from within our own ethnocentric biases, we can't see how people would allow themselves to be wasted in this way, why they would not take the initiative to better themselves, save themselves, take on the capitalist individuality that says "*I* will make it out of this." But in fact part of their problem is that they have tried to do this, as have most Indian peoples. They've bought the American dream in part and taken on greed for money and material goods. Life on an Indian reservation—almost any reservation—is a despairing imitation of white middle-class values. In this respect they are like all other minority groups in ghettos in America, and this explains why Mark has a CD player instead of the more modest possessions we would not have begrudged him. If he is anything like the Indians I lived with, he also has a color TV, though he may well live in a shack or trailer without plumbing and without siding.

Their own dreams have evaded them, and so have ours. Mark and his brothers and sisters have been nourished on memories of a culture that vanished long before they were born and on the promises of a different one from whose advantages they are forever excluded. Does Mark really believe he has won the sweepstakes? What he received was obviously one of those computer letters that invites recipients to feel personally addressed and to believe that they have won something. Without the education that could teach him to read its language critically—or to read it adequately at all—he has been deceived into believing that a deux ex machina in the form of the Baja Sweepstakes will take him out of his and his family's despair. This is the precise aim of computer junk mail, to feed off poverty and despair. And it works on its intended victims in the white American lower classes, the urban ghetto, the Indian reservation, where people need something to believe in. Mark will probably win a camera or a mixer in the end and recognize he's been the recipient of yet another *Wasichu* scam. But his booby prize will probably also keep him buying expensive CDs from this company for another two years.

In 1890, the year of the final defeat of the Sioux at Wounded Knee, the

Ghost Dance was sweeping the plains. Begun by a few leaders, especially the Paiute seer Wovoka, the Ghost Dance promised its practitioners among the warriors that the buffalo would return and the white man would be defeated. Ghost Dancers believed that their ceremonial dancing and the shirts they wore would make them proof against the white man's bullets. Among the Sioux warriors at Wounded Knee, the willing suspension of disbelief was complete. It made the warriors reckless and abandoned, throwing normal caution and survival strategy to the wind.

A tragically inverted form of the self-delusion embodied in the Ghost Dance is practiced today on Pine Ridge and other Sioux reservations. The original Ghost Dance had beauty and vitality as well as desperation and despair as its sources. Now many Sioux men who would have been warriors in another time behave as though liquor and passivity will not kill them. Mark chooses to suspend his disbelief in white promises and to wait for one hundred thousand dollars to arrive in the mail, even though he must surely know, in some unfooled far corner of his mind, that this will never happen. His belief is how he maintains hope while he stays on the reservation, probably doing the very things that killed his brother last winter, that could kill him this coming winter, leaving his mother alone with small children gone dead in the eyes.

Frank (not his real name) was my husband's best friend on the Seneca reservation. He was raunchy, hard drinking, outrageous in behavior and looks. His hair was long and scraggly, his nearly black eyes were genuinely wild, and his blue jeans were always caked with dust and falling down his hips. His wit was wicked, his laugh raucous, dangerous, infectious. Frank was merciless toward me, always making white-girl jokes, telling me maybe I better go home to my mama where I'd be safe from all these dark men. He wanted me to feel a little afraid in his world, told me horrible stories about ghost dogs that would get me on the reservation if I ventured out at night—and then he'd laugh in a way that said hey, white girl, just joking, but not entirely. He alternated his affections toward me with edgy threats, made fun of the too-white way I talked or walked, took every opportunity to make me feel foolish and out of place. He was suspicious that I was just slumming it as a temporary rebellion, maybe taking notes in my head, and that I'd probably run for home when the going got too tough. Of course he was right, even though I didn't know it at the time. I liked him a lot.

A few years ago, my son, Bernie, went through a period when he chose to remove himself from my world and go live in his father's, from which I'd taken him when he was three. I didn't try to stop him, even though I knew he was hanging out with people who lived dangerously. I used to lie in bed unable to go to sleep because I was wondering what tree he'd end up wrapped around with his dad. He was a minor, but I was essentially helpless to prevent this. If I'd forced the issue, it would only have made his desire to know this forbidden world more intense. He lived there for months, and I slowly learned to get to sleep at night. Mothers can't save their children. And he had a right.

The day I knew he'd ultimately be okay was when he came home and told me about Frank. He wondered if I'd known Frank? He'd never met him before this because Frank had been out west for years. Now he was back home living in a shack way out in the country, crippled with diabetes and other ailments from drinking, barely able to walk. Frank would have been in his midforties at this time. Bernie and his dad took rabbits to Frank when they went hunting so that Frank would have something to eat. During these visits, Frank talked nonstop about the old days, reminding Bernie's dad of all their bar brawls, crowing to young Bernie that the two of them could beat anyone when they fought as a team, recounting the times they'd dismantled the insides of buildings at four in the morning. He told his stories in vivid, loving detail. His gift for metaphor was precise and fine, his memory perfect even if hyperbolic. He recalled the conversations leading up to fights, the way a person had leaned over the bar, who had said what to whom just before the furniture flew.

Bernie was impressed with him, but mostly he thought it was sad, this not-yet-old man who looked like he was in his seventies with nothing to remember but brawls. I told Bernie to value Frank for the way he remembered, the way he could make a night from twenty years ago intensely present again, his gift for swagger and characterization, his poetry, his laughter. In another time Frank would have been a tribal narrator, a story catcher with better exploits to recount. He would have occupied a special place in Seneca life because of his gifts.

My son left the reservation valuing and understanding important things about his father's world, but not interested in living in its grip. He lives in Florida, where he's a chef in a resort, and he's going to college. A month ago his daughter, my granddaughter, was born. She is named Sequoia after the Cherokee chief who gave his people an alphabet and a written language. Bernie took her to the reservation on his recent visit north and introduced the infant Sequoia to her great-grandmother. I hope I'll see Bernie's father some day soon to say hello, and maybe we can bend together over our granddaughter, for whom I know we both have many hopes.

Just before we leave Wounded Knee, I walk over to Aunt Lena's Comanche and point to the tribal sign that tells the story. "It says 'Massacre' there, but it used to say something else." I ask her if she knows what it said before. She looks over her shoulder and laughs. "That's funny," she says, "I've lived here all my life, but you know, I never did read that sign." We're miles down the road before I realize that I never finished reading it myself.

THE BEAR WITHIN AT YELLOWSTONE

Slough Creek, Yellowstone National Park

I believe in magic. I believe in the rights
of animals to leap out of our skins
as recorded in the Kiowa legend:
Directly there was a bear where the boy had been
—Maxine Kumin, "Credo"

H's cottage is illuminated, but her porch light is off. All my antennae are up, *he could be behind any bush, the next tree* though every vestige of common sense insists, *there's no one there.*

The forest is only what we choose to see, out of our fears and myths. Most of the time, it is dim and unknown. We hear the keening of hawks and eagles, the buzzing of cicadas mating, and we think there is danger. We attack without reason. . . . And so, where was the monster, after all? Where does it reside? Did it ever live among these boughs, these leaves?—Gabrielle Daniels, "A City Girl Discovers the Forest"

The Slough Creek area of the northeast corner of Yellowstone is the organized campsite farthest from civilization in both miles and amenities. Here there's just a pit toilet and hand water pump, no stores, no phone, and a warning sign at the registration stop informing you that this is back country and your safety is *not* guaranteed by the U.S. government, even if you do what you're supposed to and keep food away from your camp. Because, says the sign, bears are not reasonable or predictable and can attack without warning or provocation. Here you agree to leave reason behind. That makes perfect sense to me, given that I've clearly left reason behind in another respect that seems to be utterly at odds with this environment.

You drive along a dirt road a number of miles off one of the highways to get here. We're surrounded by meadows and hills and other creeks and, oddly, a high-desert sagebrush area that could be New Mexico or Texas—we're in Wyoming officially, but it looks like Montana. Our tent is pitched on the river, only a dozen or so feet from the bank, where trees hang on for dear and tenacious life, shallow and stubborn rooted. It's lush and spare at the same time, like the way you have to live here: steak dinners, pit toilets.

Slough Creek is really a healthy river, a good sixty feet across at this point, running deep and cold. Hikers are advised not to attempt fording until mid-July. This afternoon I saw four strong young men try to defy that advice. They didn't make it. We're in a walk-in site, so our van is parked up a hill and we carry everything in. A trail runs by our campsite and along the river, and other trails pass near, including the one several miles to a lake that my camping mate is on now and that I'll take as a day-trip tomorrow.

The flies and mosquitoes are bad but tolerable. The weather is as fast changing and unpredictable as any I've encountered anywhere, here or in the Rockies or in the desert of Big Bend. One moment the sun is shining and it's serene and calm; the next moment the sky darkens, the wind whoops around the tent, and everything begins to blow away. Rain threatens, doesn't come, comes for a few moments, leaves. It rains in the sun, it shines in the rain. Just since I've been writing, the sky has grown dark and the wind has blown hard no less than half a dozen times. My page has been nearly ripped from my hands repeatedly, and I've had to batten the hatches twice for rain—with Mac gone hiking, I have to be alert and ready when the afternoon storm comes. You get used to the false warnings after a day—you don't go inside the tent in the certainty of rain; you hold down your paper, wrap your shirt around you, keep writing. There's a dozen false alarms for every real storm. Then again, you want to be ready. Any warning could be real. Just when you're certain you'll see nothing but birds, squirrels, the mink with the nest on the far bank, it could be a buffalo or a moose. Or a grizzly. A bear was reported here five days ago, but the serenity makes you doubt the likelihood and tempts you to leave out your food—until night. Last night late I realized my pack in the tent contained candy, gum, perfumed oil. So I got up and put on my clothes and trudged back up the hill to lock it in the car. (Nobody ever expects the Spanish Inquisition. Nevertheless.)

This fragile, tough, yet easy wilderness has thus far asked little of me except that I enjoy a powerful river and a stunning view, do some trudging, shit in a hole made palatial by legislation for the handicapped, and tolerate flies. The sky is big, the river's wide, and there's nothing I've got to do except think about starting a fire later for dinner. The wine bottle is nested among roots along the riverbank, keeping cold. The birds are singing. Who says it's good-bye to sweet reason? After this morning, I do.

Right in the middle of making a fine camp breakfast (bacon, eggs, cinnamon rolls, tomato slices, tea, orange juice fresh squeezed), I got a very large, very physical, anxiety attack. I guess that's the current middle-aged middle-class American name for it—when for no apparent reason, and with no warning, your heart starts beating fast, you're filled with (oh name it) a nameless dread, you gulp and gasp, you're immobilized, miserable, scared—and all of it so physical that you wonder if you'll stay in one identifiable piece. That's what happened to me. It was quietly, internally overwhelming. I didn't want to worry my partner, and was aware in a general way of what it was, so I just sat down to wait for those wings in my chest to stop beating.

Right while it was happening, Mac wanted me to look at an alternative campsite, one with better features than ours, that had just been vacated. Rather than tell him what was happening and ask him to make the decision himself, I said, "I want to enjoy a quiet cup of tea first. I'll look at it in a while." And of course, although the camp area is sparsely populated, that very campsite was taken ten minutes later. Mac didn't guilt-trip me at all, but was clearly wondering why I arbitrarily insisted on my tea and do-not-disturb sign just then, when time was of the essence.

I felt spoiled and corrupt. Here I am in wilderness that is the very definition of the unspoiled. I am privileged as few people are to enjoy it and be in it, relieved of all problems and responsibilities. I am given this gift of solitude and purity—and what do I do? I have a full-blown neurotic episode right in front of God and the squirrels and the river and the tough old trees. What a ridiculous way to bring civilization to the outback, what an insult to the animals who have just survived another Yellowstone winter (many didn't—their carcasses dot Hayden Valley), an affront to this place where, if we come, we should experience a grateful and heart-deep peace.

And besides, there was no reason for it. It wasn't reasonable at all. Everything's okay, everything is good. I am happier now than at any time in the past two years. Why did it happen? How can I be so out of tune with the fine place I have come?

> *Warning*: Many visitors were gored by buffalo last year. Buffalo are wild animals. They can run faster than you can, and may attack at any time. *Entering Grizzly Country: A Risk*: Although there are certain dangers associated with wilderness, you have come here voluntarily. . . . *There is no guarantee of your safety*. Bears may attack without warning and for no apparent reason. Respect the wild country and its inhabitants. Follow all rules and regulations.

I must have seen two hundred buffalo in the last three days. I have wondered at their size, their perfect design (they can run faster than a racehorse) despite a form that seems to human eyes unwieldy, their literally ruminative demeanor. They're scary because they're unfamiliar and huge—but their cousins the cows hold no such fascination for us. Why not? It's probably in large part their wildness that fascinates, like the differences between wild horses and domesticated ones or between, at another remove, pet dogs and coyotes. Wildness right there at the surface; barely a moment beneath quiet cud chewing is a wild animal.

Every time I come to Yellowstone, I both hope for and dread an encounter with a bear, especially a grizzly, though I've yet to even sight one. Yet when I'm in the country where they live—one of the few places our rage to tame has left them—I am always on the lookout. The edge is always there. However carefully I've respected the rules that should keep them away, they might come, either to give me a safe glimpse of the most wild or to devour me, and I can't know which.

This is connected to what happened this morning. An anxiety attack brought about by being in bear country, a disguised fear a bear would come to my camp and eat me all up? No, not a bit. I don't think I'm going to encounter a wild bear here at all, damn it. What I did encounter, while wary of the wildness just beneath the surface in my outer environment, was the wildness within myself, the power of the unconscious making itself felt in my legs, my lungs, my entire body.

What happened to me is not so very out of tune with the wilderness at all. I'm only a complex animal myself, and when I enter this ecosystem, I affect it and it affects me. Maybe the demons that live in me, as in everyone—unpredictable, unreasonable, prone to attack without warning or provocation—are more likely to come to the surface here, where the civilities of ordinary life are suspended, where the normal distractions don't defend me against my fears, here where there's nothing I have to do, no one I must care for, no daily responsibilities to meet, no phone to answer, no memo to write, no family crisis to confront.

Yesterday as we drove here, we stopped at a valley overlook and gazed for a long time at the scope of it. Antelope ran on the hillside. Everything was green and golden and quiet. I was filled suddenly and surely with a peacefulness, a silence so good that I thought it surely must hold. The peace held through the day and into the night, when I suddenly rose to pack away my bag in the car, aware that I must "respect the wild country and its inhabitants." Only in this sense was my faceless, powerful attack of fear and dread connected to being in bear country. I consciously respected the possibility of the bear outside. Unconsciously my body and spirit must have been preparing for the bear within.

After my anxiety went wordlessly away, we took the Slough Creek Trail toward Lake McBride. The trail runs right past our camp, and for the first mile or so it's easy enough. Like most back-country trails, it was made by animals more than by people. Animals know what they're doing back here. They make their trails along the literal path of least resistance—around fallen trees rather than over them when possible. The trail runs along by the water, which grows suddenly wild as you travel upland and upstream. Within half a mile you can't hear a thing but the roar of water over rocks, and the view is miraculous—white-water cascades, dappled valleys, blooming meadows.

Animal scat everywhere, but the only large animals we saw were dead, the corpses of elk who didn't make it through the winter. Half a dozen lay in varying states of decay along the five miles or so we hiked this afternoon. I find them compelling and, at a certain stage of return to the elements, beautiful. Some of them today smelled awful, looked grim, were covered with flies and signs of scavenging. Others were beyond decayed flesh, their bones beginning to whiten in the sun.

The most fascinating corpse was a huge mass of golden winter fur forming a blanket in the light. From a distance that's what you could see—shiny fur covering an area maybe five by seven feet, surrounded by green grass near running water. But when I got up close, I could see the flattened remains of the stomach, the legs lying in a position of repose, the black hooves, the head thrown way back. This one was sufficiently decayed that I approached it, looking at its fine bones. I wanted its antlers. I tugged to see if the head would break off—an encouraging crack—but the inside was still black ooze. No. Not that one.

The sense of the natural cycle impresses itself on you with every step in Yellowstone. We were trudging the trail, enjoying the river and the rocks and these signs of both life and death when the trail stopped. From what the map indicated, this trail should lead, in another mile or so, to a valley Mac had hiked yesterday by another route. But it stopped dead at a wall of boulders, and scanning the far shore we saw nothing but rock wall. We began climbing the huge boulders to the side of and over the water, hoping a trail would reemerge just after the next outcropping. And then the next one. Twice we almost turned back because all we could see was more rock, precipitously steep with gaps that could drop you into white water. The brambles were thick and sharp and we didn't have hiking boots suitable for rock climbing as serious as this. I had no Ace bandage on my bad knee, and somewhere in the sweaty mess before the serious rocks, I'd lost my watch. The mosquitoes were bad and we had no bug stuff. In short, we were having an adventure we were not prepared for. Adventure *is* bad planning.

You can get in the mood for a mild adventure if you let yourself. We looked at each other, each checking the other's face for signs that we should turn back now. It was clear that we must have missed a switchback, that we were indeed in the Yellowstone outback ill-prepared for the circumstances, and that although there was certainly a fine valley with a clear trail leading back *somewhere* up ahead, we didn't know where. The dark sky threatened rain again. But each of us found in the other's face the determination to keep going, see it through, find the valley. So we went on, me needing a hand just once when I was concerned that my less good leg wouldn't want to make it over a steep gap. I didn't like to ask, especially since Mac had to come back up a steep rock face to help me—but I knew we'd be in real trouble if either one of us got stupidly hurt, leaving the other to get him or her out of there.

We took turns leading. I'm glad I was in front when abruptly, over the top of a big rock, I spotted the green cup of the valley, the evergreens calmly presiding, the river running quiet, the snow-capped peak in the background, the rock wall surrounding Lake McBride now comforting instead of forbidding. I felt the thrill that hikers seek in the back country, made better because it was hard and uncertain to get there. In a way, the thrill came cheap—not days of trudging well-marked trails with a heavy pack, but a mere few hours of bad planning with nothing but a bottle of water. The valley lay magnificent in late sun. The hillsides weaved in ridiculous bloom. We came out on an old stagecoach road, the scat comforting because it meant people. Bless horseshit.

On the hike back home there was no adventure, just stunning beauty and a quiet you can't get anywhere near a paved road. When the thunder began, we walked briskly to stay warm and get off the high ground we had hiked to the valley. The next valley was our own, and we came across country rather than by way of the road, having by now a fine disdain for the beaten path we'd been so grateful to find. And during all of this, hazardous though some of it was, I felt no traces of the fear that had haunted me back at camp.

I wonder how common these irrational attacks of anxious misery are among people who know back country far better than I? Something like this happened to our friend Susan Puretz while she was canoeing the Yukon. She had better reason—she was in circumstances of major physical risk, and her attack was longer and far worse than mine. She could attribute her anxiety to her surroundings and to what was being asked of her, far more than I could. But what Susan was afraid of, what I was afraid of, may have as much to do with the civilized lives we left behind as with the wilderness we were, for a while, gratefully joined to.

Later I ran into a young man at the water pump who was wondering what trail to take. Although I'd only been in this corner of Yellowstone for a few days, I knew just what to recommend. Is the trail hard? he asked. No, I said, the trail is easy. When it ends, keep going.

LOSING TIME AT LAMAR

Yellowstone National Park

In the dream, I cower among tall grass, or beneath bushes, or behind trees. The place where I hide changes, but the terror never does. I hear the bear slavering and growling, its footsteps drumming the earth. It is looking for me. It sniffs the air, and I know it smells my fear. It will find me. Then it will tear me apart and eat me.—Sherry Simpson, "Where Bears Walk"

How I meet a male bear.
How I am careful not
to insult him. I unbutton
my blouse. He takes out
his teeth. I slip off
my skirt. He turns
his back and works his way
out of his pelt,
which he casts to the ground
for a rug.

He smells of honey
and garlic. I am wet
with human fear. How
can he run away, unfurred?
How can I, without my clothes?

How we prepare a new legend.
—Maxine Kumin, "The Rendezvous"

am fiercely clocked. I'm a scheduler. I am comforted by slicing time into its seconds, minutes, hours. The sound of a clock that chimes the quarter hours is healing to me. I like the neat division of time, imaginary and illusory though I know it to be, into manageable chunks. I need it.

So I couldn't stop thinking about the watch I lost today somewhere in the first mile of a back-country hike at Yellowstone's Slough Creek. Near dusk tonight I set out alone on the trail to see if I could find it. Before I left I promised I would stop when the trail ended and not attempt the first part of a steep rock climb alone in fading light, not because I couldn't make it *up* safely, but because coming back down would be dangerous alone toward dark. I didn't find my watch, I only half kept my promise, and as usual I met the enemy and found out I was she.

This is my bad-manna watch that always gets lost and always comes back to me. But this time it's not going to. It belongs to Yellowstone now, something in between garbage defacing the wilderness and a gift, a sacrifice of one person to the outback. But before you will understand about this watch, I have to explain how keeping time operates in my life, to clarify why I would go seeking it toward sundown alone, when the ranger had just scared our new camping neighbors with bear warnings—and when I myself had risen from a warm sleeping bag the night before to stow my packs of sugarless gum in the van in case a bear might have an interest in something as inert as NutraSweet.

I always wear a watch, consulting it frequently. My mate lost his watch five years ago, and when he told our friend Nancy, she said, "Maybe someone's trying to tell you something." Taking it as a sign, he never replaced the watch, never missed it, and began to extol the virtues of a life not tied to clock time. You get in better tune with natural cycles. You pay closer attention to the position of the sun in the sky. You actually think about time, in its restrictive senses, not more but far less. You realize that a lot of the time, it doesn't matter what time of day it is; and when it does, you can count on clocks in buildings, or even watches on the wrists of office colleagues or strangers in the line at the bank.

I always resisted Mac's efforts to help me change my relationship to time. It became for years a metaphor of our struggle on this, that when it was time (there it is again) to relax, he'd try to get me to take off my watch. For a long time I did it, but finally I felt he was judging my relationship to time and not accepting something essential about me. Eventually I proposed that we simply accept each other's very different orientations to time. He agreed, though sadly, because the implications were large in personal and relational terms.

But *this* watch began subversively to take his side by falling off me. I don't like these new digital gadgets, much prefer a simple face with marks and minute hands. It used to fit well, but when I lost weight it began to slide around on my wrist. A couple of years ago the clasp began to loosen, becoming steadily worse until now it comes unhooked probably a dozen times a day, and if I don't catch it and reclasp it, it falls off. It leaves my wrist altogether about once a day. I've lost it for longer periods many times. I've found it in the car after it's been gone for a couple of days or in my bookbag where it fell off while I was digging. Once it was gone for almost a month. It turned up in a hunk of clay at the studio where I make pottery. Once my friend Norma Hartner saved it for me for a couple of weeks when it was found while I was out of town. It's the watch that won't die.

When we took our hike, I looked at it on my wrist at the beginning, noticed what time we left (11:35 A.M.) and briefly thought I should take it off and put it in a pocket for protection. I'd decided against it because I wanted to see how long it would take us to get to the valley. When I discovered it was gone, a few minutes after the trail ended and we began rock climbing, I went back as far as the head of the hill we climbed at trail's end. But it wasn't there. I'd been making jokes the whole trip about the watch that won't die, pretending I wished it were gone. When I lost it for a few hours somewhere in, I don't know, Nevada maybe, I pretended gladness. Well, there, at least *that's* over. But the next time we stopped the car, there it was gleaming on the floor between the car door and the seat. I spoke of its neurotic attachment to me, like a scruffy stray that follows you home and won't go away once you've fed it.

But now my watch really seemed gone. What chance was there of recovering it from a mile of difficult, root-ridden, fallen-treed, pine-needled, scat-covered, carcass-strewn trail in Yellowstone back country? Neurotic watch? Only a neurotic owner would set out with the aim of recovering such a thing in such a place. So I pretended, to myself and to Mac, that I just felt like an after-dinner solitary hike, that I had this hankering to sit on a rock in the cascades a mile up. I knew, and he knew, that this silly woman was after her watch, her lost and unrecoverable time.

As I leave camp, the new neighbors in the next site ask what I think about bear danger, say the ranger has just given them a grim lecture. Nah, I say. Bears have been around West Thumb the past few days. One was sighted here last week, but unless there's a new sighting I haven't heard about, no bears around here. And I think of my own recent ruminations about the bear within yourself being the one you are more likely to encounter.

So I set off. The first quarter mile, no problem, and of course also no watch. I round the bend away from the campsite and pass the last lone fisherman. Hello, they biting? Only a few nibbles. Pass an elk carcass, then another, stinking quietly. Around another bend. It's very still out here. I accidentally flush out a Barrow's Goldeneye in the grasses by the water and feel its wings whoosh the evening air. The sun is just starting down, slashing the hillside of fallen trees. No fire damage here. I can hear my own footsteps breaking pine needles. I alternate my eyes between the good rough trail—careful of roots, watching for my watch—and the surrounding hills, the meadow on the far shore. It's quiet.

Dusk is good animal-sighting time. They emerge from thick cover to graze the meadows, wander down near water. Maybe I'll see a moose and some mule deer. There's a moose who grazes at dusk near our camp. I always watch for animals in Yellowstone early morning and dusk. You have to be quiet so you won't spook them. Maybe I can walk more quiet if I walk slower, but it's getting a little chilly and a brisk pace is better for body heat. Still I'd like to be quiet so that I might encounter an animal, yes. Who comes out at dusk? Moose, buffalo, mule deer, bear. Grizzly bear. Unpredictable, unreasonable. If you encounter one, it probably won't be at all interested in you, probably move off, unless you accidentally get between a mother and cub, or surprise one. That's what bear bells are for. I bought one to wear out here, but I forgot it back at camp. You want to be quiet to see the other animals, but make noise if you're hiking in bear country to signal them. Their sense of smell is good, but if you're downwind you can surprise them unhappily because their eyesight is bad. So is mine.

Now I'm nervous. I hear the woman asking me anxiously at camp about bear here. The ranger warnings. No. The rangers are necessarily alarmists, they have to be, it's their job. They want you to lock up your water coolers, for Chrissake. It's ridiculous. There's no bear here, it's fine, I should be enjoying this hike. The sun is glistening lower over the trees, angling onto the water. The tree cover is thickening. I can still see just fine, but no watch yet. Is that it there under that clump of pine needles? No. But what do you do if you encounter a bear? Review what I know. Maybe it would be best if I sing or whistle, since I'm not wearing a bear bell.

It's not advisable to hike bear country alone, especially if you're inexperienced, as I am. Travel in pairs. I whistle, making up a tune as I go.

I'm not nervous, really, am I? I'm just having a sensible precautionary thought or two. Right. That sound? I stop, gaze behind me. A bird. This is silly. But in grizzly territory, you always have that slight feeling of gazing over your shoulder. It's good, that slightly exciting edge. It's a mean life that has done away with fear, said Aldo Leopold. But this isn't fear, really, is it? This is just a sensible review.

Well, first, if you encounter a bear, remember he doesn't want to deal with you any more than you do with him. Less, in fact, since he fascinates you, you pay money to see him in captivity, or to hope to see him free, but safely from your vehicle. He isn't fascinated by you unless you have food. Otherwise you're either irrelevant or irritating. Well, yes, but they're also curious animals. You don't run away. That might confuse the bear and turn you by behavior into prey. (This two-legger smells of fear and is fleeing. I'm supposed to run it down.) You retreat slowly. If retreat isn't working, you look for the nearest tree to climb. Grizzlies don't climb well. Okay, trees, plenty of trees here. Could I climb one? Not a chance. These pines have no low branches. My boots aren't that good. I feel stupid whistling. Pretty soon the water will start rushing, making noise. I can begin to hear it past the silence. It will be nice to be distracted by the water. That's what I came here for. I want to sit down on a rock. Maybe find my watch. Of course when the water is rushing, the bear won't hear me ahead of time. And I won't hear it. And the light's getting dimmer. Now then. So if you come on a bear by surprise and you can't retreat slow at a distance and you can't climb a tree, you don't run, you stand your ground.

Could I do that? I've stopped whistling. The stream is noisier now around this bend, it's starting its happy blunder over rocks becoming boulders. I'll practice. I stop in my tracks, stand there, pretend I'm seeing a bear twenty feet in front of me. Even conjuring up the picture scares me. (Is that my watch there? No. Eyes up for bears, down for watches.) The trail is moving rapidly upland, and a few more steps take me to the point where I can hear nothing but the roar of white water. Neither the bear nor I will have any advance notice if we encounter each other now. I step out onto one of the boulders flanking the rapids, stand still, try to enjoy the spectacular view, but when I am quiet for more than a minute the mosquitoes organize a convention. They leave you alone if you keep moving, but even a pause brings an advance expedition. And besides, I stopped on this rock earlier, so of course I am looking in front of me for my watch, and over my shoulder for the bear, who is now approximately the size of

Connecticut in my mind, and whose appearance feels more like a certainty, less like a remote possibility.

When I finally come to trail's end, I stand gazing up the steep incline to the top, where rock-climbing begins. I promised I'd go only this far. Deep sigh. I have figured all along that the watch is most likely to be on this incline, because I had to reach up for branches to grab and pull, and that would have placed a lot of pressure on the weak clasp. So really I should check up the hill. But the reason I promised not to is that getting *down* the hill will be difficult, alone and with mediocre tread. Well.

I've got to go up this, to the top, bear or no. I've come this far and what if my watch is right here, and I hiked over a mile for it and turned back ten yards from where I would have found it? I scan the ridge, calculating alternative and gentler routes down off it and back to the trail. Yes, there's a route, there or perhaps there. I begin up, grabbing branches, slipping once, watching for my watch, which is not here. I pull myself up at the top, fully expecting a bear on hind legs at the edge. Which is not here. I wander the ridge for a while. That's that for my watch. Between this time and backtracking this afternoon, I've covered all the territory in which it could have fallen. The obvious conclusion is that it fell off into the rapids from one of the boulders when I took my shirt off this afternoon. And now I've got to get back to camp, which begins with getting down off this high ridge. First I'll find the way I came up, then take a route through the brush and rocks a little to the left where the incline looked gentler from the trail.

But I can't *find* the way I came up. How is this possible? It's got to be here somewhere. It's amazing how different it all looks from the top, in the midst of thick undergrowth and entirely without a trail. I really cannot find the bugger. And what is that noise in the trees farther up the ridge? Okay. Remain calm. I'm really quite safe. It's amazingly easy to get disoriented and lost in back country—a greenhorn can obviously manage it in mere minutes—but I have the advantage of the river. Follow the river. Just find a way back down off the ridge and to the trail. But every place I try I find a really dangerous drop-off, or when a likable piece of rock leads to the water, it leads right over the rapids, and I'm gazing at a twenty-foot drop into hell.

And then of course there's the bear. It's hungry and it's had a bad day and its stress level is high and it hates me and it's going to go out of its way to find me. But I'm becoming resigned. Obviously I'm going to die out here. It will be tragic. I will have had such a short life, though certainly a productive one. All that wasted potential. I feel sorry about Mac and the kids and my mom, all of whom love me and will miss me. I hope it's not Mac who finds my grotesquely mangled corpse. Park officials will theorize that I haplessly came between the grizzly and her cub. There was no warning because of the water. It's awful, but these things happen in national park back country every few years. Remember that young woman torn to shreds in her tent? The grizzly will be pursued and "removed from the population" by park officials. People will tell the story. Slough Creek is where that woman got mangled to death by a grizzly last summer. They think she tried standing her ground and then tried playing dead, but it didn't work. She was hiking alone at dusk because she was out looking for something she lost on that trail, a ring or a necklace. She died for a trinket. Slough Creek isn't usually heavy bear territory, but it just shows you their range is big, you can't predict. I will be legendary at my college as the man-hating feminist professor who got killed by a bear in a freak accident. A female bear. Clearly not a feminist bear.

I begin bushwhacking and climbing down rocks that are steeper and less safe than the return route I am trying to avoid—which is long lost anyway. I get scratched and bit by bugs while I'm disentangling my legs from brambles. And somehow, after what seems a long time, I come back out on the trail considerably downstream, brushing crud off myself and cursing. There's a few minutes during which I'm so irritated I don't care about bears or watches. I feel as if I might just smack a bear across the muzzle if she looked at me wrong. Walking briskly now back along the trail toward camp, even the sky gets lighter and less forbidding, and I see that I've still got well over an hour of light. Soon I can hear again, because the rapids have ceased and the river seems noble rather than savage.

✳

Somewhere along in here I spot three people hiking upstream, a father and two young boys, one perhaps ten, the other younger. As they pass me, the man says, "See any bears back there?" and I say, "No, darn it." I'm feeling suddenly both safe and silly. I ruined my own hike in our first and greatest national park, where you ought to find peace if not God, by scaring myself and by pursuing lost time—losing more of the precious stuff in the process. Camp is now less than a half mile away, and I begin determinedly to enjoy my walk. (You *vill enjoy* your *valk*, Frau George. Ve haf vays of *making* you enjoy your valk. Sign ze paper.)

And so I am caught genuinely unawares by the sound of deep, faraway, nearby—what *is* it?—snorting? My blood freezes. I get the willies right into my toenails. I look around, but it's too dusky to see well very far into the woods. I begin to walk faster. It comes again, nearer or farther away I can't tell, but it is an animal sound, a wild sound, dangerous. I stop again, start again, clip along. Sure, you thought you were safe, didn't you, just because you're headed down toward camp, toward tents, people, civilization. Civilization? It's merely downstream, that's all, this area is all wilderness, the nearest real settlement is at Tower and that's almost twenty miles away, and even the nearest (and only) paved road is several miles, so what makes you safer here than upstream? You could be dead meat here as well as there, and isn't it just perfect that you were almost back to the illusion of safety when—when I almost step in an elk corpse, a juicy, stinky one. I'm so busy scanning the woods with my eyes that I'm not watching where I'm going. I see it just in time, and veering in horrified disgust, I lose my balance and nearly fall in it rather than step in it. (Always a woman of excess, she couldn't be content with merely stepping in a rotting corpse, no, she had to get right in it and roll around.)

Something about that near miss slows me down and rights my mind, and when I hear the next frightening sound around a bend, it's more definite than anything I've scared myself with so far. Again that involuntary shudder. The animal must be large to make all that ruckus of stomping and branch breaking. When I round the bend I see, in perfectly plain sight, not one but three of the most dangerous wild animals on earth, human teenagers gathering firewood. In the meadow across the river a moose grazes quietly. I sit down on a fallen tree, mentally exhausted, to watch it.

Back at camp now, I'm writing by lantern light. It's a sweet night, with a chill in the free air. Just before dark I shared a deer watch with Emily, the little girl camped at the next site. Everything's fine. I'm sorry about my watch, but it's okay. Now neither Mac nor I has a watch, so we'll just have to do crazy things such as going to sleep when it's dark, waking up when it's light, eating when we're hungry, drinking when we're dry. There's no other choice when you don't have your watch to tell you it's lunchtime, dinnertime, bedtime. The time I lost wasn't the watch, but the waste of looking for it among imaginary beasts. My watch belongs to Yellowstone now. I commend it to earth and water.

❋

The Watch That Won't Die has returned. Taped on the door of the only campsite john this morning was a note that read: FOUND. WOMAN'S WATCH. SITE #1.

I had to go real bad, but I didn't care if it ran down my leg. I raced to Site #1, where the man and woman saw me coming. He was smiling as I approached. He looked familiar. Yes, the man with the two boys that I passed on the trail last night. He said, "I figured it was you. When we saw you last night on the trail, you looked sort of preoccupied. And I thought it was unusual to see a woman out alone at dusk on a trail like that. You must've been looking for it." I skipped any momentary desire to set him right about women alone on trails. I wanted my watch. And besides, he's entirely right. He's dangling it from his hand, and I take it from him, call it sweetheart, kiss its simple, functional face, ask it if it was scared out there all alone, tell it Mama loves it.

I ask where they found it, tell them I'm going to weave them a hand-made basket or make them one of my pots, thanks simply isn't enough, they'd never believe why. Their names are Al and Dorothy Keen, and given the eyesight that found my watch at dusk, and how I feel about them, they are keen indeed. They're from Gladwin, Michigan, a perfect place named for people who have made me so glad, have let me win back a loss. Al explains that thanks is enough, and that anyway, he didn't find it, his little son Adam did. Adam? Oh innocent lovely one, oh first man in the world, namer of the wild animals in the Garden of Eden, of Yellowstone. What planet are these wonderful people from, Disneyland? Where when I wish upon a star, my dreams come true? Is there some religion I could please convert to now? Is Jungian synchronicity eligible for tax-exempt status? But Adam won't want a basket or a pot, so what can I do?

When he rises from sleep and we meet in the parking lot, I am clutching some money for him, and hugging my watch. Adam is five years old and gives new meaning to the term thoughtfulness as applied to humans under the age of consent. He's an observant person, so it was he who saw the watch at the bottom of the incline where the trail ends. I'd looked there but at the moment I might have spotted it, I assume I was glancing for bear attacks from above, probably recalling in loving detail Clint Walker's Homeric encounter with a grizzly on an old episode of "Cheyenne." Paws the size of Pontiacs. No wonder I didn't see it. It seems that Adam is not only unusually observant but also a person of deep social responsibility, because when they got back to the camp with the watch, Adam wanted to knock on all the tent doors until they found me.

He looks mostly at the ground or away toward some far philosophical plain, but occasionally he glances at the five-dollar bill I have secreted in my hand. He may be my magical Adam, but he's also human, civilized, practical, and American. Remembering that his father had already indicated a preference for my mere thanks or, at the most, sending Adam a special present I would make for him, I explain the choices to Adam. I tell him I know he'd be content with my thanks, but that his finding this watch means more than he could know to me. I tell him I have already written a story about it and that he has changed the ending, which makes everything else different, too. So, I ask him, would you like some money I have here for you or would you like me to send you something special?

Adam has said barely a word, so deeply immersed in thought is he, and now his silence becomes profound, quieting the very birds. He looks toward his father beside him in his peripheral vision. He looks at the crisp corner of paper in my hand, held discretely at my side and out of his face so as not to cloud his judgment. He looks at that impenetrable distance. "He's a thinker," his dad says. More silence. I didn't have to think this hard to get a Ph.D.

Finally he says, almost inaudibly, "Send me something." I wonder what went into this decision, the political complexities with which Adam has groped in these moments—his knowledge of what his father prefers, the moral dilemma, the issues of immediate versus deferred gratification (his looks toward the money were full of quiet longing). And is there, waiting in some store at home or perhaps a shop right here in the park, some item Adam has been dreaming of that this money would buy him? Maybe a leather-encased toy knife with a plastic blade or a wooden box that says "Yellowstone" to keep treasures in? Or a T-shirt with a big bear on it, the bear he didn't see on his hikes? Who knows what small Adam has to relinquish to do what his fine folks clearly want?

Or maybe, given his ruminative nature, his longing for distances, he really does prefer to have something unknown coming someday in the mail. Either way, this Adam has already emerged from the innocent garden into the wilderness of choice, consequence, politics. He'd long since fallen from eternity into time by the time he recovered my lost time for me.

SEX AND DEATH AT DEVIL CANYON

Pryor Mountains Wild Horse Range, Wyoming and Montana

Devil Canyon is well named. It's where we let wild horses, those we have not killed or tamed, run free—and where we've tamed or perhaps killed a wild river. Wildness and domestication perfectly, justly combined under the jurisdiction of the NRA, which stands in this case for National Recreation Area instead of National Rifle Association. It's where we no longer let people with rifles kill wild horses—another story altogether—and where, in the name of national recreation, we've killed another living thing.

We searched for wild horses here in the Pryor Mountains Wild Horse Range of the Bighorn Canyon in Wyoming and Montana. It's lucky I saw some wild ones unexpectedly in Great Basin, because here in the range set aside for them, we spotted very few. The herd is about 125 and the range is large, but barely big enough. America has left little to the wild things we have domesticated, removed, displaced, or killed, and this land is rocky and otherwise useless. It's hardly fit for navigation, let alone grazing, except for bighorn sheep. I'm glad to see it just so that I know firsthand how cramped is the freedom we grant other living beings. It reminds me of Indian reservations all over the Southwest, vast stretches of earth not worth exploiting.

The land may be bad in terms of ease and vegetation, but it's still very beautiful. The Bighorn Canyon cuts a deep swath into and through the valleys, buttes, mesas. The most startling sight here is the canyon, a part of the Bighorn surrounded by the horse range and the Crow Indian Reservation. I've seen a lot of canyons, overlooks, mountain waters, surely

America's biggest and most spectacular—the Grand Canyon, Canyonlands, the Grand Canyon of the Yellowstone, Yosemite—and I've never seen anything like this. The river that carved it is absolutely still and perfectly green. In such a barren landscape the quiet created by steep canyon walls, some of red rock with still waters at the bottom, was positively eerie. I have never been in a quieter place. It was unearthly and somehow not good, not right. An occasional wind rumbled from a far corner or an appalling depth, overtaken again by the quietness that says very little lives here. While another place might have had many of the same qualities and felt entirely positive to me—or this place might feel entirely positive to another person or to me when I am another person—this time, the silence and nothingness spoke to my own grim silences.

The feeling was not all negative, because when you are experiencing a deep strain of numbness or emptiness, you like sometimes to have it echoed back by some power or force or place or object. It was compelling because I know that this unnatural natural stillness was created by us, by people who dammed the river downstream to create Bighorn Lake, drowning another 150 feet of canyon wall. It's not the travesty of Lake Powell by any means, and I don't know how much real harm was done—but the rushing water is now a still backwash, a turgidly gorgeous emerald snake so weirdly eternal in tone that Rider Haggard's She might have risen from it lush and naked and not surprised me much, or might equally well have crumbled into ancient flesh and disappeared beneath its perfect surface.

The rockwalls of the canyon were as compelling as the water to me, but for different reasons. I never speak of it out loud, so I'll try to speak it here. Steep walls always draw me toward them, and when I look over the edge, any edge, my stomach and legs fill with that feeling that's somewhere on the border between nausea and sexual arousal. I assume that in this respect my height willies are just like anyone else's. The generic ambiguity—is it sex or death being signaled, felt, feared here?—used to bother me, but no longer does. Sex and death are tightly bonded in the limbic ring, in everyday life, in the kitchens and bedrooms of all of our dailiness, and I figure that anyone who achieves adulthood and doesn't realize this shouldn't be permitted to cross the street unaided. But I'm being ingenuous in part. I realize that for most people, eros and thanatos are fell opposites that have nothing to do with each other. I've found this out in classrooms, kitchens, and living rooms all of my adult life. I've realized it in tentative conversations with friends about this kind of edge—the gaze over any drop-off. The friend shudders, steps back. I shudder, step back.

"Ever notice uh how much that feeling has in common with uh sex?" I ask. The friend looks at me as if I'd just suggested illicit relations with small farm animals. "In common with *what?*" "Sex. You know. Sex?" Short silence while friend considers whether I should be permitted to keep company with decent people, much less educate America's young. "No." End of conversation.

But it's there for me, that connection, and I persist in thinking I am not unusual in this. You peek over the edge: buttery thighs, the momentary frisson, the tickle and prickle in the belly, the whump. I will qualify my blanket assertion about sexuality this far only: I cannot know if sexual arousal feels much this way in men; I know that it often does in women.

But more clearly and obviously the feeling that we get when we lean over the edge is connected with death—both the fear of it and, I think, the wish for it. We back off quickly because of that distressing combination of wish and fear—or because the intense fear of it, of falling off any edge into any void, is combined with the surprising, briefly horrifying, quickly repressed desire to do it, to take the leap and get it over with. (Life, friends, is boring as well as lovely. Too intense, too flat. We must not say so, according to John Berryman's *Dream Songs*.) This brief connection of fear of and wish for death experienced at canyon overlooks and in high buildings actually meets with less resistance in people I've talked to about it than does the connection to sex. In fact, some people close to me have mentioned it to me, and if you bring it up to people who repress it, they look puzzled, but they don't act as if you're pond scum.

It makes perfect sense that a gaze into canyon depths would arouse feelings connected to both life and death, even if you think they're simple opposites. You're always surrounded when you're in wilderness land by evidence of both processes. Life seems pulsingly near, big, important, lush. And yet you feel the necessity for death in the natural cycle, your own creatureliness confronts you, the certain knowledge—even the comfort—of your insignificance and your mortality. There it is. You lean over, curious like all living creatures (if curiosity is broadly enough formulated) to see beyond what you know, into any hidden depth, hungry for a knowledge manifestly without clear use or goal or purpose, except that in humans that desire to know has produced civilization, art, beauty, achievement. What's down there? You want to know, and you feel yourself rushing with the life urge, the precious vitality, the tricky energy.

But what confronts you is also threatening and dangerous. Like any other fragile living thing, you could fall over the precipice. Your step, you realize, is far more precarious than that of the animals who live here. The best Reeboks don't put you in the same class with the bighorn sheep, and even they sometimes fall. Any edge is dangerous and you're suddenly as vulnerable as you are alive—and intensely both. So you back off quickly, quickly, wanting to shed that bump in the belly, the vertigo, the temporary imbalance in the inner ear.

Ah, but if you just let yourself go? Fall in? Wouldn't the exhilaration of flight be fine? Why climb the mountain? Because it's *there*. Why leap over the edge? Because it's *there*.

Here in Devil Canyon, my usual feelings about the edge are strangely intensified by the sheerness of the cliff walls, the narrowness, but especially by the quiet of the water below. More than any other such place I've seen, it brings together the life and death forces. The river snakes around like the serpent of eternity with its tail almost in its mouth. This simply means it's old. The power of long-term geologic process is evident in the depth and curve of the carving. And at the bottom, the river itself must support some life in the manner of a pond, thick perhaps with algae— but it's not a pond, no ducks and frogs live in it, you doubt its hospitality even for fish. It's a dead river. It makes you long to get down there somehow and float on it, but you know your life raft would be a tomb. You'd go nowhere. There's no renewal, only endless turbidity. And still you desire it, the essence of natural passivity, a once free-flowing river's death wish, a process beyond the pleasure principle, hastened ironically by humanity's dedication to that principle—which on this dying planet is linked inexorably with killing our surroundings in order to live in temporary ease and plenty. Our own life wish snakes around itself to embrace our ultimate death wish.

Perhaps all of this is why I found the place so disturbing, much in the way Mrs. Moore in *Passage to India* finds the Marabar Caves unnerving. The silence is too much. The occasional sound—the ooo-boom—in the caverns of the earth, or the bleak wind rumbling through an unseen side canyon, speaks of great spaciousness confined. Nothing that we can know—in the depths of inner earth, of the canyon walls, of our hearts— can answer the need for meaning here. There isn't any. If you meet the buddha on the side of the road, kill him, because there is no buddha, no guru, except ourselves—and in some places, at some moments, we know that we have no wisdom.

My father killed himself when I was a young girl by jumping from a hotel building in Cleveland. Like the child of any suicide, I carry that leap with me into my life. Over forty years later it returns to me when I approach any edge. In addition to the responses I believe are common in everyone, I carry my own personal burden about it that always takes the same form. How did he do it, I wonder. What kind of despair makes a person embrace the fall instead of playing—and I think it is a form of play—with the notion of it? How could anyone do this thing?

I don't think of it judgmentally, nor even with keenly felt grief, because the wound is old and tough. I look at the drop, calculate its relation to eleven hotel stories, and then think of my despairing, determined father on that window ledge at the moment of his leap, think of him hurtling into the falling and smashing on the ground below. In the translation from building to cliff, pavement becomes ground, window ledge becomes crumbling stone, the sight of passing windows the view of sheer cliff, the people on the sidewalk the insects and squirrels, the objects on the street the stones and shrubs of land.

I have this personal reason to be compelled by falls from high places, but it's only a special case of what I believe is a collective fascination. Consider the American film and television industry in the late twentieth century, screen as dream machine, the literal projection of massive cultural forces that connect my personal story to our collective one. I have reason to see it: America is in love with death by falling. Typical prime-time TV on the major networks will give you several juicy falls. Ads for the cop shows and action programs can yield two or three separate previews of horrible descents, usually off buildings; often the ones who splat are bad guys (innocent victims sold separately, but also by falling). Action films must have at least one death by fall. Even PBS has gotten into the act, with "Mystery" and "Masterpiece Theater" often containing fall shots. We seldom let them really fall or leap, of course. We *push* them over. We are also fond of dramatic landings onto burning cars or innocent bystanders. The sound of the smash landing and the look on the face of the corpse are minor genre specialties. One night while switching channels watching junk TV, I was subjected to half a dozen death falls.

I know that my father's leap into eternity has affected fundamental events in my life, and so I always wonder in the face of it, puzzle it, work it over. Sometimes I speak to him from those high places, as one should always speak with the gods of one's life, whether those gods are personal and ancestral or culturally mythic. Gods live in high places, or fall from them to dwell in depths, showing us their feet of clay, dust to dust, ashes to ashes, we all fall down. From their heights they speak to us and teach us vital things—teach us, perhaps, that there are no gods except the ones we create. Our creation of them, personal as our fingers or collective as a million voices chanting to us from the wide earth's dream bogs, is no trivial matter, it does not make them unreal. They are real, and it's we who grant them their power to affect our lives, direct our fates—we as lonely individuals, we as communities. Among our biggest decisions individually and collectively is whether to kill them or to let them live when we meet them on the side of the road, in our peripheral vision, in our longing hearts. I kill my father every time I meet him—or, rather, I let him die. But each time I rise to a height again, there he is, leaning over my shoulder. He does not whisper "leap" in the winds of a canyon or a skyscraper—the voice that does, I believe, is larger than his, collective, species throated. "Learn" is the word that escapes his wind-dry mouth here in Devil Canyon.

PART 2

WORDS YOU

HAVE HEARD, IN A

LANGUAGE YOU

MIGHT KNOW

DISRUPTING THE GAZE; OR,

HOW I TURNED CHICKEN

Burning out on pornography,
Forty-second Street, New York

C onducting the Gaze" was the name of a conference on pornography several years ago, one of many throughout the country in which scholars gather to civilly discuss this savage genre. Entire herds of us earnestly watch pornography and then talk about it in theoretical terms—deconstructive, psychoanalytic, Marxist, feminist. For ten years I participated in such conferences and made professional presentations that were psychoanalytic and feminist. I also published theoretical articles on analyzing heterosexual porn. But then something happened that made me unable to do this kind of research. When conference people would call, I'd say, "I'm sorry, I don't do toilets anymore." What made me stop is not the sort of thing one speaks about through microphones at conferences.

When it happened, I was on my normal New York trip: catch a Broadway play, check the exhibits at the Met, look up my Manhattan buddies, go to a Thai restaurant, see a film at Rockefeller Center, and go down to Forty-second Street to the porn theaters, bookstores, and peep shows. For women the last items would not fit, but for many men of the American middle class the list should sound quite familiar. You simply don't write down that last part, and you don't mention it to your wife or your kids or your girlfriend or your Aunt Mabel when you get back.

To analyze hard-core porn, the female critic has to perform a dizzying mental act, one roughly equivalent, if it were physically possible, to putting her head up her own anus, coming out her mouth, and then talking about it. I am perfectly serious about this metaphor. I don't choose it for its shock value, but because it's accurate, because in porn all body cavities become identical, interchangeable. Media proctology is not comfortable, but I got very good at it. I could continuously "read" pornographic images not only in books but also on film. Not only on film but also at live shows. I could be one of the viewers at the private windows in the back rooms of Forty-second Street shops, where women danced naked, came right up to your window and looked in your eyes, stuck their breasts almost in your face. Not a problem. I'd look at them, smile, take my notes. It's a dirty job, but someone's got to do it—both their job and mine, I suppose.

My direct gaze at pornography was always based on the belief that reading it was a vitally important activity for humanists, and especially for feminists. I did my research in urban combat zones instead of shopping mall dream factories. My eventual plan was a study in which I would link the underworld of hard core to the overworld of American cinema—but not in the simplistic way represented by viewers who claim that, for instance, a Vogue lipstick ad is as harmful, in exactly the same way, as an image from a snuff film. I'm a First Amendment feminist, so I'm among those whom the politicos can accuse of a misplaced sympathy with the rights of exploitive male pornographers. It was lively activity, this debate, this analysis. I almost enjoyed it.

"Gazing" is a psychoanalytic and film theory concept. Cinematic spectatorship (by which I guess I do mean watching movies, yes) is voyeuristic for all of us, whether we are male or female, analytically or unreflectively engaged, just having a good time or taking notes. One problem for the female watcher is the tension between identifying with the female as object and distancing or alienating yourself from her image. Female viewers are doing exactly what straight men do outside of the film frame, on the streets and in the bars and workplaces of our mutual lives—they're watching women, they're spectators, subjects gazing at an object. Women at movies are complicit in the production and objectification of other women. For feminists, it can be a problem even watching movies at the mall.

Judith Mayne says that women viewers vacillate between "masculine" and "feminine" positions when they watch movies. When I first read that, it clicked for me. Yes, that's what I do. I vacillate between looking at women on screen as objects I am observing and as people I identify with. It's hard to do both at once. I'd say the movement is as much a vibration as it is a vacillation. It always felt that way to me. Film theory is primarily based on work in conventional mainstream American cinema or European cinema or legitimate alternative cinema. The cinematic world inhabited by the female spectator of pornography is more deeply alternative, but this doesn't make the mainstream issues less relevant. It deepens their application. So I am writing now from that place in between the "masculine" and "feminine" observer positions.

After ten years, I had to stop conducting, choreographing, assembling my gaze altogether. The focus became too sharp, and then it dissolved. All the montages and homages organized in my mind's eye—and I use the term deliberately, strategically—became overwhelmed by one single image. As a spectator from the outside, I failed utterly to distance myself from the primary power of this image. The story of how I came to end my career of porn watching is disgusting. There is no way to reduce its graphic dimensions. This writing should now bear a warning and a rating: R. Reader discretion advised. Adult language; nudity; adult situations; graphic violence; sex.

On my last porn trip I was interested in the playfulness of heterosexual hard core. A crude form of good-humored parody signals porn's relationship to mainstream Hollywood cinema, with subversive intent. *Every Which Way She Can, Eight to Four, Rambone Does Hollywood, Indiana Joan,* and *Flashpants* were hard-core titles in the 1980s. One reason I thought this parodic aspect of hard core important was that some feminist analyses claim that core porn is humorless as well as viciously misogynist—a misrepresentation that I did not then, and do not now, believe to be true. Analyzing the sources of the humor might be very important. While I have no doubt that such things as snuff films exist—anything possible to be imagined has at some time happened—my own research failed to turn up a single one, with the exception I will now relate.

With me on this trip was my friend Nancy Luce, who had never seen any hard core, straight, gay, or bisexual—the last a misnomer anyway in most porn, because it's usually one man and two women, with the women warming each other up for the man and then servicing him together. I explained to her the ground rules of moving through the neon and into the shops and theaters in the combat zones of any American city: keep your gaze directed firmly ahead; never make eye contact with a man; never look embarrassed or uncertain; move with a sense of purpose; and, if possible, have a man with you. Our male companion, my veteran body and soul guard on those expeditions, stood outside the booths where we pumped quarters into slots in return for a few minutes of hard-core loops. You feed the machine a quarter, while standing inside a tiny, stuffy booth with one stool. If you want to keep viewing, you feed another quarter when the screen goes dark. It's the only form of silent film still shown in America, except at art houses. (It's been replaced, of course, by videotapes.)

We were looking for a certain kind of specialty item that day: animal porn. The image of woman and horse has mythic power, reaching back to the minotaur and the satyr. But each film of women with horses I had seen, and I'd seen quite a few, was a comic, pathetic failure in which a scantily clad woman slinked around a bored horse, who was always eating hay instead of her. I'd seen more earnest erections on my uncle's farm when I was a child than I ever saw in barnyard hard core. I mention our quest, and my admittedly blasé attitude toward it, to indicate that my threshold for disgust was by this time very high, my toleration of anomaly fairly generous, my skin very thick. Bring on the palominos.

Next to the picture of the horse film was one called *Chicken Love*. Thinking to see noble-nostriled prancers dallying with blondes, we accidentally chose the wrong booth. When we dropped the first quarter, we saw a man on a bicycle riding into a farm scene. In the middle of a barnyard stood a woman in a garter belt. Debbie Does the Chicken Coop, I said to Nancy. Was this standard fare, she asked? I told her it was a new one on me. We fed the machine another quarter.

The scene that followed is still hard for me to think about. The man took off his pants, after some perfunctory necking with the woman. He seemed about to engage in sex with her, when suddenly one of them—and I do not remember, interestingly, whether it was the man or the woman—picked up a passing chicken. It ended up in her hands, and while the camera focused closely, she spread the chicken's legs, and after sucking the man's penis to erection, she helped him insert it in the chicken's ovipositor. The screen went black, and we scrambled for another quarter.

I do not remember exactly what I was feeling just then. I know that I was concerned to maintain my confident, veteran, seen-it-all pose in front of my friend, who was appalled. The screen came alive again. The camera focused solely now on the man's penis and the chicken's body cavity. He fucked it—no other word will do—slowly at first, and then he began to pump harder, until finally he was moving like a machine, almost, but not quite, too fast to be believed. The screen went black again. We were both distressed, speaking in earnest tones about the harm this violent activity must be doing to the chicken. Any violence I'd ever seen on film had been clearly, even comically, simulated. This was real. What would happen to the chicken? We had two quarters left.

The image flashed on again. He was still fucking that poor chicken. Finally the man ejaculated, removing his penis from the ovipositor for the obligatory come shot, which, as I explained to Nancy, has to happen every time in porn to aid in the suspension of disbelief, so that the spectator can see that the orgasm is real. Then the man—sort of dorky looking, even with that big equipment, or maybe because of it—tossed the chicken aside, and its body left the frame.

Where is it, where's the chicken? we both asked frantically and out loud, right there in the porn shop, two women huddled together in one of those booths the size of a latrine. We were completely uninterested in the afterglow scene between man and woman. She had holes in her pantyhose. She'd held up that poor chicken for that man to screw. We didn't like her much better than we liked him. And we didn't care if the manager came to tell us it's only one man to a booth. Where's that chicken? Finally the camera returned to it. The chicken's body was discarded against the barn wall.

Then the man approached it and knelt down to it. The screen blackened again. We had one more quarter. That chicken is dead, I said. He fucked that chicken to death, he really did. Nancy said, no, the chicken wasn't dead, probably it was just stunned. It would be okay, the chicken would be okay. One quarter left. In our concern for the welfare of the chicken, we dropped the last quarter on the floor. Nancy leaned over in the cramped, dark, stuffy booth to pick it up. We were both having trouble breathing, partly from lack of oxygen and partly from a strange, at that point still unaccountable, sense of anxiety. From the floor I heard her groan. What is it, I asked, can't you find the quarter? Yes, she said, she'd found it—in a puddle of semen that her fingers had already touched.

The appalling grotesqueness of the situation, and our sense of disgust, came not merely from the slimy fact that her skin had made contact with the bodily fluids of a stranger in a sleaze joint in midtown Manhattan, though that was bad enough. (Check your finger for cuts, are there any breaks in your skin?) Something more was involved, and we knew instantly what had appalled us: some man had found this film sufficiently arousing that he had masturbated to it. If one man had, many had. There was, of course, a market for this kind of film.

We inserted the horrible quarter, dripping with anonymous come— where could we wipe it? on our clothes? you don't take purses stocked with toiletries like Kleenex into porn shops—because we had to see how it ended. Insertion is the right word. We were, at that point, complicit, if we had not been before, and we knew that the distance separating us from our faceless precursor in the booth was slighter than we liked. We were about to discover that it was slighter than we could have imagined. Our only conscious motivations at that point centered around desiring to know whether or not the chicken was dead.

There on the screen now was the man, once again leaning toward the chicken. He touched it for a moment, and then, and then—this was the worst part—he inserted his middle finger into the ovipositor area, which still glistened with his own semen. For a few awful moments, he fingered it, almost gently, almost caressingly. Then he withdrew his finger and turned away. The camera focused again on the chicken's whole body before moving to the man remounting his bicycle to ride off. It's dead, I repeated. That chicken is dead meat. No, countered my friend yet again, you don't know that for sure, it might just be stunned.

All the way back to the hotel we argued about whether the chicken was alive or not. Our tones were earnest. We laughed now and then, for comic relief, about the ways our conclusions about the chicken reflected our basic attitudes toward life—I'm the pessimist, she's the optimist. And the spectacle we presented to ourselves was laughable: two decent women stuffed in a Times Square booth three feet square, arguing passionately about the vital signs of a chicken, scrounging for a come-soaked quarter. But mostly we were not amused.

The image haunted us both. We cut short the porn tour. I didn't have the heart, the stomach for it anymore. Late that night she, the braver of the two of us about facing up to the enemy within, asked me if I had felt any erotic response to the images. Erotic response? Of course not, I said, not to this. Horses, yes. Rough stuff used to do it for me when I was young and stupid, God help us all. But not this. Why? Did she respond to it? Not to the fucking, necessarily, she said—but to the fingering at the end. Something sort of personal about it. Something that would have required assuming a kind of consciousness on the part of the chicken to receive it.

Oh, I said. That. Oh. I don't know. It's possible. Couldn't we talk about something more pleasant? Gall bladder attacks? The deaths of parents? Birth defects?

That is the last time I entered a porn shop. I believe I will never go back. It is important work, but I leave it to those with anesthetized gag reflexes and, I hope, more of that distancing ability I used to have, the kind that permits caregivers to deal with seriously mangled or terminal patients. There's a burnout factor to be contended with in this kind of gazing.

Reflection upon that image, which I still cannot entirely exorcise, has led me to interesting questions, troubling conclusions. I was as jaded a porn watcher as I could have been, yet this single, almost ridiculous image completely disarmed me. Why? I have watched women, real women, engaging in outrageous sexual activity of almost every imaginable variety, including a good bit of poorly acted, clearly simulated violence toward them. Some of them must have been acting under duress. It never reached me. To the degree that I felt I was invited to identify with the constructed object, I suppose I was sometimes insulted, but I never—how shall I say?—I never took it personally.

Always the image provided an opportunity for me to engage in ostensibly detached analysis. I could move with ease in that in-betweenness, maintaining productive spectator tension. It took a level of remove as distant as possible—from homo sapiens to Gallus gallus—for me to take it personally, to experience an actual identification that produced unmanageable disgust, to feel completely implicated, to know that I was gazing upon the image of my own subjugation, my own annihilation.

I have often discussed with Luciana Bohne, an editor of *Film Criticism,* a concern of many feminist film watchers. We become so enamored of finding the patterns, laying down the interpretive and theoretical grid, we find so much pleasure in doing so that we forget to feel implicated as object, in favor of engaging the image as subjects. Our critical and theoretical voyeurism makes us forget just how in between we are, or ought to be. I make no mistake about it now. The spectacle presented to me in that booth was woman as ovipositor, woman as hole, woman as absence. The chicken was the clearest possible stand-in for the pornographic woman who handed it over to him. She participated in her own death in that gesture, as I and my friend perhaps did when we pumped quarters into the machine. The slight but undeniable sense of arousal we experienced, well cloaked by nausea, indicates the depth of the female spectator's unwilling complicity in her own èrasure. It's nearly hard-wired into our circuitry.

And we were not innocent of vacillating between the position of "female" object and "male" subject in a potentially dangerous manner, for we also identified with the "male" by consuming the image, inserting the quarters, paying to see it happen. What was I really appalled by? What was I aroused by? I am afraid I know the answers, and they are the same: annihilating submission. (What are the male masturbators aroused by? Do they identify with the male penis or with the female ovipositor? We cannot assume it's the same for all of them.)

I used to find pornography personally unharmful. I am now suspicious of that complacency. I used to be content at one place in between. Now I occupy another. I'm starting to take it personally. I now participate in take-back-the-night marches and speak publicly on the harmful aspects of porn. I still don't advocate censorship, except for visual child porn produced by the clear violation of a child's civil rights. It's education I believe in now, as I always did. My own education in this has reminded me that ovipositor is mouth, vagina, anus. Only recently did I remember that at the end of *The Story of O,* the most consummate, erotically disturbing, attractively repellent literary pornography of the twentieth century, the main character, O, is trussed up as an owl before her death.

WOMEN IN THE WOODS

St. Mary's, Pennsylvania

When I tried to push his hand away he grabbed my wrists and pinned me against the bridge. Beneath us were jagged rocks. When I looked into his eyes they offered neither tree, nor shade, nor soul. . . . I knew for certain that after he raped me he would crush my head against the rocks and send me off to the sand-choked sea without a trace.

Suddenly, from somewhere deep inside me, a voice came bellowing out. . . . This sound wasn't anything human. It was the shout of a wild animal, a mama wolf protecting her pups, a murderous howl. The cry boomed and echoed through the land as a chorus of NOs: all the NOs I had ever cried, the NO I had wanted to shout to every man who had ever asked too much of me, the NO of every woman who has ever been violated, the NO that for years had been stuck in my throat, damping the power of my voice. The NO was loud and deep and dark and it came from the earth itself, from the spot where I'd bled in the sand.—Natalia Rachel Singer, "Alone in the Sand: Landscape and Feminine Desire"

How many women fantasize about trips to the woods—or the mountains or the desert—with their women friends? Sometimes my wish is to be with just one trusted woman. Sometimes it involves two or three or four with whom I could read, write, speak now and then, be quiet much of the time. We would take long walks, cook for each other, sing songs, dance—but for me the core of the fantasy is actually the privacy you can experience only in the presence of those you know very well and trust completely. It's a being with others that does not violate being with yourself.

No phones, no kids, no lovers or mates or sexual entanglements, no employers or clients, no deadlines, no committee meetings. Many women feel like we're constantly failing someone. Wouldn't it be fine, for a few days, a week, to fail no one, including yourself, and also to succeed at nothing, except reading some poems, resting, laughing? Once I became determined to *do* this, after fifteen years of fruitless fantasizing, I looked for women as deeply needy as I felt—ones willing to disappoint others and deal with the often considerable consequences. But most of my old friends are professionals with kids and husbands and aging parents. They are caretakers of the young and the old, with immense networks of responsibility, as am I. They all said no.

Three years ago I found a group of younger women who had been escaping with each other annually for several years. They were old hands at it. Chris's family has a "hunting camp," as it's called, in the foothills of the Allegheny Mountains of Pennsylvania, on Little Bear Run near the town of St. Mary's. She and our mutual friend Deanna went there every August, joined by whatever other women could be pried loose from their chains of love and guilt.

The first year I joined them was a difficult time in Chris's life, when she had suffered emotional exhaustion bordering on collapse while unearthing memories of childhood sexual abuse in which the identity of the abuser still escaped her consciousness. She was then voluntarily celibate. Coming out of a severe depression, she was discovering destructive patterns she had made for herself in relationships with men. Chris needed a ceremonial retreat that year more than any other: "I wanted to clear my decks, separated from contact with men, to figure out what my problems and issues are." Because she lives in a household controlled by a strong father, "the haven of a women's place" is important. "I had stripped away all of my power moves for walking in the world." She even had trouble leaving her house. Like many such women, she acknowledges anger toward men.

Deanna needed an escape from the gendered world for other reasons. She is the sexual assault coordinator for a women's services organization that helps victims of domestic violence, rape, and abuse. Every day she counsels the survivors of childhood and adult violence. She somehow keeps her astonishingly receptive, unembittered, and finely tuned emotional balance about gender issues, despite the fact that she also experienced a sexually violent episode with a man. She must deal daily with "women's and children's powerlessness in the face of violence." St. Mary's was a place she had gone before to get away from the phone as well as the pain; it was closely associated with calm, peace, and safety. "I carefully choose who to go with, knowing that they must respect my boundaries." She was also close to the inevitable end of her relationship with Adam, who was about to leave for the Peace Corps after having lived with Deanna.

And I needed this retreat. I was in the throes of grief following the dissolution of my almost twenty-year partnership with the man I thought I would always be with. Ours was a feminist relationship, and I was disappointed to discover what I felt was its subtle, enduring sexism. My partner, an activist and feminist in the public and political arenas, was unwilling and perhaps even unable to help me change destructive patterns in our lives, and I had discovered, to my own genuine astonishment, my deep anger about this.

I am also wary of a professional hazard. As a professor of women's studies, I continuously rehearse the history of patriarchy for new generations of students and must be tolerant of their retrogressions, women and men alike. I have battle fatigue in the war of the sexes. The swords that should have been beaten into ploughshares long ago are newly sharpened by backlash. My ex-partner sometimes says that I hate men. I do not think it's true—but I guard against the poisonous potential. In St. Mary's I hoped to examine myself on this issue. I did, but not the way I wanted to.

As we traveled the mountain roads to our retreat, we never once spoke or thought about danger. A few people were concerned about our going to such a remote place—no phones or amenities for many miles—but we dismissed their anxiety as silly. This was Chris's childhood homeland. Despite the fact that it was called a hunting camp, and that some of the camps are hunting bases, her associations with the family cabin were all safe—and female. St. Mary's was where the women and children gathered on the weekend, as many as four generations. They washed dishes and their bodies in the fresh spring water, sat in the meadow and talked, played cards while the kids splashed in the creek. The moss surrounding the cabin was thick and verdant. This place was all about safety.

We passed other camps on the dirt road, most unoccupied, on our way to the very end, where Chris's camp leans against the deep forest. We unpacked the car and hauled our stuff over the footbridge and up to the one-room cabin. Chairs hung on the walls, the linoleum was old and cracked, an ancient fridge racketed to life when we turned on the electricity. No stove—all cooking is done over the firepit outside—so our first job was to find wood for the night fire Deanna would build. There was plenty of kindling, but we were looking for logs and finding none. The late afternoon shadows were deepening.

Just down the road was an occupied camp with two men in attendance and a yard full of wood. We went to their camp and introduced ourselves, asking if we could buy some. "No, you sure can't," said the amiable older one, "but you can have some." The predictable dialogue of protest followed, all parties knowing how it would end: we'd take the wood for free. The younger man, perhaps in his thirties, was probably at least the second generation of owner in this place where camps get passed from parents to children. Denny was friendly and neighborly. The camp was elaborate, with toys and swings in the yard area suggesting that Denny was a family man likely to be joined here by wife and children on the weekend just beginning. He insisted on helping us haul the wood to our camp, where we offered him cookies. He declined, saying he had to get back to work. Deanna the firebuilder set to work. It gets cold suddenly in the Pennsylvania mountains.

That afternoon and evening were among the finest I can remember. We read, rocked on the porch, made leather and bead earrings, ate Chris's fine outdoor feast, and sat around our fire for hours with our feet propped up. We talked about the men and women in our lives, laughed ourselves sick and silly, sang Patsy Cline and the Indigo Girls until our throats ached, drank wine. A couple of times men walked by the camp, and we waved. One man with a young boy stopped to chat briefly and asked if he could camp up the way on Chris's land. She said sure. I didn't know what time it was when we tamped down the fire and went inside to throw our sleeping bags on the floor; later I'd find out that it had been around ten. I remember checking the backdoor lock—a habit when you're a woman who lives in a city.

When it started, I was still sleeping. Chris and Deanna woke to male voices close by, raucous, loud, aggressive. Lying on the floor, they said nothing to each other at first. Both noticed that the light coming from the fire, less than ten feet from the cabin, was way too bright. Perhaps we'd screwed up, and these men were here to help? What the hell, had we started a forest fire? But as they listened to the voices, their hearts first dropped in disappointment, then slowly began chanting with fear. It started vague and diluted, but the men's increasingly drunken talk turned to direct references to us, the women inside the cabin. The metaphor was hunting camp "hospitality."

What kind of hosts are they, those women? Ten o'clock on a Friday night and they're asleep? One of the voices said he was horny. Another said something about pussy. Deanna and Chris started to count voices, thinking, how many are out there? There seemed to be more than half a dozen, most fairly young, one definitely older. Deanna and Chris both recalled the earlier check on locking doors. We were mostly unclothed in our sleeping bags. But surely they wouldn't try the door. They were just drunk, just messing around, soon they'd be gone.

But they didn't go.

When I finally woke up, it had been going on for a long time. Then they started calling out our names. I heard my own name. How could they know our names? Had they been spying on us from the woods while we were at our fire? Had they watched and listened long enough to hear us address each other? Was one of the men who had passed by earlier among them? Had they heard what we were talking about? What had we said to each other, in our assumption of privacy? And then their feet stumbling purposefully to the doors—first the back, then the clump of boots up the steps, across the porch to the front. We were under full siege. No phone, no help, miles from the nearest town. All the other camps were deserted except for Denny's. I kept hoping he or his father would hear it and come to stop it all. Only men can stop men when they're like this.

Then the voices talked in drunken slurs about how they could hear us earlier, laughing and singing. Furtively creeping on hands and knees to the windows, we could see their shadows lit grotesquely by the fire. Yes, at least half a dozen men, maybe more, and a dog. They called us party animals. Someone said something about our brushing our teeth outside earlier, and we knew they had been watching us.

It went on and on, the fire snapping, the men getting louder and drunker. Someone left to get more beer from the truck we now realized was parked near the camp. Then a voice said something about the girls at their own party earlier, how they'd left early and the guys hadn't got laid. Then something about the "rules of the valley," the "way we do things here—if it's your camp, then you get to go first." They were speaking of us as interchangeable holes for sex—for gang rape. They probably also had guns in the truck. All the men around here had guns.

Inside we began to strategize. Please just leave, Deanna was thinking. She remembers the overwhelming feeling of just not wanting to deal with this. Chris was action oriented—she did want to deal with it, because she's the physically strongest one of us, the one who works out. "I felt like the protector person—I'm bigger, I'm stronger, and this is my camp."

The voices grew more aggressive. The edge got nasty. Who were these women from the city, from New York? (They must have seen my license plate.) Who did they think they were? "They've had parties down here before, they never invited us," someone said. (Perhaps a reference to other years my friends had come here?) The talk came back to getting laid, to who was going to go first. They were drinking more, the fire was brighter and higher. "We know you're awake!" they yelled. "You're lying in there pretending not to hear us—come on out now!" It had changed from calling to yelling, almost imperceptibly. The stakes were rising.

We were in genuine danger—and so far from the car that we could never make a break for it. Chris eyed the crowbar on the wall, wondering how far she'd be able to go with it. Could she poke eyes out with it? make herself do that? She decided yes, she could. When Chris stood up to find it, one of them shouted, "You in there, we can see you!" To us she said, "There's a crowbar here. I could try to get it." Deanna said, "Chris, that's not a good idea." She knows more than we do what happens when women defend themselves against male violence, and when she thought of Chris wielding the crowbar in rage—which she'd be capable of doing—she also thought of the men wresting it from her and using it on us.

We plotted possibilities for getting away if they broke down the door. Chris thought of the cow pasture. "If they get in, we could grab hands and start running, I could lead us to the pasture in the dark." But we'd never make it individually in strange woods in the dark, and if Chris, who could do it from familiarity, held our hands, it would slow us all down too much. Undoubtedly, these men knew their woods very well. They'd hunted other prey around here, and with merely human eyesight to guide us in the dark, we'd be no harder to bring down than small game. And like trapped game, our hearts were now thumping in fear. Our extremities were trembling.

Deanna wanted to wait it out. If we wait long enough they'll get bored and leave. But outside their voices were on that edge of aggression that can easily turn all the way over into anger, and if they got *really* angry, we were going to be hurt. Images of stories she's heard in her work life came to Deanna's mind as we lay there, reminded that we were women, reminded of our powerlessness in the face of male violence.

Deanna thought, am I going to be able to remember who they are for identification? She was trying to secure as many details as possible—but having worked in the court system for years, she later said, "I knew I wouldn't have as many as necessary." Chris, familiar with police procedures from quite another angle—her father was a state policeman—had seen their vehicle, and she was trying to remember—Ford? Truck or Bronco? I, more recently awake and disoriented, had no direct experience with these matters and was thinking nothing so coherent.

But both Deanna and Chris, even though they were marshaling evidence and details, knew that unless the worst happened, there was nothing any authorities would do even if we reached them. Though we'd been violated, they'd laugh at us. We'd spend our entire next day talking to some officer who probably knew these men, maybe even hunted with them. And what were we doing out in the woods anyway? Chris had heard her father talk about rape cases and crisis counselors—yeah, they all go weep together, it's so touching—that was his attitude. This sort of assault isn't even close to priority ten. If we got out of this unscathed and reported it, we'd just be a bunch of whiny women.

While Deanna and I were both by this time immobilized by fear, Chris was less so, because, she says, "when I'm afraid, I can't do anything—I was trying to talk myself into being infuriated, because that's the only way to *act*—so I was thinking, those fuckers, I've had it." *Feed this rage* is the thought Chris kept repeating. "I've been violated enough, ever since I can remember, this is not happening again. I can't even remember what happened to me when I was a child, I'm not going to add one more layer to this."

Deanna kept weighing the possibilities. "Are these people who turn to violence? or to talk? How do you tell the difference?" Chris asked, "What's shaking the floor, is that the fridge?" "No," said Deanna, "that's my legs." I think we laughed, but I can't remember. I was too scared myself. Deanna was angry as well as scared. "How dare they have this ability to threaten me? Even if they think it's fun, it's not, I'm really scared."

And then it happened. Without warning, Deanna was on her feet, throwing open the door. Blocking off fear from her abdomen so she could talk, she strode out on the porch, and in a voice of confrontation I've never heard before, one that came from deep within and made her formidable and powerful, she began. "Get out of here! We're not here to entertain you, you get the hell out!" The men stopped, looked at her, briefly considered, then laughed uncertainly. But she wasn't done. "I said get out of here! Who do you think you are? How dare you wake us up? We came out here to get away from people like you! Now go!"

After a silence during which the echoes of Deanna's voice filled the forest around the camp—the silence in which it would all be decided—one of the men said, "Well, welcome to Pennsylvania." Deanna came in on top of him: "That has nothing to do with anything! I said get out of here! We came here for peace and quiet somewhere we don't have to be afraid and you're taking that away from us! We're always exposed to that and this is a place and time not to deal with that. You go right now, and you don't come back!"

Chris had positioned herself on the stairs so that they could feel the threat of her own formidable size—tall, muscular, she looked in the fire-light like what she was: a woman who could not be easily shoved aside. She was determined that if they made a rush on the cabin, they wouldn't get past her. She moved to the middle of the stairway. I stood in back, realizing that Deanna's voice was so fearsome that if they didn't heed it, we were sunk.

But they did. Slowly they began to move off, mumbling imprecations, calling us bitches and cunts. We watched their forms disappear into the night, beyond our sight. We waited a long time before going back in, try-ing to turn ourselves into animals so we could feel the air. We could still hear their voices a distance off, and sometimes it sounded like rising an-ger. We double-checked the locks and tried to go back to sleep, but the woods were dark and we didn't know if they'd come back, maybe having decided they weren't going to take being humiliated by these bitches.

In the dark, we debriefed. For Deanna, these men had "pushed all my buttons about not being able to predict behavior. I didn't want to go to court, have a rape exam, talk to cops." She'd been wondering where the men would hold us down when something rose up in her. She knew the identity of the voice that came through her on the porch. It was her moth-er's. "A lot of what got me to go out there and have my mother's voice come out of me was the fear that Chris would turn it physical, and what would I do then? I was afraid she'd start after them, knowing that I couldn't, and she was ready to. If I had waited and just lay there, I kept feeling the in-evitable would be physical confrontation, whether it was their coming in on us or Chris's responding with violence—so it felt like I had to do some-thing." That mobilized Chris: "Deanna was the mouthpiece. I would be the body." And I? Long ago and far away, I had once been these women's teacher, perhaps sometimes a role model. Now they were mine.

We fell asleep toward dawn, the men's voices still echoing through our trunks, our minds restless and fearful. In the morning, we talked. "It was Denny. The older one was Denny," Deanna said. This genuinely shocked me. "No," I said, "it wasn't, it couldn't have been, he's a family man, a good guy, you could tell that yesterday, he gave us wood, he helped us." I don't know why it was so important to me that it not have been Denny. Chris agreed with Deanna. "It was him."

It was one thing to be assaulted by complete strangers, but somehow another thing to be violated by a neighbor. Hospitality between neighbors had been the ethic under which we'd interacted with him—and, ironically, the metaphor for rape used at the fire, the "rules of the valley." During the siege, I wished Denny would overhear the voices from his camp and come to cut down our enemy. But he was our enemy.

So our intruders did have an identity, or one of them did. We had one more night to spend here, one more precious night before going back to our daily lives for another entire year. For safety's sake, must we leave? Should we go to the police station and spend our day there? No. We would not be driven out. Why should Denny get away with this? We knew who he was and where he stayed—we began to think of revenge. Perhaps we should wait until dark and then go over to his camp and make threatening noises from the woods. But that was out of the question—sometimes men in these woods might really shoot first and ask questions later.

Instead, we team wrote this letter, knowing that even if he wasn't there, we could leave it on his door. We decided to educate him on what he'd done, but not to let him know how frightened we had been—just in case the letter angered him, we didn't want him to have more ammunition to use on us, and the knowledge of our fear, as opposed to our anger, would give him that. We were going to do something that appealed to his decency, something that might shame him, so that this would not happen again, to us or other women, at Denny's hands. We enclosed money for the firewood and the crumbling cookie we'd offered him the day before, took it to his now-empty camp, and put it on the door.

Denny—
    You were with those boys last night.
    Do you think such behavior is harmless? Neighborly? Just good clean fun? What on earth were you thinking? Do you suppose being drunk is any excuse for harassing women in the middle of the night? For participating in highly insulting comments about women and sex—men in the dark woods talking about being horny and wanting sex and trying to open closed doors?
    We do not know who the important women in your own life are, the ones you cherish and care about, but surely you have some. How would you react if they were away in an isolated place where persons

strange to them woke them with the sound of loud, drunk male voices at their own camp fire? Would you feel angry on their behalf by the violation of their peace and privacy? Would you sympathize with their anger at such a midnight confrontation?

Are you aware that *this kind* of threatening behavior happens only to women, and regardless of how many of them are present? Can you understand that, aside from being personal harassment, your actions are an intolerable affront to the community of women and their sexuality?

In some ways, the worst thing about it was that *you* were there. We liked you and trusted you because of the neighborly generosity you showed us earlier in the day. We thought you were a good person. We were grateful for your help and your friendliness. You thoughtlessly destroyed that ability to trust you. It is such mindless uses of power that engender a deep wariness and distrust in women for the opposite sex. You do not seem like a man who would want to be part of the reason that women must distrust men. You know better. We thought you were a grown-up.

We don't want your firewood free. (It *wasn't* free, was it? We paid dearly for it in the night.) Here's five bucks. The wood is worth more, but we have to fix the chair that your pond-scum rowdies wrecked.

Diana and Chris and Deanna

P.S. Here's a cookie. Don't choke on it. If you want to talk to us about this, you know where to find us—in the daylight, where we can *see* you.

Of course Denny never showed up. But we spent a safe night, stayed out at our fire, refused to be driven in by fear. The next day we left, bumping along the dirt road of empty hunting camps. At home one of our men, with the best motives, tried to get through to us that going to the woods wasn't safe, that perhaps we didn't understand how bad it might have been, that we were really in danger of rape, maybe of more. He urged us not to take this chance again, told us that we, of all people, should know that we do live in a patriarchy where men are violent toward women, that he didn't want us to be a statistic in that record, that to be realistic we must not place ourselves where even the ordinary constraints, the force of the social contract, did not apply. And the Pennsylvania deer-hunter forests were such a place.

We have considered all of that. We know it's true. And yet we cannot live always in fear, denying ourselves the liberties of our humanity, our freedom of movement. It was important to us to return to the woods.

✳

It is two years later. Deanna is still working in women's services, still helping other women heal and wondering how staying in this profession might be wounding her own spirit; but she is strong, her heart still intact, her smile still so beautiful it stops strangers. I continue dealing death blows to my own demons, who sometimes seem to have the gift of eternal life. But some days I am downright happy.

Chris has remembered the identity of her childhood abusers—more than one. Discovering their identities was a process that involved a great betrayal of love, trust, and authority over the child she was, the adult survivor she has become. She is healing and is about to embark upon the riskiest adventure she has faced since confronting the men in her memory: she has permitted herself to trust again by trusting us, her female friends; found that affection and fidelity of heart is not always betrayed; discovered in herself a secret so startling it always brings her to tears when she lets herself know it: *she* can still love. She has fallen in love with my oldest male friend and will soon be leaving to live with Richard in Santa Fe.

We three women have cemented our bond with a ceremony we called our "celebration of befriending" and our "marriage." We did it in the late summer of this, the year that will probably take us all to different lives. We are going to St. Mary's once again before we part, bringing with us our finest friend, Susan, who officiated for us in our vows of friendship, and my granddaughter's mother Mary Ellen, a young woman just awakening to feminism. We haul our packs and bags over the footbridge to the grass, where I walk Mary Ellen in bare feet through that moss as thick as feather pillows.

✳

For the next four days we weave baskets on the old porch, build fires to cook over (fire veggies, soups, Tex-Mex), haul in the chairs just as the rains come, accompany each other to the outhouse (so the monsters that live at the bottom can't bite Chris in the butt), sing our old songs (Patsy and Van and the Indigos and Janis and Joni and Gordon) and our new (Toni Childs, Tori Amos, John Gorka). We read out loud and we write in our journals—perhaps to our lovers or children, mostly to ourselves. The sun comes and goes, as does the talk of sex, so raunchy or else so awful that we could never speak it in the city. Bike rides. Mushroom picking.

We confess the things we did as kids that still haunt us—the roadkill Mary Ellen put under the pillow of a girl she didn't like; my emotional torture of pets; Chris's shoplifting binges. (Deanna was either hopelessly good or else she lies; Susan had left by then or she'd have topped us all.) Our sins are mutually known, completely forgiven. We offer each other the absolution we cannot offer ourselves alone. The creek makes it sound like rain all the time. When it does rain, it is fearsome, thunder that brings us up out of our chairs, lightning that scorches the cabin. All of us weep for our losses, or for those of people we love, at some point during these days, except Susan, who wants to but cannot. Sometimes we swaydance with each other, coupling off. Dancing with her makes me miss Susan, whom I seldom see. We used to dance when we were housemates.

The last night we stay up until three. We can't stop laughing. I ask for someone to sing us to sleep. Deanna stills us with Janis Ian's old "Lullabye," her clear voice sounding over the murmur of the creek. "Lie down and don't you wake til morning, / Close your eyes all through the night. / This is a lovers' lullabye."

On the final morning we go to the creek and Mary Ellen, tentative at first but now at home not only with us but with the woods, assigns survival parts in case we get stranded here for, oh, say, a year. We throw our hair into the creek at the rapids, feeling it pull the roots downstream.

✳

Mary Ellen asks, in the safety of last-day light, whether any of us was a little scared around the late-night fires, surrounded by the darkness that could have hidden men like those who assaulted us. We all answer that we were not afraid at all, and I see that what I am saying is absolutely true. After the first day, when we told Mary Ellen the full story—the sound of a chainsaw roaring in the background from another camp—there'd been no talk of fear, of men in the night. We always checked the locks on the doors, one of us quietly asking if the back had been double-locked, but no one said, "What if they come again?"

I had thought of that night only once, when I crossed the creek alone and walked up to the woods, thinking about the demons and lovers and good men and bad men in my life. As I came back over the footbridge, I heard voices from Denny's camp—not those of decent men who could hurt people under the influence of mob psychology, testosterone, beer, and desperation, but those of children—querulous, intimate, sober, strong, male and female. I knew I was essentially in a world of these children's voices, offering safety even from a distance, and of women who take care of each other's spirits.

Speaking it to Mary Ellen, I knew my function in this. Deanna was the fearless voice of women in the night. Chris was the body of women ready to fight. And I was the story catcher, the one who, in our tribe, would tell what happened so that others might learn things that are useful for the spirit and the body to know. I was speaking for all of us when I said, No, we aren't afraid anymore. We reclaimed the woods when we faced them down. These woods belong to us.

WORDS YOU HAVE HEARD, IN A

LANGUAGE YOU MIGHT KNOW

Amtrak Christmas, Erie to Manhattan

I t takes about eleven hours to travel by train from Erie, Pennsylvania, to Penn Station. I told my companion we could look forward to hours of rambly, rumbling tracks, vibrations of calm suffusing us, making us sleepy, asking of us only the vacancy of mind we long for. But this is what happens instead: I am coming in and out of a half sleep, feeling crazed from two weeks of sleep deprivation and night sweats and dreams of death, when I wake to Dirk saying, *Lord, someone is giving him mouth to mouth resuscitation.* My head swivels around. A few rows back a man is lying on the floor of the train car, a woman bent over him blowing into his mouth. Then someone with a knowing voice is saying, *It's taking too long for him to come out of it. Someone get help!* Dirk and the man across from us are up moving, uniformed personnel pour in, and then the car is teeming with people asking if there is a doctor on the train. A crowd surrounds the man on the floor so tight that I don't see how he can breathe. I am having trouble breathing myself, because something feels familiar here.

He is screaming out words and sounds, calling in what seems another language—we are in Turkey, we are in India, we are at the least in Italy, here in my dreams those sounds between language and anguish. Then it is distinct, it is English, he is saying, *I'm okay, I'm all right, it's all right. Let me up.* But they don't. Something here feels uncanny, as if I'm on the wrong side of a window I've looked through before. *What is it, what's wrong,* I ask someone who's been in the tight knot of people around him. She says it's seizures. He is having a seizure of some kind. My response is so loaded that it's physical. It is all I can do to stay in my seat. If I get up, if I push my way through, if I say anything, I will end up at the center of all this, and I cannot do that right now, not even for a fellow epileptic. This is why I feel that odd sense of having almost been here before. I am an epileptic who has been in remission for years. My last seizure was three years ago, but over my lifetime I have had many in public places. I know what it is like to be this man on a floor coming to consciousness, or trying to, after a seizure, surrounded by people who will not leave you alone, who refuse your pleas that they back off and let you breathe, that they do not call hospitals and authorities.

The car is still full of people when they begin to stop the train. They are sending medics into this rural New York State dawn on Christmas morning. I drift in and out of something like consciousness, something like anesthesia, listening to a woman say, *They're doing it all wrong if it's seizures, they have him on his belly and he's hit his nose and it's bleeding.* When he comes to enough to say, again, *I'm all right, it's all right, don't stop the train,* they tell him to just calm down, that the ambulance will be here shortly. The medics pull up beside the train with the ambulance. I can just make them out in the gradual gray. It's too late to intervene, but I am hoping he can do the trick that convinces the ambulance staff he's okay, so he doesn't have to get off the train here in Nowhere, New York. He has just come back from the nowhere of a seizure, and soon he will be in a car with a siren screaming to a hospital in a strange town on Christmas morning, when surely he, like all of us, was going somewhere. I whisper to my travel mate, *He's all right, you know, if he's an epileptic he's really okay by now.*

I never saw it happen before. I was always on the inside, where he is. This is my first look at the kind of havoc I have caused, because before I was at the core of the bleating crowd hanging over my body, frightened I am dying, I am possessed, I am having a heart attack, they will have to see me leave this life, they cannot deal with it, they don't know what to do, they cannot let me alone, they cannot watch, they cannot, above all, turn away from the spectacle of the woman with limbs flailing, eyes rolling back in her head, taking down furniture as she falls, or sometimes just going rigid, skin turning gray, surely, surely dying, perhaps dead.

Or so I have imagined the scene, judging from their faces later, their halting words, their answers to my questions. Always I come out of it in these stages: before *Where I Am,* there must be *Who I Am.* Before *Who I Am,* first *That I Am. That I Am* is what must be established. Once I figure that out, eyes still closed, I hear their voices from universes away, chattering like aliens in space. They have taken me to a ship and I will never see my home again, if I have a home. I exist for that while only to long for a home.

Remain with your eyes closed while the voices clarify slowly, become human, begin to form words you have heard before in a language you might know. Then you know that you are someone who once knew some words with which to reach others. If you could make your mouth work, perhaps you, like they, could talk. It will not move.

Bide your time. Stay here drifting, in and out, increasingly aware you are not dead and so you are also not free—there must be explanations. When you open your eyes you must meet other eyes, surely human, and convince them that although they just saw you jerking like a shot deer, you are now perfectly all right. For them you have come from the womb of the touched. You are a believer speaking in tongues or a demon possessed by evil energies unspeakable, from fires burning hot as their childhood fiends. You have done this right in their faces, they are implicated, and you do not know it. You are the only one who was not there.

The train has fully stopped now, and down the tracks they tell the tale in the other cars—there's a man back there having some sort of a fit. Meanwhile inside your face mask, you prepare. Soon you will have to open your eyes, you cannot delay it much longer. To convince them, you will have to give your name, rank, serial number. Otherwise they will lop you off the train. Increasingly yourself and able to decipher, you count to ten behind your eyelids. Yes, soon.

I am in a doctor's office, perfectly fine, checking out in a line half an hour after he has done some unspeakable procedure to me in an examining room. I smile and joke with the woman behind me. That is all I know before the tunnel, the rushing wind, the focused, bitterly riveting buzz in my head that is my firm signal, past the point of no return. I do not know how long passes. I do not know that my body has thrown itself all over the floor space, my hand has gripped a chair and pulled it over me.

I am in a yoga class, calmly stretching. The tunnel, the din, the wind, the dying, the coming back to meet gazes serious and stunned. I open my mouth to form the words, finally know that yes, I am saying the right ones. But they cannot possibly believe me. I have exploded and reconstituted in mere minutes and I am claiming I am fine? It could not possibly be true. I am Dracula's Renquist. I am a crazy woman in a snakepit. My head swivels all the way around on its stem. They want to cross themselves, to call the exorcist.

In a restaurant, eating chicken after pottery class, it happens as I wend my way to the bathroom. I come to consciousness on the bar, where they have placed me while they call the ambulance. Waking wet, I wonder if I have peed, but it's only beer from the bar. Over me my friend's face congeals and forms, recedes and comes in. He is terrified, and to help him through it I say, before I really feel it, the simple chant *I'm all right, it's okay*. He says, *You were dead, I saw you dead, you were twitching and then you stopped, you went rigid, you didn't move, you were gray, your eyes were gone.* (Versatile, I do grand mal and petit, catatonia, rigidity.) *You were dead,* he says again. Then the dead woman rises from the bar, because I see the medics with the stretcher, and I know they are about to take me to the hospital. If that happens it will be hours and dollars before I can get free. I sit up straight, name my name, prove myself sane. I tell them where I work. I prove that I know what day of the week it is (Wednesday, pottery day, I remember just in time), recite the date, tell them who is president, what year it is. This is exhausting work. I just want to go home. I am all right.

In between bleats of something, not pain, called out from the afterbirth, he says again: *I am all right.* Unwilling to make myself a center, or to take the chance that I am wrong, I sit still in my seat, honoring him the only way I can—by not turning around to stare. I form the words in my own mouth that he is forming in his, trying to send him strength. *I'm all right, don't make me get off the train.* But the ambulance is here, they are helping him off. I did not wish hard enough or speak to the saints of intervention loud enough. Now they are putting him in the back. He insists on walking to show them that he can—a little unsteady but it's genuine walking. He will waste half his Christmas proving his human balance. As for me, I belong not safe in Penn Station but in the dark back of an ambulance with a man I don't know, speaking in tongues, speeding toward another oblivion.

A WOMAN RALLYING FOR THE ROAD

Pro-choice march, Washington, D.C., April 1992

Professionally and personally, everything in my life seems to have aborted. I'm pro-choice, all right. What's happened to me is about choices—the ones I've made, the ones I haven't. I'm liberated, I choose my own roads. Right now that's Interstate 79 to Interstate 80.

My work life just degenerated into accusations by colleagues and administration about my professional behavior. I'm thought to have organized a feminist boycott of a male colleague in order to punish him for his attitudes toward women and his vote on a personnel matter. It never crossed my mind to do anything so openly incendiary at my workplace. Even if I'd thought it was a good idea, I'm much too tired to organize. That takes time and energy. I attend political events planned by others—such as this march in Washington—but I don't instigate action. This colleague is completely irrelevant to me, and I to him; as far as I know, we bear each other no ill will. This perception of my secret campaign against him was constructed of whole loincloth by other people. Yet the reverberations have affected my life for almost a month.

My delicately recorked personal life in the trenches of the gender wars has also popped open again, spraying pheromones on everyone in sight. My relationship of the last couple of years has ended, at this very moment, this weekend, a few hours before I left on this trip. Dirk is moving out while I'm on my way to Washington instead of coming to march with me, as we'd planned. I'm in Somerset, Pennsylvania, near the West Virginia border. I'm picking up my part-time daughter, Krissy, and granddaughter Ayron from a bus, then driving on to Arlington tonight, where we'll meet

Bernie and Mary Ellen and Sequoia (my son and his partner and grand-daughter). We'll march tomorrow in Washington, three generations of us, without my absent lover. I feel like I don't need to be with a man. Hell with him. Yes. Straight to hell with the whole notion of pair bonding. It's for the birds, literally, and not many species of *them*, at that. With humans it just doesn't work for long, and most of us know it. We engage in a massive, collective hallucination that it does. Our need to do so must be very great, to sustain such a level of denial of the obvious.

I've been driving from western New York through Pennsylvania thinking about what it's like to be, for the first time in my life, a woman alone on the road. I've chosen it. I've chosen to end three relationships with men in the last three years. One of the relationships goes back twenty years, one three or four, this new one almost two. Somehow the endings all came in about the last three years. I find myself choosing life without a lover, with nobody waiting in the wings—or nobody I want to be with. I still love one of those three men like an incurable disease, another like a badly wounded brother. This third partnership is too new to know what I love him like. But I do love Dirk. Mac is a jagged whole-body scar. Without him I was temporarily quadriplegic. A man named Jeff is last year's torn ligaments healing; I cannot let him be part of my life, not ever again. It was too destructive for both of us. With Dirk the pain is immediate: I just finished hammering my own thumb. The welt is rising.

What's it going to be like not to be on the partnered highway I'm used to writing and thinking from? I'm usually the passenger with the notebook. For years my companions were the indefatigable drivers. The road alone is new, and I'm driving exhausted. I've almost had two car accidents in the past two days. I've been to see an old friend widowed three years ago who has just started a new life near Pittsburgh. She's still gutted by loss. Then I went to a women's studies conference in Greensburg. I left there today simply *full* of unsavory revelations about myself. The conference ended with seventy academic women in a circle, each stepping forward and saying out loud the thing she most fears in life. Now, these kinds of ceremonies give me the shudders. But, I thought, there are times for this sort of thing, my dear. I didn't know if I could do this, nor what I'd say. Where's the door? The moment of panic, and then, and then I did it, I stepped forward and found myself saying, "I am afraid to be without a man, I am afraid to be alone," in front of seventy strangers. And it's true, of course. Having said it out loud, I can't deny it.

I haven't been able to eat or sleep for about ten days with any regularity, averaging between two and four hours of sleep a night. I've had two meals, maybe three, in that time. Mostly I force myself to eat standing up at kitchen counters—a bagel here, a banana there, a hunk of cheese, a fingerful of peanut butter. I'm losing weight I can't afford to lose. I'm working long hours, half falling out of bed at six o'clock, going strong until late afternoon, tanking up on coffee to keep working till midnight, falling back into bed, unable to function but also unable to sleep yet from the caffeine, yawning in and out, achieving REM sleep shortly before the alarm goes off.

So when I got on the road without a co-driver, although I was awake and alert, I knew I was not altogether safe. One's mother wouldn't want one on the road like this. The most unsafe thing about traveling alone is trying to figure out where you are by using the road atlas while you're driving. For immediate danger to your life, it's worse than eating chicken skin. You go off the road while trying to see what that sign says, especially when you've got night vision problems. The near accidents taught me something about sex and driving that I think applies to my professional and personal relationships. It's a road tale and a gender parable. In the first near miss, I had checked my rearview mirror before shifting lanes but hadn't turned around. A guy in a truck was in my blind spot, and I started to pull into the lane. It was close. He shook his fists and made violent gestures at me as he passed by, yelling behind closed glass those imprecations I could not hear.

Today the same thing happened in reverse. Another man in a truck started to pull in front of *me*. My immediate response was to hit the brakes, and to think, hey, mister, whew, but it's okay, I understand—I was in your blind spot, wasn't I? I knew he was embarrassed and chagrined and scared. My response was automatic to understand that we all have blind spots. I know some women do shake their fists and some men don't, but this pattern of driver response is pretty clearly gendered. Men are enculturated to respond with aggression and women with empathy. Estrogen surges. Testosterone triggers. I keep telling myself that that, too, is not anyone's fault. Isn't that feminine of me.

I began to look at everyone I passed on Route 76, to see how many women alone were behind the wheel. Of course there would be women going home from work, but that stretch of road was more remote than a commuter belt, more like a superhighway, a trucker route. I saw a lot of men in cars alone, some men with women, and some women with children, but I didn't see any women alone in that twenty-mile stretch, not one. That's probably an uncharacteristically pure sample, but I wonder: on the roads of America, how many of the people traveling long haul from one place to another are women? I think not many. We've got to learn to travel alone.

I love and I hate the road. I hate driving long haul—the exhaustion, the flatness, the way it goes on and on, especially out west. But I love the sense of not knowing what's around the curve, the next granite outcrop or waterfall beside the road or sudden field of absurdly wild flowers or urban landscape of factories or nuclear power plants or towns with wonderful names like Husband or Mars—both of which I went through yesterday. A Husband from Mars. I once had one of those. I'm wondering how living alone and driving alone are going to intersect. I'm wondering, while looking at a flat, dead, not-quite-spring-yet sky, why I find myself not able to see or to feel spring coming? I'm wondering when that sense of resurrection and possibility will hit the spirit of my life, as well as when it will come on the road. In travel I often feel the newness first, the flat sameness next, and then I start to enjoy the open-ended flux. This is an intense time and a flat time for me. The road feels both intense and flat.

Because I'm on my way to pick up family, I'm about to become one of those women driving with another woman and a child. We three will join another woman, a man, a child. Then all of us will join half a million women and men and children in our country's capital to tell the government that women are sick of the control of their lives residing in the hands of rich old white men in high-back leather chairs. It's deeply lunatic, that arrangement.

But the old white men built these roads, and they're beautiful. The network of American highways is among the great accomplishments of American men. Men have been the primary engineers, the designers, the people who actually built those roads, the people who fix them. I'm parked in the back of a Day's Inn right now, looking at what's driving on the road— semi after semi, their rigs night bright, always mysterious. These roads are driven by men in trucks, men in pickups, men in cars, moving cargo from place to place. There's benign power in that. Men have created the network that ties one place to another. Men have been best at linking places together, moving the frontier one more settlement out. Women have been best at building connections among the people in those places. Stirring my coffee here, getting ready to go to the bus stop, I am starting to feel good about men. I'm celebrating our differences, I'm politically correct, I'm appreciating diversity, all right? We can all get along. We need not ruin the planet because of our fear of each other, our desire for each other.

I pull up to the bus stop, down a remote side street, ten minutes early to wait for Kris and Ayron coming here to meet me from Pittsburgh. If the bus gets in early, I don't want them cold and waiting and nervous in a strange town. There's a guy waiting for the bus. He comes over to my van. I'm not even parked yet when he begins to approach. His name is Tien, he's from Taiwan, he cooks in Chinese restaurants. Sweet young man. He used to study folklore and is now unemployed and living somewhere around here. He talks a lot. Fine, I'll be polite, I'll listen. I don't really want to. I want my last few moments of alone. I can barely hear myself. My life is a mess. I can't think. I have a headache.

"Where you going?" he asks. I say, "A march for women's rights in Washington, D.C." He says, "Can I come and march for woman right, too?" I say, "What?" He says, "I would like to come with you, I would like to go to Washington, D.C. and learn about American woman right, and march for woman right with you. May I come? Will you please give me a ride?" Feeling like dogmeat about this, I graciously explain that I cannot, that I am going to have a full van soon. I thank him for his interest in American women's rights. But he will not give up. Now he is saying, "Can I call you? Will you give me your phone number? Can I come and visit you in Erie, Pennsylvania?" He says both city and state. I say, "No, I really don't have time in my life for new people. It's nice having a conversation with you here, but that's it." Still he will not stop. He keeps pressing—for contact, for friendship, for a ride, for a phone number, for my address.

I get crisp and he finally seems to get the idea. He says, "Well, it was nice to talk to you," and reaches out to shake my hand. I return his shake. But then he grabs my hand to his mouth and kisses it. I say good-bye, roll up the window. He thought the bus was coming and when he realizes it isn't yet, he starts to come over to my van again. So I pull out quick and park up the road at the donut shop. I can't even occupy a public place to pick up someone from a bus without some guy. . . I don't even need to complete this sentence. Every woman over eight and under eighty knows this story, and so do all the men in our lives who must hear us gripe about it. It's the cultural difference as well as the gender problem in this case, because you want to be friendly to immigrants. You want to be welcoming them, you don't want to be paranoid and ethnophobic.

And yet, though the styles differ, perhaps men are men the world around. Tien was, in a sense, putting the make on me. In the workplace, it would be called harassment. Here it's just business as usual and there's no recourse. *I'm so tired of it.* I hate fending off the moves and I hate being afraid. I had that feeling when he kept pressing, and I realized that one of his hands had been in his pocket for a long time. *That* feeling. Is this a psycho-pup who's going to pull a knife now? That's paranoid. And yet if you are approached by somebody who, rather than making conversation, tries to push his way into your life, then you start thinking that way, if you're a woman. A woman on the road alone is in danger, and she knows it. My last business trip alone to New York, I was followed all over Grand Central and Penn Station. I was followed in the subway because I was carrying all my luggage on my back. I appeared, and was, vulnerable. I could be stolen from, I could be pickpocketed, I could be assaulted, I could be raped, I could be killed. I felt the shadow of that fear, even with this nice man.

Asian men aren't as threatening in size, an issue I've discussed with my friend, Michael Ichiyama, a Japanese-American psychologist who studies the position of Asian men in American patriarchy. But the feeling still says: stranger, can't trust him, male, can't trust him. Women feel this on the road intensely, that vulnerability when they're in a strange city or even when they're in the relative protection of a van. And we feel it at home. We fear the intruder. The intruder can take the lethal form of somebody who breaks your ribs or the annoying, *almost* threatening form of somebody trying to push his face into yours, be with you, get close to you. I hate them both. I'm a friendly person. I reach back when reached out to. But not for this. Life keeps teaching me that I can't be friendly. When I saw Tien approaching my car, should I have put my window up and locked my doors? Yet now I feel I should get back down to the bus station because what if the bus has come and Tien has decided not to get on it, and Krissy and five-year-old Ayron are being harassed by him. I keep thinking the bus would have to pass by here, where I am parked. It would come on Route 76. But I don't know for certain; I don't know how much longer I should wait before I go to see if everything's all right. But if I drive back to the bus station, Tien will come to the van again.

As soon as I pick up Kris, we won't have to worry if we stop to get something to eat and somebody hits on us. We can handle it. But Thelma and Louise were together and that didn't prevent violence. That was a fiction, but the actuality it imitates is the same, except that you don't get to shoot the son of a bitch. That kind of thinking, for Kris, is not theoretical, not far-fetched, not remote. Kris was asleep when a man broke in and raped her own mother, just down the hall from her. She was ten. It's not remote for me either. It's funny how fast urban life makes you leap to violent possibilities rather than to merely irritating ones.

Now I wish Dirk were here. I admit it, I wish I were on the road with a man, because then this wouldn't have happened, not in this way. Even if Tien had approached the van, I wouldn't have been afraid. He'd have understood that I belonged to this male, he'd have understood the universal language of possession of the female. Now there's just this little kernel of fear. The bus station is down a dark side street. It's closed up and nobody's around. It's not a clean, well-lighted place.

If I go back and the bus isn't in, it's so cold that Tien's going to try to get in the van. Then what am I going to do? While I am thinking this over, a human form takes shape along the road, coming toward me. It's Tien. He's found me, a half mile away from the station. He comes to the window of my van and says, "Do you know where the bus is?" Right then, fifty yards down the road, the bus is pulling in to the tollbooth. The station is down the road the other direction, but I do not, cannot offer this man a ride. "There it is, right there," I say, "better run." He runs, I drive, the bus pulls in slow and backs up. When the passengers begin to come off, I feel at last safe because there are bus fumes and a male driver right here.

Krissy is a young woman of strong opinions. She comes stomping off the bus issuing me orders, right in front of the driver. "Don't you *ever* put me on a bus again!" It's good to hear the voice of a woman who is not feeling at all vulnerable. She's furious. She has a travel horror story involving missing a bus in Erie and chasing it to Pittsburgh with Dirk. She's snarling while Ayron is trying to say hello, when I realize that Tien and the bus driver are having a disagreement. Tien wants to get on the bus and the driver is saying, "You don't have the right ticket to get on this bus to go here." I say to Kris, "Get in the van *now*, get in the *van*, hurry *up*." I herd her, still bitching, into the back of the van and come as close as I can, under the circumstances, to peeling out. I can see what would otherwise happen. Tien would end up standing in the dark, in the cold—by this time it's snowing—alone and begging for a ride again. I would feel guilty, empathetic, responsible. We must be gone before this can happen.

Yet just beneath the irritation and the small kernel of fear, that sense of guilt and responsibility comes to me anyway. Tien is just a harmless man who doesn't know the rules of this culture well enough to know that his behavior is improper. He was really just pressing for hospitality and doesn't know that this isn't socially acceptable. Another voice in me gives a cynical cluck and says, you're a sap. He does know. An American man would have gone about it differently. He wouldn't have used the same sort of ingratiation. The style would be different. But American men at bus stations do hit on women for money or a ride or conversation or sex, and none of it is acceptable or safe except conversation, if that.

After we're safely away from the scene, I'm so relieved that I wish we could stop somewhere for a while, any roadhouse. I'd make Krissy dance, which she hates to do on command. Ayron and I feel different about that. Ayron will dance anywhere and she's great at it. I am pleased that she's so free with her musical, lovely little body, completely without inhibition. I hope she'll be able to stay like that, but I doubt it. Earlier I wished Dirk were with me because I wouldn't have been afraid. That fear makes me wonder about how I'm going to get enough dancing in my life, now that I'm alone.

Bars are almost the only public places in America where people go to dance. When I go to bars with my male friends who don't dance, I'll dance with any man who does. So few American men dance that we can't bear to say no when one asks. My contention is that a dance is a dance, and that's all. You shouldn't fear being followed around or pursued or hassled, to say nothing of being raped in a parking lot, because you agreed to dance. But my men friends have always said I am wrong. They tell me I don't understand: for a man in America, a woman agreeing to dance with him in a bar constitutes automatic encouragement to hope that the other dance will ensue. I find this notion batty.

If women have the right to say that a friendly dinner does not establish a claim to anything more, even less should one expect any repercussion from anonymous dancing. But every time, my male friends have been technically right. I may hold to my ethical position, but when I dance with a stranger in a bar, he always presses for further contact, just as pushily as Tien. Usually I'm with a group that includes my lover, so it's just a matter of establishing that I belong to this man, am associated with him and protected by him. That generally takes care of it. Like I said, most men understand the territorial rights of other men to a woman's body. They often do not understand a woman's rights to her own. Now that I am going to be a woman alone and unattached, I'm going to have to deal with this, if I want to dance. The kernel of fear will take root in my stomach, lodging near the irritation, sometimes winning. And I cannot take my five-year-old granddaughter to bars as my dance partner. That's called child abuse.

Krissy's own road story involved not only chasing the bus *to* Pittsburgh; she also almost missed the bus *from* Pittsburgh. She screamed in the cavernous bus station at personnel who were letting the bus pull out, even though she was there in time to have the required tag attached to her luggage if anyone had waited on her. She missed, by moments, being a woman with a five-year-old child ditched in a strange city in which she had no acquaintances, no money, and no way to reach me to say that she wouldn't be halfway across the state at our meeting place when I picked her up. She simply pitched a hissy fit until they stopped the bus. We went on to Washington that night, exchanging our stories of being women alone, a little scared and without male protection.

By an amazing road synchronicity, we arrived at the prearranged hotel meeting spot, in the middle of the night in Virginia, at the same moment that Bernie and Mary Ellen arrived from Florida. They'd been traveling with a U-Haul and two-year-old Sequoia on the road for two days. We'd had no agreement on a meeting time. We'd said we'd get there when we got there, sometime before morning, from our starting places 1,500 miles apart. To pull in at the same time made us all believe in God. We stared at each other from behind our vehicular window walls, incredulous, exhausted, happy. In a quiet way, it was among the finest moments of my life. All of my young darlings had homed in on each other as if we all had continental radar, synoptical sight. The omniscient narrator of our family's life story had seen us all driving toward each other, south from north, north from south, in the middle of an April night, our sleeping children in our arms, our intention merely to be together.

Mary Ellen and Bernie were strung out on caffeine and hadn't slept any more than I. We were facing a day of hard physical activity and intense mental energy—the Washington rally of half a million people, with two small children in tow, followed by another three hours of driving before we could hit a motel to rest. So we should have gotten right to sleep. When we got into town it was 1:00 A.M., and we were losing an hour. We had to be up at 7:00. That would have been five hours of sleep at best.

But we stayed up all night, silly and strung out, having our family reunion there in the hotel room until 5:00 in the morning. Just as one of us would say, *This is it! sleep! I mean now!* somebody would start giggling or, far worse, farting, that fail-safe instigator of family hysteria. Sequoia and Ayron were wired, jumping all over the room, sensing that the adults were a-binga-bongo and posed no threat to absolute freedom. In the bath-room Sequoia charmingly told Ayron the life stories of two of her new dolls, and then they drowned the dolls in the toilet. Perhaps a shampoo was intended. When we all dropped off to sleep, dawn light was seeping through the curtains like poison.

The march was an amazing experience. Estimates ran as high as three-quarters of a million people, and whether it was that or half that, this was certainly the largest mass of humanity I'll ever be part of. We marched to-gether for reproductive freedom, for women's autonomy and independence. Those things are dear to my heart always, but especially now, with three generations marching. Or, rather, two generations marched while carrying or pushing the third, whose freedoms we feel it vital to secure. Our chil-dren are in hundreds of people's photo albums from that day, in part because both girls are beautiful. And we're an awfully photogenic rainbow coali-tion—we are white and honey blond, black and caramel, Native American and African American, Irish and English and Polish. Everyone loved our little ones, probably because they didn't have to carry them.

Sequoia, too young to understand, was a stunned and fascinated spec-tator of the throng of faces of which she was a part—and then she became a tired and grumpy spectator. Atop her daddy's shoulders or in her moth-er's arms she was bewildered, but interested, and utterly at home. Else-where, in stroller or on foot, she was mercilessly analytic, furrow-browed with thought. Ayron, at five, chanted with the crowd one hundred zillion times, "Hey hey, ho ho, George Bush has gotta go," periodically stopping to ask us again who George Bush was. She got to dance on the Mall with lots of people watching her. In the end, she joined Sequoia in very vigor-ous protest not of George Bush but of us for not getting out of there when she got tired.

Peter, Paul, and Mary, Gloria Steinem, Bella Abzug, Faye Weldon, Jess-ie Jackson, all sang or spoke. The march route took hours. We had a wonderful time. We had a terrible time. It was not a mistake to take the little ones, but two year olds and five year olds involved in a six-hour on-your-feet event when they're already wired and hungry and cranky was almost too interesting. We felt proud to have them there. We felt closer than we have as a group for years, because we've gone our separate ways. At one point, I said I wished Dirk were here, and at another I said that Mac would really have had a lot of fun here, too. Krissy turned to me, hands on hips, and said, "Hey. You're with your kids now. Enjoy being with your kids."

Point taken. It was most important to be there with the people I gave birth to or helped to bring into the world or helped to bring up, my blood and bones and heart. I was standing up for my own freedom, and that of my son and my daughters and my granddaughters, so that their lives have a chance of being less dependent on the power of men outside of us and more in cooperation with the men on the inside of us. There were many men in the march, and that sense of solidarity with them felt right. We need each other. I am proud that my son, Bernie, felt that this was a necessity for him, that he feels common cause with women on the issue of control of their bodies is a high priority in his own life. When a man makes this issue his own, he gives back to women a small part of our own bodies.

Mary Ellen was fascinated by the White House. This was the first time she'd seen it up close. She's a thoughtful person who knows how to really experience primary events in her life. There is a freshness in her perceptions that mixes finely with her savviness. She's never too jaded to *feel* what's happening to her. So it was she who reminded us of what the White House represents for Americans. This is where the decisions are made, this is where the power brokers reside. She was much enamored of the idea of throwing in a tennis ball that said, "Free Barbara Bush!" The White House lawn was covered with hundreds of message balls. They made one massive statement: This is the voice of America, and the face of America, on reproductive rights. Two-thirds of the American people believe in reproductive rights for women. Listen to our voice.

At the end of the day, our feet were sore, our backs aching from pushing strollers and carrying kids and backpacks. We were so exquisitely exhausted that our very spirits ached. We were near weeping with weariness and inability to cope *anymore with the children,* who my children had, yes indeed, chosen to have. They wore signs saying so: I AM MY MOTHER'S CHOICE. We were thinking about adult doses of Nyquil for them, perhaps tranquilizers. Rubber hammers. Separate motel rooms. Could we please put this two year old and this five year old in there, close the door, and get some sleep? See if they're alive in the morning?

Coming home, I drove alone again. Kris is helping Bernie and Mary Ellen drive to New York State, where they're moving. From now on I will see them much more than I have the several years they've lived in Daytona Beach. It will be good to have my family near me again. We will have a sense of wholeness, even if the daddy-man they've loved these many years is no longer with me. Hey. You're with your kids now. Stop thinking about whatever man isn't with you. The grown son who has come home is a wonder of a person. He and my healthy herd of male friends should be enough male company and protection for any woman in her right mind.

But I am not sure that I, that many women I know, *are* in our right minds about men we love the other way. I do still fear being without that primary partner, the lover/other, the (un)like mind with whom a woman may suspend disbelief and curl up in the yolk of the Platonic egg, fairly off her head with stuff about eternities and mountains falling to the sea, whatever she may otherwise declare. We must learn how to be alone, open to the surprise of dedication and loyalty in ourselves and others, but not expectant, not needing the other in order to feel fully alive, and unafraid, and ready for the road.

THE ROAD TO ST. MARY'S

Route 948, western Pennsylvania

I'm in the triangle formed by Erie, Pittsburgh, and State College, trying to get to St. Mary's to relax with my women friends before the fall semester starts. I'm late. Did you ever notice that locals always grossly underestimate the distance and the time it takes to get from one place in their world to another? You'd think the locals would know, but they never do. In Erie you ask someone on the east side how long it takes to get somewhere on the west side, and they often say, "fifteen minutes, tops." It's at least twenty. Or you ask how many miles it is in the country and they say "a couple" when it's five. A while back, I asked how far to St. Mary's and the guy said, about two hours. I know it's at least half an hour more than that. So how do people get anywhere on time? Is everybody late? All the time?

I'm *always* late. I told the women I'm meeting at the hunting camp that I'd be there around nine. I won't arrive until noon, and to do that I'm literally throwing things around. I just vacuumed the bejesus out of my van. Within twenty-four hours I've managed to fill it with detritus from one end to the other—sleeping bags, garage sale items, loose change, McDonald's bags, cups of both styrofoam and fine pottery, coffee spilled on the dashboard, orange juice, gum, nail polish, bandages, jewelry, earrings, plastic bags with vitamins melting in the sun, toothbrush, Chapstick. I am a slob. In my heart I'm an orderly person, so it bothers me that I wander through life with ketchup packets on the floor, one of them usually squishing out on the carpet. I've got soured half-and-half cream packets here, wrappers from tapes and batteries, an old poem, a copy of my first book. I've got plastic, I've got cans of beans, a hairdryer, a T-shirt. I've got a cooler. My shorts and underwear are drying, or dying, in the back. I've got a wet bathing suit where I spilled water from the steamer I was going to press my other clothes with, but I forgot the cord, so it won't work anyway. There's sticky black gunk on my toes from walking in bare feet. My feet are always dirty. I'm a fundamentally clean person, but I only get a chance to bathe two times a week because someone's having a break-down in the kitchen or a cat is dying or I've just found a lump on my breast or the water heater *and* the fridge just quit at the same time, and the pa-pers aren't graded and I'm supposed to give a lecture on the seventeenth century in three hours and I can't remember what century we're in right now.

I've turned off a main road and headed into the mountains south of Warren, near a town called Sheffield. The smokestacks of Warren are behind me now, with their terrible beauty like helicopters in Vietnam. I can feel the forest closing in. You know when you're coming into deer-hunter country in Pennsylvania. Major towns disappear. The village of Barnes is mostly churches, bars, beer distributors, lawn sales. A friend from this area said to stop at the lawn sales because the mountain people are poor and they don't know what they have—you can pick up amazing stuff for next to nothing. As a lawn sale junkie, I've never before troubled myself with the ethics of wanting to pick up something for nothing. And it's true, I've already stopped at several lawn sales where very good goods cost a fraction of what I would pay in Erie or Buffalo. I bought an old hurricane lamp for three bucks. It would have cost at least thirty in the city. Here's another church and a sign for "Operation Jump Start." Now Route 948 to Ridgeway.

For a while I had a semi up my tail. The metaphor felt literal—on a narrow stretch of highway, he filled my rearview mirror, careening and trying to pass me in a two-lane no passing zone where I was already driv-ing over the speed limit. Years ago in an episode of the "Twilight Zone" TV show, a riderless, driverless truck relentlessly pursued a person in a car. This felt like that and reminded me of my fifteen years of thruway commuting in which I'd come home at night on an isolated stretch at ten or eleven o'clock, just me and the big trucks. In those days I drove a VW, so I felt even smaller. Most of the truckers were fine road companions, unobtrusive giants running alongside me, but a few messed with my mind on purpose. Once three truckers sandwiched me, one in front, one in back, one on the side, blasting their horns, swerving close, trying to frighten me. It worked. I was plenty scared. It was one of those moments you carry for a lifetime.

A sign here says Rock Bottom. Is that like Low Shoulder or Bump? Did you ever notice that when road signs say Bump, there's seldom a bump? Valley View Camp here, near Joe's Refuge, looks like a junkyard. I just passed a roadside log storage place—this is logging land as well as rich in steel and coal. You can really feel the autumn here. It's still steamy August in the city, but in the mountains already is that crispness. September comes to the mountains in August. Curvy roads here, but folks move right along. I'm headed for Chris's family hunting camp. (Now I'm entering Forest County, Howe Township.) There seems to be an unwritten rule about how primitive the accommodations must be to qualify as a camp. Often there's electricity, but no telephone and no gas, just a wood stove or a coal stove or propane. Many people live in the area year round, but much of the local life is at the hunting camps. Chris's family place is a few miles outside of the town of St. Mary's on the edge of the Allegheny National Forest. It's my fourth year for the annual August women's trip.

A few summers ago, we spent a night under siege at the camp by a herd of men with trucks and guns and beer and a dog. When I saw my own story about it in print in *Ms.*, I couldn't believe I wrote it, or that it ever happened. The women are all there right now, waiting for me: Deanna, Chris, Susan, Claire, Christelle. Susan is the one feeling most ragged this time. She's been the editor of a Civil War press for about a year and can't stand it much longer. The lively industry of popular Civil War books is run by people who tend toward both racism and sexism. Appropriate that a military truck is in front of me now, here at Route 66, that mythic American roadway. One time when we drove here we encountered truckloads of military men, either active duty or national guard. For miles we were behind a truck stuffed with guys in fatigues with buzz cuts, whooping, hollering, gesturing. They looked like kids heading for Boy Scout camp.

This is the first time I've driven here alone. I usually come in a car with Chris, who knows these roads well from having grown up here. Passing an antique shop now. Fishing Licenses Sold Here, Night Crawlers For Sale. Here's a billboard for Stroh's—We Bring More to the Party. Maple, oak, suddenly more pine, becoming coniferous as I drive deeper. Behind me, the traffic has dropped to almost nothing. Welcome to Elk County—Eastern Gateway to the Allegheny National Forest. A trailhead here, lots of Slow Down, Big Curve signs. I'm looking for a place to pull off to let the driver behind me pass. I'd like to be entirely alone for a while, anonymous, just a person in a car.

At the hunting camp I will wash my face and hair in a cold mountain spring and tramp in moss so thick and soft that you can sink in up to your ankles. The camp is just one room with an old linoleum floor, a rusting fridge, an outhouse, and a spring. We'll cook over an open fire, tell stories and laugh, talk about sex, sing, sleep really deep, drink wine. I can stay at St. Mary's for two days, but then I'll have to leave for a conference at Penn State to discuss women's studies. From State College I'll return to Erie just in time to teach my classes. My son, Bernie, is graduating from the police academy this week. (Here's Ridgeway Church of Christ.) I'm supposed to be three places at once. I'm always behind. I do everything half-assed and it seems that everybody is always disappointed in me.

Rose's Christmas Store, wild turkeys for sale, rugs and quilts. I've entered and exited the Allegheny National Forest five or six times the past hour. One of my anxieties is that I've never driven here alone. Many of the roads don't have names, and Chris's directions sounded like this: "You take the third dirt road on the left for about a mile and a half and then you should see another one on your right and then you should see a logging camp. Turn right there. . . ." I'm a little concerned. Here's Johnson's Poultry Farm. If you don't drive, you don't know how to get there. Beware Elk. Entering Borough of Ridgeway. Sweet mountain town, white fences, logs in yards, a few brick homes, urns with flowers, mailboxes on the side of the road, the American flag everywhere. This is patriotic territory.

The rest of the women will be relaxed when I get there, and I'll try to unwind. Leaving home last night, I was getting ready to go to a reunion, this camping trip, and a conference at the same time—packing for three different kinds of events in a three-day trip is confusing. Who am I today? Here's a cemetery on my right. Hello, dead folks. I know I've forgotten something. I'm going to be wearing sneakers or hiking boots at the conference, or dress boots in the woods, whichever I remembered to bring.

I just stopped at a secondhand store looking for a bookcase, and by God, they had what I was looking for. There was some junk on the bookshelves and the lady said she'd "red that off" for me. Pennsylvania talk. Here's a pretty girl talking to some boys outside the fire station. Getting close to my destination now. Although I'm not going to relax for long here, just to be with these women is enough. I'm not really comfortable with much of anyone these days. I'm almost desperate for privacy. Yet I'm also hungry for my women.

Last week, there were twenty-five messages on my phone machine after I was gone for less than two days. At least six of them were important enough to respond to within the next few hours, three vital right then and there. One was from the Chautauqua County Sheriff's Department in New York State. I was being questioned in connection with a murder across the street from my summer cottage. I called back. The detective asked what time I left the cottage yesterday and I couldn't remember. I've been staying out there trying to read and work, but I'm also back and forth to Pennsylvania every couple of days—it's less than an hour between my properties in New York and Pennsylvania. I only had a few hours of sleep and as usual I was feeling like some form of plant life. (Clearcut woods here, trailer court, little wooden boxes with flowers in them, funny lawn decorations, a bathtub Mary.) I had no idea what time I had left the cottage that day, so I got out my calendar, which informed me that I'd been in Erie for the past day and a half, and therefore not at the cottage at all on the murder day. I didn't remember where I was because I'd been up until midnight with visiting folks from France, having menopausal hot flashes and dripping sweat onto my dinner plate while trying to make multiculturally clever conversation.

So I told the detective I wasn't there at all, that I left on Thursday, not Friday. He asked what time? Once again I had no idea. My neighbor was shot by his son while he was on the tractor. He was mangled so badly that at first they thought it was a farm machinery accident. Not until later did they find the bullet wound. (Martial Arts Company, Emporium 19 miles, East Johnsonburg, 9 miles west.) I must've sounded mighty suspicious, not knowing when I'd been there or when I'd left. It's a good thing they think they know who did it. When I got off the phone I left for the cottage, to be alone and to write. But moments before I arrived, there was a car accident out front. An old lady, confused by all the lights from the police investigation of the murder, stopped in the middle of the road and the guy behind her plowed right into her. I didn't get anything written that day. I'm empathizing with the old lady.

✳

I'm quietly departing the camp, where I've been for two days. Leaving woods and no phones and heading back to civilization, I have that feeling I get when I return from backpacking—disorientation, not quite sure how to drive the car, how to maneuver in and out of traffic or interact with people. I'm approaching the town of St. Mary's. The woman behind me in a black car is putting on makeup on her way to work. She's stretching, looking in the mirror, applying lipstick. I do that. I don't wear makeup, but I do think, "Somebody should do something with this hair," and primp its mass fruitlessly. I'm on my way to the conference in State College and I'm dressed in woods clothes and sneakers. Passing a lot of John Deere equipment. The year-round homes of many people in this isolated area are surrounded by heavy equipment and jacked-up pickup trucks.

I've been listening to the tapes we recorded by the fire in the woods. It's untranslatable—old friends laughing, dancing, singing, bitching. I think about trying to convince people, on the basis of these tapes, that these are the deepest women I know. We sound brain dead. We sound that way because we need comic relief, and we are healthy enough creatures to find it where we can. And these are indeed the deepest women I know—resonant, thoughtful, compassionate, committed people, all of whom live out their convictions about human connections in the face of their own and others' isolation. The collective experiences of this group of women might well have rendered them unable to live with trust or openness at all, yet they do, fighting back the pressure to shut down, to cut off love at the root where it was poisoned.

Most of the women in this group are survivors of sexual violence. Two were raped as children, in circumstances so harrowing, involving such violation of their essential humanity, that I cannot recount their stories lest I contribute to their pain, which remains private. One endured her rape when she was grown and did not have a name for it at the time. One who was not herself raped has lived for many years with another child-hood rape survivor so crippled she cannot return warmth, causing my friend to live in a lightless house, shades drawn both between the house and the world, and between the women themselves.

Most of us are lonely in the purest sense, surrounded by people but unable to find our own lonely other, or having found him or her, having to leave, or being left. One of us has dealt with domestic violence in more than one relationship and knows what it's like to be beaten, to depend on police to protect her from one man intent on hurting her, another intent on killing her. In the backgrounds of this collective entity of laughing women are guns and knives and razor blades, both actual and metaphorical. We all work in the trenches of the gender wars, helping not only ourselves but also other women and men when we can. No one meeting us or encountering us together would guess for a moment that our own lives have ever included such personal violence. We appear amazingly normal, whatever that means. When I think of an America that is impatient with the victim stance, I know that such backlash is a case of mistaken identity, that hardly a single "victim" I know has rested in that place, but, rather, is daily engaged in not mere surviving, but thriving. What sort of collective cultural meanness of spirit would deny such people their struggle?

We're good humored about it, though. Yesterday we invented a board game we figure could make us all rich. It's called Blame the Victim. We thought of all the things that mothers, fathers, or lovers say to make you feel bad when you are already miserable. You land on items like the Family Loyalty Quiz, which you *always* fail. You can also unload guilt on your opponent. You collect guilt points and if you get too much, you can commit suicide. If you get a suicide card, you can also use it for an attempted suicide in order to get attention.

Recently Christelle, a new member of our group, sat in my kitchen puzzling over Carson McCullers's "Ballad of the Sad Cafe," in which a powerful woman is utterly defeated, her strength drained from her. What to do, Christelle asked, with that ending? Since she herself has suffered a great deal, and suffers still, I knew she knew the answers. We work hard. We don't give up on ourselves or on those we love or on the hope for a peaceful planet. And most especially, we rest from our labors, in laughter gut deep and light and lovely, taking clear and present delight in our mutually entangled lives.

THE BEACH AS NURSERY

Pawtuckaway State Park, New Hampshire

We were almost the only people here, until the site next door was occupied by a group of kids who transformed the woods into a singles bar. No mean feat, but they managed it. Here is one of the most beautiful state park campgrounds in the Northeast. Small lakes are ringed by ample sites with minimal infringement, not even garbage cans. Glacial rock formations rest among low pines, through which we could see them setting up camp. I tried not to loathe the young and the restless when they started playing loud rap music. They got tanked up on beer in the shortest possible order, tossing empty cans into the forest surrounding their site. Then they started *breaking trees* to get firewood—young men jumping on limbs yelling, Break, mothafucka! The crack of live wood. Get off those trees, mothafuckas.

We went to bed around midnight. I woke up many times in the night to the continuous beat of rap. Humba, humba, humba, I'm bad, I'm bad, I'm bad. The last time I heard voices and music was 5:30 A.M. In the morning the rhythms of rap music were replaced by those of parenting. The family beach at Pawtuckaway, where we went to escape our neighbors, is a study in men trying to learn how to be daddies. It's also a live laboratory of the human female body before and after birth. Coming through the steamy parking lot onto the beach, I gravitated to the family area. We took a picnic table next to a mom and dad with twin babies and a toddler. The man, in his thirties and not too shabby in a muscle shirt, was trying to do his share as a weekend, holiday-beach dad. He was charmingly clueless. The mom had all three hanging on her pear-shaped, full-hipped body most of the time.

When she rose to take the toddler to the beach, the daddy said, "What do I do again?" She explained patiently how the twins were to be fed. He inquired once more regarding a fine point as she tried to leave. "I said, they split the jar of veggies and each get a bottle of juice," her vacation veneer thinning slightly. "Oh, okay, I've got it." She walked away with the toddler. He tried to deal with both babies, one a little cranky and wiggling down into the double stroller. "It's time to eat now," he offered cheerily. I managed to refrain from extending help. It was good to see him doing his new-age bit. He beamed over at me when I said they were cute. "Yes, these are my twins, they're six months old today." Then one of them spit veggies down daddy's hand. It was sort of orange. At one point the mom came back, sighing long sufferingly when he made one of those helpless gestures. He made another. She said, "Oh, that's right—you've never changed a diaper."

Interesting piece of information, that. He's got two six-month-old babies and a toddler and he's never changed a diaper. He seemed to be into taking lessons if she were willing to give them. But she wasn't into spending her beach time playing teacher. She changed the diapers efficiently on both and then breast-fed one while the toddler bounced on her knee. He kept track of the other one, then she traded breasts and toddlers and he kept track of the other, coochie-cooing in its face.

Looking around the beach, I saw this scene duplicated by dozens—men trying really, really hard to be good dads, men fathering their children. Two men alone with toddlers nearby seemed completely competent. Maybe they were new-age fathers or male single parents or a gay couple or dads used to giving moms time off. But most of the men here didn't know quite what they were doing. They were slightly out of their element. I know this sounds patronizing. Where have I been? Things have changed? It's different in the 1990s? I don't think so, not really, not much. Anyone who thinks they've fundamentally changed lives in the world of low-cholesterol, high-income, alternative culture. Step down to the corner bar for a piece of reality.

The beach was filled with women of all shapes and sizes and ages and dispositions doing the work of mothering, accompanied by children of all shapes and sizes and ages and dispositions. Children hung off their limbs and their shirts. Mothers navigated heavy buggies and wagons full of toys and kids through deep sand, trying not to pull the arms out of the sockets of young ones who want to go one way when mommy's going the other way. Woman as caretaker, especially of the young. I watched the ease with which women give their bodies over to the young. I saw some exasperated, end-of-the rope moms, but many more patient ones, encouraging their young into the water for the first or second time. I watched which parts of mothers' bodies get stepped on, heads and arms and legs and breasts, while their progeny clamber over them, spilling sand in their eyes.

Half the beach was occupied by the female body after giving birth and half by that body before birth. There were exceptions—mothers still thin and lithe, pudgy teens with no stretch marks. But the segregation of families and singles was striking. On beaches you can clearly see that the human female form is a curriculum in diversity. After the age of consent, the collective female body is of course massively distant from the cultural ideal. The ideal stands out on a family beach like this, a public display case of flesh and cellulite and hanging breasts and fat and loose skin and wrinkled skin and just about everything *except* the regularity and uniformity we are taught to desire. It all looks pretty good, and fully human.

Leaving the beach, I hear an NPR report on fathers. Contrary to general assumptions, fathers spend almost no more time with their children now than they did twenty years ago. A few minutes more a day is all the entire gender revolution has produced. Most of those average minutes per day are accounted for by dads in their thirties in privileged socioeconomic and educational groups—this from a study that says fathers spend a third of the time with their kids that mothers do. (Three years after divorce, over 40 percent of children have little or no contact with their fathers.) The research concludes that fathers in their thirties seem to like being parents more than their younger or older counterparts.

Then a psychologist analyzed the data. Despite the fact that dads spend relatively little time with their young, children seem to bond with their fathers and to regard them as very important. American children want very much to have their dads respect them and fight even harder for the approval of fathers than of mothers. The psychologist's profound conclusion was that the lesser time spent by fathers with children makes the male parent more glamorous by virtue of being remote. No, really? His final point: there is no problem making sure that children bond to the father, even in cases of little contact or approval.

If "bonding" means attachment that becomes desperate because of remoteness and the impossibility of pleasing, if it includes striving for approval that never comes, then indeed we have no national problem here. The psychologist also said that mothers protect the territory of parenting from fathers, keeping kids from spending too much time with their dads.

Was *that* what I saw on the beach today when the mom tried desperately to escape, but the dad couldn't figure out how to feed and change his babies, so she finally gave up and did it? If so, her passive-aggressive, competitive manipulations were way too subtle for me. I thought she was just tired.

I live around that world of thirty-something parenting that accounts for the best of fathering, according to this research. Yet even in my world, fully involved fathering is not really the norm. It *is,* however, a well-developed fictional construct. Many of my colleagues are fathers of small children. Some of these fathers spend the vast majority of their time at work, including evenings and weekends. I got a strange verification on this from a female police officer on my campus. When I come to the office at odd times, I often see the office lights of the same male professors. I asked whether this was a pattern. At several colleges where this officer has worked, there's always a contingent of professors well known to be in their offices nights and weekends—always male, always married, always fathers.

This anecdotal data doesn't seem a mystery to me. The fathers need to get away from the kids to concentrate on their work. In an era when the father's study is a thing of the past, they're going to ditch the kids with the mothers in order to do this, regardless of whether or not the mothers work outside the home. My own theory is that many men invent or create work they simply must do in order to be away from home. Kids can be noisy and boring and irritating. Of course there will be wonderful exceptions. I just spent time with a friend whose husband does more raising of their child than she does. We all know of fathers who are genuine co-parents; I work with two or three. But they are still rare. What I see more often is the *myth* of the feminist father or equal parent.

I've talked in times of extremity with the women involved in several of the living experiments that exemplify this myth. It's one that women often help to perpetuate. It was vital to them to have a different kind of marriage and parenting situation than they themselves grew up with. Before the babies came, their lovers and husbands promised full co-parenting. When it didn't turn out that way after all the vows and good intentions, the women had as much invested in the story they'd told their friends and families as did the fathers themselves.

Many fathers continue to deceive themselves about how much parenting they do, in part because their women don't make them confront the actuality of old patterns into which they've both slipped. Very well, then. It's sometimes a mutual, collective self-deception. I'm not sure why this cover-up is going on, but I'm sure it will need to be exposed before any further and fundamental change in American parenting can occur. And I'm weary of being labeled a male basher when I venture to say we're creating this cover-up. I said *we*, not just them. I know the reasons for the situation are complex, having as much to do with economic as with psychological and social factors. It's not male bashing when someone notices that elephant in the living room—or, as the case may be, *not* in the living room. It's just acknowledging a reality. With luck, he's also not in the singles bar. He might, as is the case with some of my own male colleagues, be camping in the forest, where he has long since outgrown breaking trees. Maybe he's hunting deer. The woman and the little ones at home are hungry.

COMING TO MY FATHER'S HOUSE:

ANNE SEXTON'S ISLAND GOD

Squirrel Island, Maine

Looking at an old family photograph when I was twelve, I saw a face I didn't recognize. Asking who this was, I first heard her story. Suicides have a way of haunting the next generation. . . . I believe I became a writer in order to tell her story and possibly redeem it.—Kathleen Norris, *Dakota: A Spiritual Geography*

Anne Sexton, more than any other modern poet except Adrienne Rich, first gave permission to her contemporaries to write about female experience in the body. I wanted to write my doctoral dissertation on her after her suicide in 1974, but could find no one who took her seriously enough to work with me. So I did my dissertation on three giant dead white males (Sigmund Freud, William Blake, and John Milton), all the while writing articles on Sexton on the side. Those essays became part of the foundation of Sexton studies, which legitimized Sexton for a new generation of college students. A few dedicated critics worked throughout the eighties to recognize Sexton's achievement, publishing and presenting panels on her work at professional conferences.

Alicia Ostriker, Diane Middlebrook, and I met annually for years to talk about Sexton, forming a conference of three to assess our current Sexton projects. Alicia wrote articles about women poets and then came her groundbreaking *Stealing the Language: The Emergence of Women's Poetry in America.* I wrote *Oedipus Anne: The Poetry of Anne Sexton,* the first book-length critical study. After working on it for ten years, Diane published her controversial and now-famous biography, *Anne Sexton.* We edited or wrote for anthologies, and with Diane I also edited Sexton's *Selected Poems* for Houghton Mifflin.

Yet nowhere in my publications did I give an indication of my personal stake in this poet—nor would I have committed it to paper for fear that discussing the roots of my personal motivations would have further discredited both her and me, making us both easy to dismiss. Every critic has a personal stake in what she or he reads and writes, as reader response theory told us a generation ago. You bring along your own baggage. But the ostensible and entirely illusory "objectivity" of the critical enterprise—still stupidly maintained—makes us lie by omission. I've lied that way for fifteen years.

Among her other achievements—including a mythopoesis of psychoanalysis, a body of work on mother-child relationships, and radical rewritings of cultural myths and of the Bible—Anne Sexton is American poetry's most eloquent translator of the language of suicide. Her suicide poetry attempts to give readers an understanding of what it feels like to need or want to die. While she said that "suicide is the opposite of the poem," she sometimes kept herself alive by speaking her poems in that special language of the suicide: "Like carpenters they want to know *which tools. /* They never ask *why build*" ("Wanting to Die").

My stake in this is clear to me. My father's suicide when I was five runs like a red line through my life and through most of the words I have written. He presides in silence and absence over this book, as over the lives of his family, who still feels the reverberations of that death nearly half a century ago. He left a suicide note before he leapt from a hotel building in Cleveland, Ohio, but it did not tell me what I need to know. So I have sought to understand him however and wherever I can. I have read his Sunday sermons (he was a Presbyterian minister), the letters home to parents and then to his brothers over a period of decades, and there simply isn't a clue.

I know that the depressions started when he was away at school at sixteen. They lasted as long as a year, sometimes precipitated by a circumstantial crisis, but this was not always the case. His darkness could come for no apparent reason; in current diagnostic parlance, his depressions were endogenous, probably genetic, and his life might have been saved by the new generations of psychoactive drugs. He became adept at hiding his feelings for months at a time even from those intimate with him, like many depressives do. He sought and received some psychiatric help over the years—he was ostensibly on his way to an appointment with a psychiatrist when he checked into the Drake Hotel, requesting a room on the top floor—but it never gave him much relief. And that is simply all I know. He told no one, not even my mother, about the details of his tortured inner life; not his brothers, to whom he was very close; and certainly not my brother, just entering adolescence when he died; or me, the five-year-old future writer who even then was wild for words.

So I sought from other writers the words that could explain how people feel when they are desperate enough to leave life. I sought them from those who struggled with that horror and outlasted it, like Robert Lowell, and from those who could not survive their own lives any longer: Virginia Woolf, John Berryman, Sylvia Plath. But I didn't find what I needed. Decorum and reticence marked Woolf's words, stunning though they were, and Plath was too cryptic. I did not find that combination of *passion* and *anatomy,* that almost Wordsworthian quality of deep emotion recollected in tranquility, until I found Anne Sexton.

All those years immersed in Anne Sexton's work were really dedicated to my father—a wonderful irony given that those who guessed my personal stake thought it was about feminism. I have come to comprehend my father and to love him even more through her words. I processed my inevitable anger at him for abandoning us through Sexton. When I look now at the introduction to *Oedipus Anne* (Urbana: University of Illinois Press, 1987), I see how thinly, yet effectively, I veiled my personal agenda in the cloak of the critic. I said nothing of my father in that book. But I wrote: "When Sexton tells her dead father that she will bend down her strange face to his and forgive him, she is speaking of what we all need to do: to bend down our faces to our fathers, living or dead, and forgive them" (xii).

Forgive them for what? In a chapter of *Oedipus Anne* titled "How We Danced: Fathers and Daughters," I introduced Sexton's relationship to her father in this way: "The 'normal' woman in Western society . . . falls in love with her father, who delights her, despises her, seduces her, betrays her, and dies. . . . Burial and resurrection of the fathers becomes a central theme in Sexton's poetry, as it is in the personal lives of her contemporaries and the collective life of her culture" (25). If the critical genre had allowed, I could have added "and the immediate life of this writer."

One reason I was angry with my father, at least unconsciously, is that I associated him with playfulness. He always seemed moderately amused when he was with me, and I know from his brothers that he had a lively sense of humor and a happy irony. I said nothing of this in *Oedipus Anne.*

Instead I wrote about American attitudes toward suicide. I analyzed suicide as cultural sin, employing Alvarez's *The Savage God*. I argued that despite the euthanasia movement, despite the fact that we no longer bury suicides separately or consign them to Dante's seventh circle of hell, we are still mean spirited toward those whose terminal illness is mental rather than physical. In this excerpt, it's clear that while my subject was Anne Sexton at the start, by the end it was my father:

> Poets are among the few whom our culture still invests with a ritual function. We ask them to speak the unspeakable for us, and when they do, we are capable of effecting a violently negative transference. Critical response to Sexton's poetry seems to me to bear this out. Particularly if the poet has exposed our pain, seen into our darkest selves, we need to purge ourselves of the violating member, to punish the one who has broken boundaries and violated taboos. . . . We are angry with Anne Sexton for killing herself, partly because she is the same poet who wrote with such commitment and intensity of the delight of being alive. (xiii)

Even though I did not write about my own personal relationship to suicide, I dedicated that book to the memory of three people. They are all suicides from my personal life. The first one, Myron Kinney Hume, 1904–54, is my father. That is all I permitted myself there. But a few years later, I began to touch the wound in a travel essay about Sexton. "Anne Sexton's Island God" appeared in Frances Bixler's *Original Essays on the Poetry of Anne Sexton*. Here are extended excerpts from it.

✷

In Anne Sexton's later religious poetry, characterized by a ceaseless search for a God she could believe in, the summer island of her childhood became the geographical locus of her spiritual and poetic quest. Her poetry was always preoccupied with legacy and inheritance, in which were subsumed her religious quest, her sense of herself as a woman, her search for meaning and identity. Squirrel Island was the concentrated core of inheritance and legacy for Anne Sexton—the place where her family came together, where the generations lived side by side, where farflung people met to confirm their sense of who they were and who they intended to remain, but did not. It was where the fathers of her personal and mythic lives congregated—from Nelson Dingley through Arthur Gray Staples and Ralph Harvey, three generations of her God. What she once called "the lost ingredient" was lost, I think, on Squirrel Island, and found there, in her imagination, at the end of her life.

Linda Gray Sexton and Lois Ames describe the family compound where Sexton spent her early summers.

> Anne's happy memories centered on Squirrel Island, near Boothbay Harbor, Maine, where the Dingley, Staples, and Harvey clan summered in seven large five story 'cottages.' Built atop the shoreline granite with the wind at their back, these summer mansions were anchored into the rock by huge chains. The family lived skin to skin with the sea. From Arthur Gray Staples' study in the 'Aerie' the only view that met the eye was one rolling wave after another.*

The sure-thing father-God she found at the end of *The Awful Rowing Toward God* resided on an island toward which she rowed in hopeful need of salvation. He not only resided there; the "island of God" *is* God. This elegiac poet created God in the image of memory. He had been transformed from the loving ragged brother of her early poetry to the authoritarian, arbitrary, alternately loving and rejecting patriarch of her later work. As she became more emotionally isolated, so did her God become more remote from us and from her, until finally he formed the body of a magical and distant island toward which she rowed with deep need, if not quite belief, at the end of her life.

Many readers have been disappointed and puzzled that the poet who earlier dreamed she could "piss in God's eye," who radically manipulated traditional orthodoxies for happily subversive ends, who dismantled Christian mythology, rewrote the life of Christ and celebrated her own sacraments in new psalms, should have capitulated in the end to a father-god who received her worshipful submission. Sexton never explained the metaphor of God as island. If I am right to track him to Squirrel Island, then the nature of his being, and the terms of her submission to him, are understandable in a new way. I pictured it as a rocky, all but deserted place, studded with few houses on abandoned rock and beach. I looked for it in atlases, but couldn't tell which of the many unnamed islands off Boothbay Harbor it might be. It was too small to be labeled, even on good maps of Maine. A few phone calls and localized atlases later, I found that ferry

---

Anne Sexton: A Self-Portrait in Letters, ed. Linda Gray Sexton and Lois Ames (Boston: Houghton Mifflin, 1977), 4. Poetry citations from *Selected Poems of Anne Sexton,* eds. Diane Wood Middlebrook and Diana Hume George (Boston: Houghton Mifflin, 1988).

boats leave Boothbay Harbor for various islands, including Squirrel, regularly throughout the year. I went there on an early June morning. It takes about half an hour to get to Squirrel Island by ferry boat. My companion and I were told that sight-seers stay on the boat as it goes around the rest of the harbor area, but that we could stay on the island until the afternoon boat came through to pick us up.

Far from being rocky and deserted, Squirrel Island is a fully developed Maine summer colony. A few summer people were already in residence, though it was early in the season. The island has no stores or food or restaurants, but it does have many residents, all of whom arrive with no cars—the island has only a couple of roads—and carry their supplies with them. I approached a formidable older woman as we disembarked because we had only the vaguest idea what to look for. We knew that two of Sexton's family houses were called, originally, Dingley Dell and the Aerie, but we didn't know quite where to find them. Our skimpy directions indicated that one was near the boat dock and one was on the other side of the island. I braved the woman's forbidding exterior and asked her a few questions.

Yes, she knew Dingley Dell and the Aerie, but she hadn't an idea in the world who Anne Sexton was, and she, Mrs. Hicks, had been coming to the island for, what was it, seventy years. Then I tried using Sexton's parents' names, Mary and Ralph Harvey. Mary she knew—she remembered Mary dancing at the Casino. The Casino? But now she'd clearly had about enough of this nosey off-islander's inquiries that were not welcome. She wasn't rude, just a bit short, and I didn't blame her. Her husband, Mr. Hicks, was more open. He said that Dingley Dell was just next to their house. They were walking up now, and they would show us. On the way up the raised sidewalk, I continued to question Mrs. Hicks as much as I dared. How well had she known Mary Gray? Well enough, but Mary was married, you see. I still don't know what she meant by that. She repeated it several times.

While walking with her, I looked around at the solid summer houses, all owned by prosperous people on the mainland. None was a typical summer cottage. All were two story and large, some positively elaborate—normal for this kind of summer colony, but such a colony was not quite what I had expected. The front yards were rocky affairs of granite outcroppings such as appear all along the Maine shore. A casino? Yes, but it had burned down. So had the bowling alley. But other structures had replaced them. Yes, Mary Gray liked to dance. I couldn't tell if the reserve and slight disapproval were toward Mary Gray, or toward me for asking about her.

Mr. and Mrs. Hicks gave us a real sense of what the islanders were like: older now, a bit austere, protective of their privacy, and affectionate toward their island home. We helped Mr. and Mrs. Hicks carry their supplies to the house, and they directed us to Dingley Dell and the Aerie. Mr. Hicks, the chapel historian, said we should be sure to stop in the chapel, which is deeply intertwined with the history of the island and its inhabitants. After he sold us his booklet for a dollar, we went to Dingley Dell.

Dingley Dell is a planner's and builder's caprice. There is nothing else remotely like it on the island. It gives substance to Sexton's family history in "Funnel":

> Back from that great-grandfather I have come
> to tidy a country graveyard for his sake,
> to chat with the custodian under a yearly sun
> and touch a ghost sound where it lies awake.
> I like best to think of that Bunyan man
> slapping his thighs and trading the yankee sale
> for one dozen grand pianos. It fit his plan
> of culture to do it big. On this same scale
> he built seven arking houses and they still stand.

The dominant form of the house is indeed an "arc" or arch—they reappear everywhere, creating a lightness of tone. Dingley Dell would easily have been the most elaborate house on the island when it was built. The family that owns it now was not anywhere in evidence, so we looked in the windows at the elegant formal dining room, the gracious living room, the well stocked kitchen. I recalled a photo in Sexton's *Letters* of her grandfather, Arthur Gray Staples, Anne, and her sister Blanche. Clearly, that photo had been taken on the deck of Dingley Dell—I could place it exactly.

Leaving our belongings on the porch, we began the trek through and around the island toward the Aerie. We stopped at the chapel. A glance at the chapel history revealed that it was indeed a mine of information.* Nelson Dingley, Jr., was the first of Sexton's direct forbears to inhabit this island. It was purchased under his leadership by an association of twelve members in 1870. He and the others raised subscription money for the chapel almost immediately, which was erected in 1880 with generous

---

*All excerpts from *Squirrel Island Chapel: 100 Year Diary 1880–1980,* compiled by Marvin D. Hicks; available at Squirrel Island Library.

funding. From the minutes of the Chapel meetings of 1880, Mr. Hicks records this passage:

> Next Sunday it is hoped to have the chapel formally, and yet heartily, dedicated to a breezy and healthful Christianity—such as the Great Founder of our Faith, who delighted in the lilies of the field, the birds of the air, and the waves of the sea, would have us cherish.

In 1882, Nelson Dingley, Jr., then Governor of Maine, was elected the first President of the Chapel Association. He was Sexton's great-uncle, but Sexton presents him as her great-grandfather in the poetry, for it was he who built the houses in "Funnel" as far as I can determine. It is appropriate that this woman so in search of fathers would call her great-uncle one of her great-fathers.

Mr. Hicks reprints the memorial service eulogy for the Hon. Nelson Dingley, Jr., in 1899. By this time, Dingley had been president of the Chapel Association for seventeen years. The island's religious history, and its secular one as well—little separation of church and state existed on the island at this time—bears his indelible mark, and tells us something about the religious past of the highly secular family that, by Sexton's generation, was characterized by the kind of Protestantism Sexton recalls in one of her early poems: Protestants are the people who sing when they're not quite sure. Yet by the end of her own life, Sexton was re-seeking the Old Testament God, whose characteristics share much in common with both the god and the mortal fathers of Squirrel Island. [. . .]

The deserted chapel was well appointed in dark wood tones and lit effectively from the ample windows that the islanders carefully planned. I walked up to the pulpit and found the nineteenth century bible presented to the church by the Ladies Association of the island, and decided to open it and let my eye rest where it would, and read aloud. My eye fell first on Genesis 28:21–22, which I read:

> So that I come again to my father's house in peace; then shall the Lord be my God: And this stone, which I have set for a pillar, shall be God's house.

From the chapel, we cut back around to the shore, intending to find the Aerie. Once five stories, now four, it is described in Sexton's "Funnel" as looking like a shoe factory. There was no mistaking the Aerie when we came to it. It looks like, well, a shoe factory. It is certainly the largest private structure on the island, though in awful disrepair, unlike the beautifully maintained Dingley Dell. Peering in the windows, we could see it hadn't been fully inhabited in years. The house sits high on a hill, with an unobstructed view of the sea. Looking at it, I could imagine it in its prime, full of children and their parents—Dingley and Harvey and Sexton and Staples people.

It was here in the Aerie that Sexton's grandfather, Arthur Gray Staples, had his study. Staples is the family figure most intimately connected with the God of the *Awful Rowing*. He was the most literary member of the family, having been for years editor of the *Lewiston Journal,* and author of several books of essays, housed in the island library. Among the family members, he could bless her most directly as a writer. She recalls him fondly and frequently in the poetry—he is the grandfather of the bagsful of nickels in *Love Poems,* who belongs to me, she says, like lost baggage.

"Grandfather, Your Wound," takes place in the Aerie, where Sexton stands "in your writing room." The island "you were the man of" is "made of your stuff." She is here, in imagination or in the material world—both Diane Wood Middlebrook and I think she came to Squirrel Island in the early seventies, not long before her death—mourning his death, his wound, and her own. She is an ocean-going vessel here, as she will be later in the rowboat of *The Awful Rowing;* he is the wooden ceiling of his writing room. She hears him speak "like a horn"—the familiar island foghorn of this sea I am gazing out at?—and the sun goes down, but comes up again in a kind of resurrection. Here is part of the text:

> The wound is open,
> Grandfather, where you died,
> where you sit inside it
> as shy as a robin.
> I am an ocean-going vessel
> but you are a ceiling made of wood
> and the island you were the man of,
> is shaped like a squirrel and named thereof.
> . . . .
> My God, Grandfather,
> you are here,
> you are laughing,
> you hold me and rock me
> and we watch the lighthouse come on,
> blinking its dry wings over us all,

over my wound
and yours.

The lighthouse is visible from the Aerie where I stood, but is no longer
operated by hand as it was when Sexton was a girl on Squirrel Island, when
she might in fact have been held by her grandfather in his writing room
overlooking the Atlantic. Compare this with the final scene of "The Rowing Endeth," after she moors her boat at the "island called God":

> "On with it!" He says and thus
> we squat on the rocks by the sea
> and play—can it be true—
> a game of poker.
> He calls me.
> I win because I hold a royal straight flush.
> He wins because He holds five aces.
>
> .   .   .   .
>
> He starts to laugh,
> the laughter rolling like a hoop out of His mouth
> and into mine,
> and such laughter that He doubles right over me
> laughing a Rejoice-Chorus at our two triumphs.
> Then I laugh, the fishy dock laughs
> the sea laughs. The Island laughs.
> The Absurd laughs.

We may regret that in his transformation from human grandfather to cos-
mic Grand Father, the figure of Arthur Gray Staples became slightly sin-
ister. It is difficult to entirely applaud this "dearest dealer." But perhaps
at the Aerie he was warm and true.

Turning back from the sea toward the derelict house, I imagined Sexton in her own island room in "Mother and Jack and the Rain." Squirrel
Island is clearly the place most identified with Sexton's own version of the
primal scene:

> On my damp summer bed I cradled my salty knees
> and heard father kiss me through the wall
> and heard mother's heart pump like the tides.

Perhaps no poet, even in this self-consciously post-Freudian era, has so
completely eroticized the family as did Anne Sexton. In "Leaves That

Talk," Arthur Gray Staples has a love affair with his granddaughter, touching her breast and her neck. Our compulsions meet in the blent air of chapels—and of bedrooms. Anne Sexton blent the air of our collective compulsions when she squarely faced the eros of lineage on Squirrel Island.

Moving back around the island to make a full circle, we found a beautiful patch of woodland, changing yet again my original notion of what the island looked like. This is the island I had originally imagined, a rocky, wooded rough outcropping. This patch of woodland is the scene of Sexton's "Kind Sir: These Woods":

> Kind Sir: This is an old game
> that we played when we were eight and ten.
> Sometimes on The Island, in down Maine,
> in late August, when the cold fog blew in
> off the ocean, the forest between Dingley Dell
> and grandfather's cottage grew white and strange.
> It was as if every pine tree were a brown pole
> we did not know; as if day had rearranged
> into night and bats flew in sun. It was a trick
> to turn around once and know you were lost . . .

These poems form the core of what I call the Squirrel Island group. They show her returning in spirit to Squirrel Island from the beginning to the end of her writing life. The network of references in this group of poems includes some of Sexton's most concentrated themes: fear of madness, sexual anxiety, relationships to the "mother, father, I'm made of," the quest for an ultimate deity.

Back at Dingley Dell, we sit on the porch, watch the birds, look back into the windows. Dingley Dell and the Aerie are on opposite sides of the island. One is merry and waggish in design and faces the mainland. The other looks out to sea, where one might gaze as if into life's deepest emptiness, its deepest fullness. Sexton seemed sometimes to be two poets, one of delight, the other of despair, one inhabited by the living, the other given over to ghosts. The Aerie looks like the Yorkshire moors. Dingley Dell is like a meadow yellow with flowers.

Before we leave, we buy more copies of the chapel history from Mr. Hicks. Mr. and Mrs. Hicks come out onto the porch to talk. It is clear that our interest in their island has won them over. From them we find out that there are no mortgages for houses on the island—one must have enough money to buy or build outright. Buy is the wrong word, after all—Nelson Dingley and the original association members stipulated that one could not own any part of Squirrel Island—one leases the property for 999 years. That seems fitting. No one should, no one can, own God.

Waiting back at the dock for the boat to pick us up, I talk to another islander. She seems vaguely to know of Anne Sexton—she thinks two island women gave a talk on her connection to the island a year or so ago, but it is clear she hasn't read Sexton and knows nothing about her. I regret this. An important poet traces her roots here, and in her work this island becomes God. A modern and at first secular poet, she returns Squirrel Island finally to its religious roots—and whether or not I like that, these people should know of it.

We pull away from the island—I call it the awful outboarding away from God. I imagine Anne Sexton leaving here at the end of her summer childhoods, going back to the mainland to school, to responsibility, to her poetry life to be, and to an early death with or without God. With one of her therapists, "Dr. Martin," Sexton used a shorthand for the feeling of loss and loneliness that often overwhelmed her: "like leaving Squirrel," she called it. I find it poignant to discover that the "island of God" may have been the island of childhood where she summered. I also find it beautiful; I contemplate that simplicity, that perfect circle of sought-after comfort, one that brings the middle-aged poet back to the finest moments of a troubled and unhappy past. Perhaps anyone's idea of heaven is some such journey into the past.

Although *The Awful Rowing Toward God* ends with what I regard as an unconscious capitulation to paternalism, at least two qualifications of that submissive gesture comfort me. Only in the final poem of the collection does her God take on his externalized and patriarchal character. Elsewhere he continues to appear in heterodox and polymorphous form: in the chapel of morning eggs, in a whore, in an old man or a child, in the private holiness of her hands, in the creation of gender or the act of lovemaking, in morning laughter. And the ocean rower is a woman traveling to land through sea. The island of the father-god rises from the ocean of the mother-goddess. Squirrel Island in its salty sea is not only the father. Her journey is through and to both mythic imagos. The God Anne Sexton sought must offer absolution, as perhaps must any god whose qualities serve the needs of a guilt-ridden culture. Absolution is to be had only from the source of that guilt: In Sexton's case, the source is both paternal and maternal, the "mother, father, I'm made of."

Although *Rowing* was the last collection Sexton prepared for press, it does not represent her last questing words. Those are spoken in poems such as "The Consecrating Mother" (*45 Mercy Street*) and "In Excelsis" (from uncollected last works), which take place in the same liquid medium as *The Awful Rowing*. In "The Consecrating Mother," Sexton's speaker stands before the sea, which says, "Do not give up one god/ for I have a handful." She should be entered "skin to skin," says Sexton,

> and in moonlight she comes in *her* nudity
> flashing breasts made of milk-water,
> flashing buttocks made of unkillable lust . . .
> I am that clumsy human
> on the shore
> loving you, coming, coming,
> going . . .

The ocean-god of "In Excelsis" is the same mighty mother. "I wish to enter her like a dream,"

> and walk into ocean,
> letting it explode over me
> and outward, where I would drink the moon
> and my clothes would slip away . . .

She stands on the shore with another woman, "loving its pulse," absorbing "the wild toppling green that enters us today." Only a selective misreading leaves Anne Sexton in the ambiguous embrace of the father-god. She resides in his island arms, but they are both surrounded and enfolded by the mother sea.

✳

It is five years later, and I am completing what I now realize is the last leg of my journey to Squirrel, island of fathers, by driving to downtown Cleveland along Lake Erie, to a modest eleven-story building at the center of a triangle formed by Severance Hall, the Cleveland Museum of Art, and one of the Presbyterian churches at which my father occasionally preached. The Drake Hotel, where my father ended his life, is now a nursing home and assisted living community. I stand on the sidewalk below where he jumped. I have not before been prepared to confront his act so directly, opting instead for displacement—several elaborate journeys to New England to trace the troubled steps of Anne Sexton as she moved toward her death.

I have a bottle of champagne in the car, and I'm armed with an alibi to get not only in the door but up to the top floor. From my brother, Elliott, who is also trying to work through our father's death, I know the location of the room, on a corner overlooking the museum pond. The pond and the paths around it provide me with my clearest memories of my father. I walked with him on weekend afternoons along the winding paths, little hand in big hand, his shoes the size of boats, carrying bread to feed the ducks that paddle close to the edge and come onto the grass, seeking food from humans. My hands trembled with excitement, and I remember my father calming and steadying me with the same hands that gave bread to his parishioners at communion. Take, eat.

I ask to see the person in charge of information and admissions. I explain that my mother is considering entering a nursing home somewhere in the area—this is, in fact, true—and that because she'd lived for years in Cleveland, and had enjoyed both Severance Hall concerts and the museum with my father, we'd like to learn about this one. I'm shown the facilities by the gracious administrator. I say I'd like to see a vacant unit. My mother, I explain, would prefer a high floor, with clear views of the places dear to her. Although the room where my father leapt is occupied, one near it is empty. I am shown into it, where I try to concentrate on the well-appointed features to which she points. After a decent interval I wander to the window. The sky is clear blue. It's not possible to be alone with my thoughts, but at the end of the tour, I ask if I might go to the balcony just above the top floor to enjoy the view. I assure her I can find my own way back downstairs.

On the balcony I can position myself just above the sill of the window from which I calculate my father must have jumped. I try to imagine what it must have meant to him, in the final moments of his life, to gaze at these three landmarks—museum, concert hall, church. The church would most have disturbed this Presbyterian minister who had lost his own parish in East Cleveland and awaited the reassignment promised repeatedly, and never delivered, by the Presbytery. Without a flock to guide and minister to, he was lost; yet his suicide note, probably penned moments before he died, said that he could no longer guide, minister to, or save anyone else, because he could not even save himself. How like a passage from an Anne Sexton letter: "All those people who write to me and believe in me! God! I don't even exist!"

Moments before he jumped, when he was already on the sill, a hotel maid opened the room door. She screamed and pleaded with him not to do it. He jumped, right then, in front of her. She gave her report to the police. When my brother and I grew old enough to want to find her, there was no trace. She was the last person to see my father alive. I wish I could have found her. Sometimes I still fantasize about it. But this was forty years ago. She might be dead. I'll never find her.

Nor will I find him. He's gone. The dead are in their stone boats, "throat, eye, and knucklebone," and they refuse to speak. Now Sexton, who understood this, who knew the pain caused the living by the silence of dead parents, is also dead, having left her own daughter, Linda Gray Sexton, with that tortured legacy that Linda, too, works out in words. I think of my father's broken body on the sidewalk below. I have seen the coroner's report. There's not much that isn't maimed, pulverized, when you hurl yourself a hundred feet to pavement. I have seen his last view on earth, striven to see it clear—the view, that is. I cannot see his soul. It belongs to him. On the ground again, I open the bottle of champagne, and I toast him: to you, Myron Kinney Hume. And then I walk over the hill to feed the ducks, who waddle toward me, hungry mouths open. My hand is steady. Take, eat, so that I come again to my father's house in peace.

—For my brother, Elliott Powers Hume

PART 3

ROAD NOTES

WEARING A HUMAN FACE

Carlsbad Caverns, New Mexico

Something must be amiss or out of place
When mice with wings can wear a human face.
—Theodore Roethke, "The Bat"

1

At dusk, three hundred thousand bats spiral counterclockwise from the mouth of the caverns, stretching a dark finger of flight down your throat. How many millennia they have done this, no one knows. They got here first. Bats look like small birds, but mice should be rodents, not walking fish. A creature that hangs upside down all day in the dark knows something we don't, don't want to. Seeing the webs of their wings, we despair. They don't care that we see our fear in their faces, or that their flapping swoop in our dreams makes our mouths open in the scream. Nothing comes out.

2

Underground, lime body parts poised in room upon room, the caverns a genital innerspace hardened to delicate stasis. Stalactites and stalagmites reach toward each other in stony yearning you feel in your trunk when touch gets close. Those who have come together form columns of vast solidity. You trust them. These bodies are faithful. Pools of shallow water complete the lie, the cave ceiling, reflected, seeming for all the world a sky that clouds glide through. You touch the columns. Calcite crumbles in your hand, a grainy smear.

3

The Big Room alone would contain ten cathedrals. There is Milan, its overripe facade almost affronting the eyes. Deep ecology is shallow. "The Caverns are exquisitely planned by an architecture profounder than ours. Respect the Earth Mother's holistic integrity. Banish your hubris." Away with the human-centered universe! Ah. Earth Mother? Is it possible to think at all without thinking the body? Thought arises from within it, returns to it, takes its shape. Awake, transcendence is a doomed enterprise. Look to your dreams, the seers say.

4

That night I dream a silk sash in muted reds and bright violets. To keep it I must give up my other belts, laid resplendent before me. I watch the sash wave. Its intricate buckle sparkles. I try it on, take it off, cast it away, try it on again. A woman wafts in and picks it up, touching it to her cheek. She puts it on, trails it smiling, says something soft in my ear as she passes, walks away.

5

Dreams do not point up and out, but down and in: excavation, not flight. Sound enters, disconnected, stupid, precise, your cave-self whispering in your sleeping ear: listen up, I'm talking to you, every word I say is true, it all means something. But what are you saying to yourself? You might as well be a bat. You might as well spiral into night, counterclockwise.

6

The ground above the caverns is brown and green, familiar. All you see is nameable, known and real. The mouth of the cave is a throat from which webbed creatures take flight at dusk, interior loosed. You want to understand your bowels, your guts, your skin. Lake Erie: in a wood box near the cliff, six baby bats, five dead, one starving, its mouth open. Nothing comes out. I rub the silky webbing of its wing, nearly transparent, between thumb and forefinger. I press the cords behind my knees, sinews above my heels.

7

Freud sat alone in his study, dreaming of Rome, fingering his collection of artifacts. His throat hurt slightly. He rubbed it where it would later lump cancer. The archeology of which he spoke unearthed the ruins of civilizations that once covered the land. He said: our sense of the uncanny is produced by the return of the repressed, something once known, long forgotten. You can know it now. What would you know again? Confronting the cave mouth, you stand before the intention of earth itself. Shapes of the interior form, but we do not form them. We feel awe in their presence, stumble around their rumbling forms, their mute iconic bodies, beloved and unknown as parents.

8

Excavated, my dream would reveal ruins of secrets I keep from myself. Milan is in there, yes, and Rome, and the time I ran down Euclid Avenue in Cleveland, weeping and lost, tripping over the belt hanging from my dress. I saw calcite yearning. I saw stately passion. I saw the bats, I heard their living screech. The uncanny: once known, long forgotten. The bats return to the cave before dawn, dumb and blind and beautiful.

THE LONELY OTHER

Gethsemani, Kentucky

Coyotes will begin calling in the coulees to the north. Soon, the monks, too, will begin to sing, the gentle lullaby of vespers and compline, at one with the rhythm of evening, the failing light and the rise of the moon. Together, monks and coyotes will sing the world to sleep.—Kathleen Norris, *Dakota: A Spiritual Geography*

Yesterday we went to Gethsemani, the Trappist Monastery in Kentucky where Thomas Merton lived and wrote and is buried. When Mac made a retreat there twenty-five years ago, the strict rule of silence still prevailed among the Trappists. One of the monks—he was clear souled and flint eyed and clean of heart and marginally comfortable talking to a woman—told us that in the days before Vatican II, you could live and work daily, year after year, beside a brother and know nothing of who he was. Now there are a few times and places in which to speak, but many of the monks still prefer silence over speech, song over the cadences of conversation. We didn't know if I, a woman, would be permitted entrance. This is still one of the stricter orders—its full name is the Order of the Cistercians of the Strict Observance—with roots in not only the seventeenth-century Counter-Reformation frenzy of penitential fervor but also in eleventh-century monastic spiritualism. Body hatred, distrust of women, runs too deep here to have disappeared utterly. But I was permitted.

I waited in the secular graveyard attached to the monastery until vespers, the late afternoon service of song and prayer. From where I sat and where I walked, I could see into the monastic enclosure, see the other, the sacred burying ground for the monks, the rows of simple white anonymous crosses. They wrap the dead in their monastic robes and commit their brothers to the earth, dust to dust, ashes to ashes. Mac went over the wall into the enclosure to walk the stations of the cross, but I did not, knowing that the friendly toleration of outsiders might not extend as far to me as to him.

I read from a letter of Thomas Merton's: "The contemplative has nothing to tell you except to reassure you that if you dare to penetrate your own silence and dare to advance without fear into the solitude of your own heart, and risk the sharing of that solitude with the lonely other who seeks God through you and with you, then you will truly recover the light and the capacity to understand what is beyond words and beyond explanation because it is too close to be explained: it is the intimate union in the depths of your own heart, of God's spirit and your own secret inmost self, so that you and He are in all truth one Spirit."

Who is the lonely other of Merton's letter? Is it the other within the heart, the secret sharer with whom each of us lives? The one internally, eternally veiled, who is continually disclosing, enclosing—the ark of the covenant I make with my spirit, the promise of both communion with and separation from the private core of pleasure? of pain? How can I, can anyone, "advance without fear into the solitude?" I feel as though I promised solemnly, before I was born, never to violate that solitude, that internal silence, never to risk finding that the presence at the center might be an absence, might dissolve like smoke before my gaze. And if the lonely other of the heart is a presence, I know it is not made of sweet Logos. Yet I have been seeking all my life to find that lonely other, to expose her to the light, to see what stuff she's made of.

Or is the lonely other the brother or sister penitent and celebrant, separated from you by the stubborn silences of skin and bone and marrow and blood? Is God in the private holiness of my own hands or in the twining of my hand with another hand, another lonely one?

I entered the second-story tribune of the chapel for vespers. Visitors are separated physically from the monks, "on pain of papal interdiction." We watch from above their lovely, isolated entrance into worship. When I saw the brothers filing into their choir stalls in white cassocks, with light streaming through the windows, saw them standing, leaning against their walls, the configurations of angles and curves of their bodies against the wood and stone disarmed me. It was something about the combination of angularity and softness, a blend of Vermeer and Rembrandt. The curves of their close-shaven skulls went straight into me. They were beautiful—the bent, aged ones you could see were a step or two away from that simple burial, and the young ones, earnestly peaceful, still exuding the exertions of the quest. I envied them the steady beat of their ritually inscribed lives, the predictability of rising at 3:00 A.M. for vigils, personal prayer, breakfast; lauds at 5:45, eucharist at 6:15; choral prayer at 7:30, a morning of work; more choral prayer, then a simple lunch, and reading, rest, and prayer in the afternoon, vespers (this), supper, compline, and bed at 7:30. Undoubtedly I romanticize it. It's a life of hard work—farming, cleaning, studying—but it is safe and steady and full of method rather than madness. Or perhaps the madness remains, and I know nothing of this.

Who are they? Where have they come from? Who are their fathers and mothers and sisters? Why—*how?*—have they renounced the world? Why—*how?*—have they renounced the flesh?

I sat there, letting the sounds of their voices raised in songs of prayer wend through me. I felt very close to them, and also utterly removed, not just because I am in a state of secularity opposed to their sacredness, but also because I am the very other they have renounced. I was bleeding hard, a menstruating woman in the balcony. While they sang below about the sacrificial blood of Christ the Lamb, I was feeling and smelling and almost tasting my own monthly sacrifice. When I menstruate, I strain and moan with it, the cramping is heavy and deep, the smell of iron comes through my cunt (oh unmonastic word), my mouth, even, it seems, the pores of my skin. Bitter, metallic, red, sour, sweet—the smells of life, pond scum, flesh, woman. We are born between piss and shit; woman's body is the gateway to hell. And these men below me traded their own flesh and mine for the purity of contemplating another icon of desire.

Their voices waft up to me. I let the unexpected, surprising tears fall down my face onto my shirt, the shirt that covers the breasts that won't feed any more babies, won't produce any more mortals whose deaths the earth refuses to mourn. The movements they make below me—opening and closing books, turning pages, coping with sleeves, bowing and raising curved heads, opening and closing eyes, mouths—are orderly, perfect, timely, quiet. And I am bleeding up there, yearning toward them, toward my lonely others. I am not really thinking. I am all feeling. I am feeling my dead father, cassocked in Calvinist black rather than Cistercian white. I am feeling his pain, enclosed in spirit and earth thirty-five years ago. Their cassocks are white, the light flooding through the monastic windows is white, my father is black, and I am red.

One of the brothers rises to give the reading from the Book of Revelation. Crazy John on Patmos. "And in those days" before the end, there will be monsters like scorpions feeding on the flesh of men for five months. Like all of Revelation, it is pure vision, unencumbered metaphoric frenzy, hell on wheels. The monsters' tails are like the tails of scorpions, their wings and legs are those of lions and birds. And their hair? What else? Their hair, of course, is like the hair of women. My hair is long and dark under its pins. It's almost too much, this is. I want to take the pins out of my hair, pull the cotton from between my legs, and stand in the tribune naked, bleeding on the floor, wailing for Lucifer. Embrace me, brothers. I am your lonely other. Only one image of woman presides below—the Virgin enthroned with the Lamb in her lap: cool, distant, worthy of contemplation.

When vespers end, visitors and brothers file out. I watch the ones whose shapely heads attracted me most electrically. Only one looks up to the tribune, and his eyes meet mine in a secular glance that turns into a gaze. His eyes are assessive, tired, glassy. Immediately I think this is a man who once knew women. Then he, too, is gone, and Mac is gone, and I am alone in the chapel with one robed monk. We stay there together alone for many minutes. I don't know if he knows I am there, or if he cares. He never turns around, never looks up. His gaze is fixed on the representation of the Virgin and the Christ child. A piece of wood cracks into our silence. His head is curved in contemplation. He is young, lean, tall, gaunt. In the secular world, he would be ordinary, perhaps homely. Here he is Beauty's very form. And then I leave the lonely other, passing confessional booths on the way down, wanting, womanishly, to hear his confession, or to offer mine to him.

SACRED SPACE, IGNEOUS PRIVACIES

Mammoth Cave, Kentucky

Submission. I am sitting on the bank of the Green River, leaning against an old, tenacious tree root. We were warned against swimming here. The river looks peaceful, but the current is strong. I mucked about on the bank a while ago, my feet sliding so deep into slime and mud that I wondered if I'd just sink in to my thighs or my throat. Even holding tight to tree roots, the mud bank took my body, and I slid through it on bare legs and back. The sliding felt good, and part of me wanted to go right into the water. But I grabbed at a root, held tight against it. The shine of spiritual peace on the faces of the monks is possible only by submitting, giving oneself over wholly to that desire—but I am committed to the tussle, the wrestle, to what Blake called "mental fight," and I love its rigors, different from the rigors of submission, as the monks must have come to love theirs. I am not their representative, but Philip Larkin's in "Church Going," in which the speaker, doubter, quester, comes to terms with his motives for stopping at a country church. He comes here because this "cross of ground" is where believers have marked birth and marriage and death.

A serious house on serious earth it is,
In whose blent air all our compulsions meet,
Are recognized and robed as destinies;
And that much never can be obsolete.

The human hunger to "be more serious" makes us gravitate to church grounds, where we know "so many dead lie round." When I teach this poem to my students, I know they are too young to feel what it means. It never *quite* works for them the way I want it to, the way it works for me. In the blent chapel air of Gethsemani, my compulsions and those of my brothers seemed so far removed from each other, but another knower in me knew they met, even if only in separation.

This morning I entered Mammoth Cave, the largest natural cave system in the world. It's a time for entering sacred space—the monastery, the grotto. This very river carved out miles of underground, spacious caverns, theaters of rock, limestone acid eaten to form interiors of strange, godless, eyeless beauty. The caverns—we were three to four hundred feet underground—wind into twisting paths, each turn-off a secret whispered into the loins of the passers. Come to me, spoke each new turn, give yourself to my darkness as to the night sky and see if I will come forth into light.

What I found most mysterious was not the stunning smoothness of lime but the hemp or fiber sandals found in the caves within the last hundred years and recently dated—about two thousand years old. They must have been left by someone among the mound-builder cultures, the indigenous people of that period. I thought of my own son, my half-blood, two-hearted boy, my child who towers over me and whom I love with the utter selflessness—and the complete narcissism—of maternity. Where will he leave his shoes? Lately I have thought of the Iroquois Indian lore I have let slip from memory, the ritual injunctions of the old Seneca women who midwifed my entry into motherhood and into life on a reservation. They said I must bite rather than clip his fingernails. I've forgotten why, but I obeyed. They said I must point his shoes one way—I have forgotten which—either above or below his head—I have forgotten which—so that he would grow up to be, or would not grow up to be—I have forgotten what.

There was a time I did not believe in the value of such human rituals. There was a time I laughed over these desperate gestures of belonging, of incantation, of placating and pleading with the spirit world beyond us and within us. I was young and strong and stupid then. Now that I am older, still strong, still stupid, I know such rituals reflect needs fundamental enough that they will not be denied. I no longer deny them. I also don't know how to enter them. Do you enter them like you go into a cave, by simple steps?

I keep thinking about interior earth as sky, just as medieval people imagined the sky as a sphere, and the stars as a canopy for earth with a vague heaven beyond it. I suppose I think of the cave domes with some sense of completion, with the surface of earth a heaven of light—and the far interior as a vague hell, like Milton's Pandemonium in *Paradise Lost*. Infinity only baffles me, though the befuddlement is pleasant. I have always realized that I have an essentially medieval mind, yearning only dimly toward Renaissance. On some firmly established, stubborn level, I am pathetically hierarchical, a firm believer, beyond my permission, in the Great Chain of Being. Ridiculous. And deeply connected, I do not doubt, to my sorrow over mutability. Just dead *wrong,* too, in every way, and I know it. But I do think I must know my shadow, my specter, and embrace her in order to cast her out. So wandering through the maze of a deep cave, I find that its dome is my sky. That perception has its temporal virtues.

Forster's *Passage to India* comes to me again, Mrs. Moore nearly losing consciousness in the caves—people press too close, and she knows something is going to happen that she will be powerless to stop. She is growing old, homesick, wise and loving and vulnerable. I always remember two scenes—in the cave, when she feels suddenly oppressed, and on the ship on her way home from India to England, when she looks at the stars at night. I recall only these scenes, cave and sky. She dies while gazing at the sky. I identified strongly with Mrs. Moore not just because she was the locus of sanity, feeling, and decency in *Passage* but because people turned to her for answers that she knew she did not have. I feel that way often. For years, not just my students, but many of my friends—who ought to know better—have turned to me, convinced I am in possession of some truth, some ultimate, that I could give them if I only would. This has happened so much for so long that I realize I must project some kind of confidence I do not truly own. It's embarrassing and irritating. And it is also in some sense gratifying—it must be or I wouldn't allow it to continue. But I'm tired of being The Rock, the touchstone, for so many people. I have contributed deeply to their misreading of this personal text, this me, for so long that I am not sure how to escape it. I have done some things to end it—my friends' pilgrimages to my home have stopped, because I have learned, now and then, to say No. No, you can't come hundreds of miles to stay at my house and just talk to me, just be with me. (Please I won't bother you, you'll barely know I'm there, they used to say—grown-up people with real lives, professions, responsibilities—and then they'd come and break every promise and trail around my life like puppies, or imprinted ducks, quack-quack.) It's difficult even to write this, to commit it to paper, because it sounds prideful, egotistical. I have somehow been taken for a medicine woman, a magic mama. It's a sure case of mistaken identity.

I need to find places and people (few! few!) with whom I can crack, shatter, rebuild. I need time to feel my own pain, discover my own pleasure, empty of the expectation that I will behave like an icon, an emblem, a bloodless root of knowledge. I know nothing. Right now, this time in my life, I am raw, almost skinless sometimes, and that is something I must allow to happen. Allow? I seem to have little choice in the matter. Deep feeling—of which I speak much and experience little—is insinuating into my igneous privacy. If I thought I was a form of pure, stopped, frozen volcanic rock, I am discovering the lie. Pure sedimentary, I am. An underground river is carving these caves.

MISSISSIPPI HARVESTERS

Mississippi Delta

Homesteaders Tom Bridwell and Marilyn Kitchell live on a hundred acres of Mississippi Delta as poets, printers, hunters, harvesters. I've had enough of contemplation and caves and images of martyrs and monks and my own blood. It's time to put a hammer in my hands, maybe stop thinking for a while. On these meadows of Mississippi green, Tom and Marilyn are carving and building and forging, growing animals and each other and things to eat, and now a baby in Marilyn. You can't get there from here. Miles of gravel, then red dirt logging road, twisting and bending toward their compound (they call it "the campus") of house, barn, cabin, print house, with homes for Tom's parents, uncles and aunts up the road. Isolation and communion by choice with the angles of the outside world to which they wish to open: the hardware store, the redneck working buddies with coolers of beer in the back of the pickup, the old-timers from whom Tom learned to build homes by himself. Tom says, "We wanted to come where there was so much work to do that we could never finish it." That seemed to me a worthy statement of purpose.

Most of us set goals so that we can meet them—or we think that's what we intend. We feel the delicious agony of disliking ourselves for not meeting our own expectations. We languish in guilt, disappointment, lack of fulfillment. Tom and Marilyn seem steps ahead of that self-defeating brand of aspiration. They know that becoming is being, that the struggle and labor will never end. They don't want it to. In the lifetime meantime, one enters their world of order, wrested from chaos, as one would enter a state of clarity itself—a clarity consisting of constant, unremitting clearing—of land, mind, spirit, trees.

A woman dressed in white emerging from the trees—that was always Marilyn, says Mac, remembering the beauty she's brought to the several wild places she has lived. Like all their friends, we romanticize their lives. It's possible, though, to do that with some recognition of the sweaty labor they endure and lean into with determined, purposeful bodies from morning to night. Last night I went with Marilyn to the night feeding and milking of the animals. Marilyn as goatherd and milkmaid, surrounded by bleating kids born recently, Marilyn with balanced, spread legs kneading and pulling udders, speculating she might have been a goat in a previous life, telling me just *how* stupid chickens are, talking to her goats, speaking about printing books of poetry here in the woods, castigating Black and Decker, the recalcitrant baby bulls who immediately start sucking each other's genitals when she finishes feeding them. The two donkeys follow us curiously, suspiciously. Kids feed on my fingers, walk through my legs. Cats jump cattishly onto barn beams. Tom has already fed the pig. Pregnant Marilyn here among her creatures could not be more in touch with the fundamental, beating rhythm of life, feeding, being fed. It is difficult not to mythologize her. And we are fed royally at their elegant table on deer meat, mustard greens, goat-milk dressing, pickled okra, potato salad, and a strange variety of pea. Here there are *hundreds* of kinds of peas.

I slept hard and well here last night, but I dreamt of Harve. Harve is—was—another of the circle of poets-potters-printers-painters-sculptors (and the occasional carpenter or plumber—like Joel, the plumber who reads Wittgenstein) that we discovered on Cape Cod and Martha's Vineyard years ago. First Tom, and then Tom and Marilyn, were the magnetic core of that summer group of which we became erstwhile members—mainlanders and academics that we were, they still liked us, and they let us in. All of these people were dropouts from mainstream culture, all lived on the margins, barely making it financially—the intellectual underbelly of prosperous cape life. All had shed their previous professional lives in theater or academe or agency photography and were living on good vegetables, strong smoke, and coffee and beer, writing their poems and making their pottery. I was used to being the magnetic core of other people's seeking, and this was the only group to which I ever sought admittance. It was a large relief to be irrelevant, but welcomed.

Harve was one of them, a student of Buddhism, a poet, a quietly charismatic person. When he worked in a deli for a while, they called him the Deli Lama. There was something knowing and hard-edged about Harve, also something soft and wild. He'd had a psychotic break a few years before we met him. It was no secret that he was a troubled man, but in the horrible division of the world into winners and losers, I'd have said Harve was going to win. He didn't. When Tom and Marilyn moved here from the cape, Harve tried to make it here with them for a while, but the heat and the chiggers beat him. He went to Naropa Institute, looking for— what? "Seven tigers—nothing unusual—never mind," as one of his poems said. Then he returned to the cape, and when his lady there wouldn't take him back, he drove to the ocean beach, and at the summer solstice he blew his brains out.

He is one of the dear dead to whom I dedicated my book *Oedipus Anne* and one of those whose decision to leave life I have been trying to understand. When I first met him years ago at a poetry reading, I read a poem about my father's suicide. Everyone seemed a bit uncomfortable with it except Harve, who let me know in the clearest possible way that he had listened with empathy to every word. I didn't know then that I would later write a book that tried to empathize both with my father's death and with Harve's own. Harve's death was especially hard for Tom, Harve's closest friend, and for Marilyn, who loved him well. Tom had taught Harve how to shoot. Even the gun came from here. That darkness has shadowed the light of their carefully constructed world.

Tom's a good hunter and a good shot. This morning he took us out and taught me to shoot—first time in my life, except for an air gun. This morning I shot off two full rounds from a heavy pistol, and a few from a big rifle, at tin cans and Clorox bottles. It was terrific. I loved the sound, the feel, the power of it. You can surprise yourself with what you enjoy. I'd have said I would not like it, wouldn't be interested. I could have shot off rounds for hours. The bigger surprise is that I could get good. Pacifist, wouldn't-hurt-a-fly, feminist me got off on shooting. I can't imagine shooting anything alive (except a human intruder intending me harm, and I've always known I could do that if I had to), but those elegant things *are* killing machines, and if you can admire the seductions of the vehicle— then could I kill an animal? No, unless I was really hungry. Marilyn hunts deer, eats what she kills.

We went into town to the hardware store and met Troy, a good guy among the neo-Nazi racist Christian fundamentalists Tom says *are* Mississippi. Tom is thinking of writing a book he'd call *Mississippi Apartheid*. The whites hate and fear the blacks, think of them as a lower order of humanity—if human at all. Tom says that's the way it still is. It's the real reason I could not love the South, to say nothing of living in it. I wouldn't be able to keep my mouth shut when the old boys started in. I went through a long fallow period of doing just that in my life—ignoring racist comments, not wasting my energy responding. My work with black students and causes in the last few years, and my deep involvement in the life of Ayron, a half-black baby who is part of me, now make that silence impossible. I will never again be able to sit quiet or even walk away when white people speak disparagingly of people of color. Mine need not be the method of struggle adopted by all people—I certainly don't expect Tom to get himself in a fistfight every time he goes to the store for feed or nails. But I can't even allow harmless old white ladies their genteelly racist-liberal complacencies anymore. Some of the old ladies I know have said, for instance, that it's "cruel" for my daughter, Krissy, to have brought a sweet, beautiful, innocent, half-black baby into a world where she'll have to face racism—not theirs, of course, think they. But it is theirs. That's a racist sentiment from its rotten, hypocritical core. I have to say so, and I do. I'll do the same thing in public places and at family gatherings and in unpredictable social situations for the rest of my life. My words are nothing, they're cheap, they're easy, but I must say them.

The last twenty-four hours, since dinnertime yesterday, have been so packed that it could have been three days since I last wrote down my thoughts. I have read Harve's long suicide letter and the letter of an adopted daughter to her sister concerning feelings about their lifelong relationship and their mother's death—two of the nakedest, rawest, most searing documents of human pain and love I have ever seen. Marilyn and I had a breakthrough as women together and have grown closer to each other in one day than we've permitted ourselves over the last many years. We've all listened to Leonard Cohen's poetry sung by Jennifer Warnes on *Famous Blue Raincoat*. We listened to Garrison Keillor's monologue on "Prairie Home Companion" and he spoke right to me and to Tom about some very fundamental stuff in our lives. We've talked about Southern racism and miscegenation, tree lines, house building, families. We've eaten too much. We've gotten a taste of Sunday Mississippi clan life up the road, drinking beer and shooting at the empty cans with Tom's relatives and neighbors.

Tom's people remember *every detail* of nights forty-three years ago, the time Aunt Pearl got the fishhook caught in her hand or the morning that they caught over three hundred rainbow trout. We're close to Faulkner country, where the past is never dead. They speak only the speakable, the presentational, but I wonder: if Aunt Pearl can remember everything that was said that day in 1937, does she also, with equal clarity, remember the touch of one man's hand on her body in the dark that same year? or the thing Pete said to her in passing that he's never thought of since, but that she has kept alive daily for decades, replaying gestures of a moment worn into the folds of her brain?

When the shooting starts—hitting beer cans from fifty paces—guns materialize from everywhere. Uncle Morris, the alcoholic his wife kicked out, comes ambling over the hill with his repeater rifle. He has a face like the map of Texas, where he's from. He shakes my hand, then puts the gun in it. I'm shooting okay, but just missing. Then a burning cartridge pops out of the rifle and lodges to sizzle in my halter top, right between my breasts. I've branded myself. It's a perfect red circle, blistering now. Guns everywhere, one still in my hand. I'm into it, but also appalled, taking notes in my head. All these people are drinking in the vicinity of guns. It's a wonder there aren't more Sunday porch deaths in Mississippi. Drinking while shooting seems to be the state sport. It's hot and muggy. Someone comes up behind me—I didn't know who, turns out it was cousin Jim—and rearranges my body for my last shot. Everything feels personal and anonymous. These are good people, real storytellers.

I leave with Marilyn to walk the half mile home to milk the goats. We are speaking to each other, hearing each other in new ways. The fineness of her—I always knew it was there, never knew how we could penetrate each other's genuine but self-protective exteriors and strategic omissions. Those barriers fell away this time. I respect her dignity and grace, and now I know more about their sources. She knows me better, too. That kind of knowing and being known feels good and right.

I keep thinking of what Tom said about the monastic, contemplative tradition, and especially of the import of Eastern religion into Western thought. Having paid his dues, he distrusts, even despises it. He calls Naropa "no-hope-a" because of Harve. Having chosen active struggle as his way of being in the world—or it chose him—he distrusts passivity, surrender. I argued with him, yet my argument was born of an essential agreement, of true friendship—not all Buddhist approaches, though, are passive. Tom is all contained intensity. The burn of some sought and elusive pleasure (or peace) fires his eyes. It will always burn there, I can see that. He knows this, dislikes it, accepts it. Sometimes I feel close to Tom, and always safe, and often understood. Our similar intensities never quite surface. They meet somewhere out in the space beyond body. Like my relationship with my friends Richard and Pat, my bond with Tom is beyond gender, and understood without any need to speak it to each other.

Tom is making rich every step I take in this, the poorest county in the poorest state in the country. What I'm learning here is worth knowing, important for remembrance. The past will be in the present, as it is now.

✳

Tonight we'll listen to the radio together, talk about old times and the future, eat good food, drink home brew. I feel stoned. It's hot and muggy, I'm shooting off guns in the Mississippi Delta edge country, I'm far from home, disoriented, my spirit is struggling with unnameable and unspeakable conflicts, only some of which are muted by the diversions of fine people and new places. I yearn toward home and toward embracing the road in shifting and unequal balance. I feel suspended above and beyond my ordinary life. Some of the time I hardly know who I am. It's always that way on the road, where the burdensome hooks of normal daily rhythms are removed from my skin, so that I wonder what holds it to my bones and what holds my bones to the earth at all. The feeling is partly pleasant, partly painful, more insistent than it's ever been. I am trying merely to accept it, to work and feel my way through it, knowing that this trip will be—they always are—an emergent part of whatever I will be, whoever I will continue to become, when it is over, when I am opening my mail, wondering about the lives of the people I love through my absence, when I am placing my feet on the terra firma of Brocton, New York, and of Erie, Pennsylvania. I am always scared—there is no other word for it—when I'm away from home. I don't know of what—of rootlessness? of being whoever I am apart from place, from stability? of carrying my mind through space and time with this strange sense of lightness? No one would know it. Tonight and tomorrow, we will surely speak of things that count, real and substantial things, but I will also be hovering above us all, half out of my body, half out of my mind, somewhere else, interrogating the ceiling beams with questions I cannot form, and hoping for answers I'll never know. For some of the people back home who count on me, knowing this about me would tip the world slightly off center.

I *do* know what keeps my skin on my bones on the road—or who, more properly. To the extent that Mac is home, I carry home with me on the road, and so I do not come apart, I do recover my heart from the ceiling. It is he who takes me to the road, to the only forms of daring and venture I allow myself outside the realm of mental fight. My ambivalence toward him for removing my neurotic indicators of stability—the phone, the obligations, the smiling hooks of children, parents, students, computers—is real, and he knows it. He also knows that so far, on balance, it has always worked. By the middle of any lengthy trip, I give myself to the road, to the mountains, the moose, the coyotes, the deserts and canyons and rushing waters, the tacky tourist towns, the maps and road signs. Helpless in Erie on the street, I am a fine navigator of America. I turn into Mapwoman, deciphering routes with skill and authority. Will it be that way this time? Probably. But some part of me is detached, walking a lonesome valley, inhabited by the lonely other of Thomas Merton's contemplation.

The days begin to lose their distinction and discreteness on the road. I lose track of the days of the week, of what state I'm in. Sunday, someone reminds me. Still Mississippi. There are long stretches of driving on such a trip—ten hours at a crack—where nothing happens except fast movement overland that whacks out my sense of time. Then in people-places like this—we are still with Tom and Marilyn—a great deal happens. Such intense compression further fools the external and internal rhythms that usually mark the passage of whatever passes for time.

The heat weighs me down. Harve's suicide letter weighs me down, that pain he could no longer endure. I have never read anything like it in my life. I have no words to respond to his last words. It's no use, he wrote. When he loves, he loves too deeply and too much. When he hates, he hates too deeply and too much. No escape for him. The anonymous adopted daughter's letter is full of longing, self-erasure, self-claiming. I'm also reading journal excerpts given to me by my bulimic student. These three pieces of writing possess one common thread—a lonely self-loathing so unroutable as to be final and a plea to be loved unconditionally. It should not be so hard to be loved. I am accustomed to thinking of the differences between humans and other animals in either anatomical or perceptual terms—opposable thumbs, brain size, consciousness. *I think, therefore of course I am.* Consciousness of mortality in particular—*I know I die, therefore I know I am.* It's reversible, it also works as, *I know I am, therefore I know I will die.*

Perhaps the definitive differences are matters of love rather than of thumbs or thought. We love, we need to be loved, therefore we are human. Yet dogs "love," show evidence of needing to be loved, don't they? Or no—perhaps they accept affection when it is given, but do not die when it is removed? Maybe they do, though—I've seen dogs I knew were lonely. Dogs aren't fair points of reference, perhaps, because they are so domesticated that we have given them our need, passed it into their DNA by breeding them for our emotional use. Monkeys, too, so close to us in different ways—wire mother, cloth mother, the failure to thrive. I suppose animals have the need to *belong*—to species, to herds, to hives. In that sense, the human need to love and be loved is only a permutation of the need to belong that's clearly experienced by most animals.

I do think there's some distinction worth making about the character of our loving. Feeling may be regarded as a form of thought, a by-product of consciousness. But might it not be the *cause* of thought, of the emergence of consciousness, as easily as its partner or its effect? Thought, perception, consciousness, rationality do not seem to me as fundamental to the qualities of "the human" as does love and its sister, hate. To put it brutally, I have encountered many people in my life who are by any measure stupid—people who, in capacity to reason, to be aware, are about on the level of newts. But these same people, blank-eyed to reason, unreflective, damned near thoughtless, can love, can need love, with the intensity of a wildebeest crossing the African plains in search of water.

These three documents show me not only how unloved some people feel, but how unlovable. As I wrote to my bulimic student in response to her journal: we all know, or think we know, that we're shit. At best that's so in Western culture, and I pridefully believe it's universally true in some way. Why do people hate themselves so much? If they do find love with a fellow mortal, can there ever be enough of it? Why are we all such black holes of need? I want, I want, we cry. I want.

CACTUS, POETRY, DUNG BEETLES,

AND WILD PIGS

Big Bend National Park, Texas

Texas hill country has wildflowers in greater profusion than I've ever seen, field upon field of burnt orange, yellow, white, blue, for a hundred miles. Good-bye to green, hello to brown. Upland wetness and fertility and tall trees yield to sagebrush and dry heat, to creatures that squat in the sun. I've been waiting for this transition. Desert land is alien. I remember feeling uncomfortable with its otherness in the early 1960s, when I first crossed the Southwest as a kid. But I've come to like it. The Borrego Desert in California is a delight. Just like going to Europe taught me for the first time that I am an American, coming to love the desert Southwest has taught me that I'm an Easterner at heart. I don't know how that works. I can see myself living much farther east, in Maine, in Massachusetts, Vermont, but probably not the Southwest. I like being here for a leisurely visit, though. It's the otherness—what put me off at first—that I like. The hunker-down heat is tolerable because it's dry.

But dry was not what we got first at Big Bend. With a trip this long, you're not really on it until you've had an all-night, toad-strangler storm or two, until your camping gear gets wet and scummy, your personal belongings have unidentifiable crud on them, you can't find the soap, there's sand in the cooler, you don't know what day it is, weird things have happened, and you don't care because what the hell. By that definition, I'm on this trip now. Coming into the Big Bend area, I saw a dead coyote hung by its feet on a ranch-range fence. Now what the hell. It'd been hanging there for a while, a good while, dried out. There are few cattle on this open range in South Texas, no sheep, and anyway, coyotes don't bring down cows. The land won't support much in the way of crops or people or animals. So how come some rancher hung up a coyote? That's a loaded cultural gesture, but I don't quite get it. A throwback to when coyotes really did present a threat to ranchers? Just rancher hatred of coyotes as useless, nasty critters, the bad rap? Who is the statement directed to—coyotes? people?

Big Bend is startlingly green, though it's Chihuahuan Desert. Freakishly green, despite ocotillo, prickly pear, yucca. By annual rainfall standards (about ten inches) it's desert. Big Bend is huge, surrounded by Mexico on three sides. It's one of the least-visited national parks (remote, not built up, not terribly hospitable for tourists hooked on comfort) and one of the most diverse. The Rio Grande on the south border is a mile below the northern Chisos Mountain section. The first night, we camped in the desert at low elevation on the park's border with Mexico, almost on the Rio Grande. It's real there—a remote Mexican village, Boquillas, just across the river that you can get to by rowboat only. The Park Service has nothing to do with it. Very few park visitors know about it. The villagers row a few gringos over the river. There's dope and firearms smuggling and wetbacks, and when it's festival time in the village, the culture clash still involves guns and fights and occasional murders. I wanted to go.

But Big Bend was having freak weather. Our first night here, they got about one-quarter of their *annual* rainfall. The campground flooded, but we were lucky—the tent held up, everything wet but not soaked through. A lot of people's gear floated away, as I discovered on my morning run. Later we found a remote river access area, climbed a steep hill till it got too hot, then came down to the river bank, Mexico just across it, in a canyon we had to ourselves—until the outfitters arrived to launch a float trip from our spot, because the usual access place was flooded out. Mud everywhere, buzzards. A lot of bird people come to Big Bend, where hundreds of species congregate. I'm charmed when Mac points out a new one, but my real and plebeian fascination is for the vultures always circling, huge and ugly-beautiful, common, black with red heads and three- to four-foot wingspans. You can feel them flying close, hear the beating of their wings. Sometimes they make a shadow flying close overhead. I like these mean-ass birds, so obvious and crass and hard edged.

Yesterday afternoon we tried to get across the river to the Mexican village that welcomes the few turistas who come. The word was that the mud on the Mexican side of the Rio Grande was knee deep, so probably no boatman. I was feeling edgy enough to try, so we drove to the access area and started down to the river on foot. Within a hundred yards, mud up to our ankles. We tried to get through it, but there was no water anywhere (the river doesn't count when it's all mud), and the boat probably wouldn't have been there if we'd managed to make it to the near shore. The village itself was flooded. I'm not that adventure crazed. I've gotten us in hip-deep beaver swamp in the Colorado Rockies, but mud is not my milieu, and the odds against getting there were high.

Risks. Chance taking. I take most of my chances in my head. I'm usually wimpy about physical risks. I have no desire to skydive or downhill ski. And *adventure* is often a negative word for me. I usually agree with Bilbo Baggins about adventures: "Nasty, disagreeable, uncomfortable things—make you late for dinner." I've still got a few risks left in me, some capacity for adventure, for taking chances. I'm still alive. But I want my risks essentially safe—no high odds, no potentially large prices to pay, no broken bones possible, no broken soul especially—and I know that's cheating.

We changed campsites last night, moved upland thirty miles from the Rio Grande into the Chisos Mountain area—cooler, maybe drier. Here we are surrounded by dramatic mountain skyline, almost red-rock peaks. Late last night we watched a lightning storm over the peaks, unnerving because we didn't know if it was coming our way—it wasn't, finally. Surrounded by this splendor I am contemplating what Aldo Leopold—writer, naturalist, Wilderness Society founder—called "thinking like a mountain." I am thinking about thinking like a mountain, but I can't do it. I think more like a river rat than a mountain. Yet it is true that when I come up against mountains, I remember that there might be other than transient human thought, might be gods other than our pale, anthropomorphized imaginings create. Leopold also said, speaking of riding a horse in a thunderstorm in the Rockies, that it must be a mean life that has done away with fear. I'm afraid of the mountain and the storm over it.

This, too, from Leopold:

> In dire necessity somebody might write another *Iliad,* or paint an 'Angelus,' but fashion a goose? . . . If, then, we cannot live without goose music, we may as well do away with stars, or sunsets, or *Iliads.* But we would be fools to do away with any of them.

Fashion a vulture? Mac reminded me that someone asked J. B. S. Haldane if his long career as a naturalist had led him to any conclusions about the nature of the Almighty. He replied that he had learned something of interest about God: "He must have an inordinate fondness for bee-tles." (One of the quarter million species of them has now landed on me.)

I'm just back from hiking down into the Chisos Basin Canyon to the floor, where you're really in the belly of the valley of the surrounding red-rock peaks. Down on the valley floor, you can just sense a shadow of what kind of world the aboriginal Indians of this area occupied—there must have been some, even if this isn't a richly archeological site. It's quiet, deep, still green. The variety and diversity of plant life in this high desert is as-tonishing. The century plant, a member of the agave group, and related to the yucca, is without doubt the sexiest plant in the world. I saw them in every stage from young to dead, from a couple of feet to fifteen, from green to dead black, from bursting wet to dry rotted. At one growth stage they look like gigantic, jack-in-the-beanstalk asparagus you could eat for days. Several other stages are screamingly phallic, just pure sex, huge purple-green pillars that look like erections ready to ejaculate. I tend to sexualize my visual field, but this was so broadly erotic that I fail to see how anyone, at least any heterosexual or bisexual woman worth her salt, could not perceive the yucca plant as male genital. I've seen film of plants that struck me as erotically charged, but I've never actually fantasized sex with a real plant before. This reminds me of Georgia O'Keeffe's flower paintings, where eros is absolute, both diffused and concentrated beyond denial, pure life force. The century plant enters my mind with the artist who lived nearly a century. The plant is Mescal by another name. This was once Apache territory. They used the century plant (so called because it blossoms so seldom) for everything—food, shelter, clothing. It was to the ancient people here as the buffalo was to the nineteenth-century Plains Indians, the very stuff of their lives. That's surely one rational way to see it as eros.

I also found the spiny cactus called lechuguilla that sends up fingers, and in the crotches of these protrusions cluster a variety of beetle. They sit on the stalks and mount each other in a quiet desert afternoon orgy of feeding and sex. They're black, with bright orange-tipped feelers, and appear to have great patience. Periodically, wildly orange wasps interrupt them and they raise a menacing leg. That's all. They make a shuddery buzz, rather frightening at first, moving from place to place. Then you become used to them, as the deer here are used to us. Tame deer—a little too tame for my taste—wander through the campgrounds unafraid. They shouldn't trust so much. Then again, what's wrong with the peaceable kingdom where people and predators and prey come together affectionately?

✳

I studied God's inordinate fondness for beetles for half the day. Coming up the Chisos Basin Trail, I saw two beetles rolling a piece of horse dung across the path. I stayed, sillier by the minute on sun and dung beetles. Group after group of hikers passed me while I watched the journey, the quest, of one team of two scarabs over a span of about eight feet. What I learned about dung beetles, what they taught me about my life and theirs, will take me years to process.

Two of them rolled a largish piece of dung across the trail together. They helped each other. The smaller one provided passive weight on the inclines, while the larger one bunged like hell with his back legs. The little one would pull the dung over on top of him/herself while the bigger one pushed. In this fashion, they could truck along on the beetle interstate at no mean pace. Then up a big hill. They'd get halfway up and fall down six inches, halfway up and fall down six inches, halfway up and fall down six inches, until Sisyphus' rock took on fecal overtones. I couldn't leave until they got up the hill. I moved stalks of desert grass out of their way. I was desperate for them. But they weren't. Just keeping on keeping on. The hand I moved the grass with is bedecked with two ridiculously large silver rings: Egyptian dung-beetle rings, scarabs, two working together on my hands. I remove them only occasionally; they are part of me, to be buried with me, no doubt, as they were with the Egyptian dead as signifiers of immortality. One Egyptian belief says the sun is a giant ball of dung rolled across the sky every day by a scarab.

Finally my beetles gave up and curved overland. I expected they were heading for a den. But no—what I learned next is that they make a den on the road. They stopped twice. First time, the big beetle scouted ahead, dug for a while at a likely submersion site, then went over to the smaller beetle guarding the dung and bumped into him/her with a signal that clearly said, "Nope, not here." On they went. A few feet later, they began to dig loose dirt in earnest for a long time. The dung wasn't yet buried, but the dirt was nice and loose and they were burrowing efficiently. Suddenly, the smaller one emerged, walked a few inches away, cleaned her/himself elaborately—and flew off.

This threw me, because I had figured the code came to this: *Okay, field buddy or mate, I know where you are, I can get back to this spot. It's inefficient for both of us to finish burying this piece of shit—so I'll see you later.* But that wasn't it. Because after another fifteen minutes of solitary burrowing, of what I thought was finishing the job, the other beetle bunged off with the dung—up and left, deserting the burrow. Now figure that. I left, too, like a dumb beetle, up the path, bewildered. There has to be a reason for this. I have asked several people who know something about beetles, but they don't know the answer. I am not likely to learn it in this life.

The poet Howard Nemerov wrote about a little bird who feeds on lion dung in the zoo. It ends:

> This goes to show that if you have the wit
> To be small, simple, cute, and live on shit,
> Though the cage fret kings, you may make free with it.

That's about dung beetles and birds and women as far as I can see. Women figure less subtly in that other famous dung poem, Andrew Marvell's "To His Coy Mistress," the seventeenth-century metaphysical make about a man trying to talk a woman into giving up her virginity. It proceeds on Hegelian lines—thesis, antithesis, synthesis.

> *Thesis:* If we had all the time in the world, your coyness and evasiveness would be no problem.
> *Antithesis:* "But at my back I always hear / Time's winged chariot hurrying near. . . ."
> *Synthesis:* Therefore, let's do it *now.*

Near the end appears this elaborate, grotesque conceit built on the dung rolling of scarabs, these beetles on my hand:

> Let us roll all our strength and all
> Our sweetness into one ball
> And tear our pleasures with rough strife
> Through the iron gates of life.
> Thus though we cannot make our sun
> Stand still, yet we will make him run.

Oh mama. Why am I afraid to run the sun? Why does it scare me? Leonard Cohen: *Like a bird on a wire, I have tried, in my way, to be free.* While watching the beetles, I occasionally looked up from the microcosm to the mountains. I can't think like a mountain, but I have tried, in my way, to be free.

In "Design," Robert Frost's speaker encounters a white mutant flower, a white spider, and a white moth—"assorted characters of death and blight

/ Mixed ready to begin the morning right." He watches the drama of predator and prey unfold, appalled, then asks what kind of pattern, of design, produced it:

What but design of darkness to appall?—
If design govern in a thing so small.

What I saw at the end of my dung-beetle afternoon was the opposite—a beautiful yellow flower with a small, matching yellow butterfly feeding on it. I asked what kind of pattern or design was behind it, and found myself answering:

What but design of lightness to delight?—
If design govern in a thing so bright.

Well? Does it? Is there design, grand and minute? Is it meant to appall us? Delight us? Or doesn't it give a good goddamn? I hope it doesn't care about anything as trivial as human perception of it—it couldn't be very grand if it did. I suppose we cannot help but search it out, interrogate its intention, create it if it isn't there, desire to know our place in it, if it is. But that's *our* red wagon—or yellow butterfly or dung beetle.

✳

I just had an adventure, and it's not even quite 8:00 A.M. Yesterday on the canyon trail, I ran into a man who had encountered one of the wild pigs that live in the canyon, called javelinas or peccaries. The pig had scared off easily. I was sorry I probably wouldn't get a chance to see one. I was even jealous. That was yesterday afternoon. I had no idea that by 6:45 the next morning, I'd have been chased by half a dozen of them. Early this morning, we heard some impressive snorting sounds down in the draw off the trail near our campsite. Before he left on his run, Mac saw one of them, but it was still pre-dawn dark. As it got lighter, I left the tent and went down the trail, following the sounds. No one else around—just me and the sounds of what my field guide now tells me, thank you, are "the truly wild pigs of the New World." I'm squatted down just off the trail, looking hard into dense undergrowth area, hoping to see one, pretty confident they'll take off when they catch my scent. Sure enough, there they were, about half a dozen, snorting and rooting around, smallish but substantial. Wild, squatty, beasty.

And then they either saw me or caught my scent. At which point they're supposed to take off, yes? But no. One starts toward me—then another—

then another—then while I'm feeling like they're ambling in my direction from several sides, I catch sight of The Boar, twice the size of the females, making lots of noise, coming at me. I'm between the boar and the females. Picking up speed now, all of them.

I want to stand my ground. I have to make a quick decision. I suddenly remember all the nature film I've seen on various kinds of wild boars. Some wild pigs are known for ferocity. Check. But pigs don't eat people. Check. And we're in one of Our National Parks—there would be warning signs if the wild animals here were dangerous, yes? Maybe. Then again, this *is not* one of your well-manicured, tidy parks—it's inhospitable wild land. Just last night I heard that so far this year, twelve people have died at Big Bend. This is only May! Three of those were drownings in the Rio Grande. Allowing for a couple of homicides and a couple of heart attacks and a couple of falls from cliffs—maybe the pigs go ape now and then? No. They're just curious, they just want to check me out. I remember how ungrounded my bear fears were in Yellowstone. But I've got six wild pigs closing in on me, I'm alone, and it's still not completely light out. I turn and run a few yards, figuring they'll stop. But my running makes them start to clip along, the sound of their collective hooves impressively firm and thunderous. So I take off in earnest, head back up the hill to the campsite, and when one backward look tells me they're coming right up after me, I don't stop until I get to the van. Close the door. Pant. Wait. Nothing.

Finally I get out and approach the hill they'd been coming up last I saw. One remains posted near the entrance to the campsite. I get up on the picnic table and then I see the boar a few feet further down, even bigger than I thought. Standoff. We stare at each other. Finally they get bored, and I realize I'm not going to get boared. They turn around and leave. Now that I've had time to check out the field guide, I'm somewhat reassured. They're nearsighted and curious, far less ferocious than their reputation. I probably could've stood still and let them check me out. But half a dozen wild pigs coming at you in the brush is not an easeful encounter. Perhaps I wish that my sense of risk taking had been a little stronger—but I'm glad to have gone down there alone instead of staying warm in my sleeping bag. Adventure enough, and it didn't even make me late for breakfast.

ALAMOGORDO AND WHITE SANDS

White Sands National Park, New Mexico

Yesterday we entered the vast military testing areas of New Mexico and Arizona. The desert land is still used for missile tests, and of course the A-bomb was first tested not far from here. (Tested? Exploded.) The car has not been running right. It's bucking again. On the phone, my son, Bernie, told me he had a dream that we were killed in a car accident and that my friend Karen called him on the phone, as executor of my estate, to locate my personal papers. He said the dream was vivid and frightening. I respect dreams enough that I am thinking of what he said. The car is dangerous. So we have stopped to have it fixed.

It is Wednesday? Still? Again? Perpetually? I'm sitting in the showroom/ waiting room of a car dealer in Alamogordo, New Mexico. I've been sitting here for almost five hours. I fully expect to sit here for five more hours. Behind me the easy listening music is pumping out of a speaker I can't turn off, and it's too high on the wall to punch it out. I have read every readable word of *Rolling Stone* and several columns of the unreadable stuff. I just don't give a good goddamn which new rock singer I never heard of has just cut an album that will change music history or which one has been recently arrested for puking on a policeman in Minneapolis, even if, especially if, they're the same person. I have read this week's *Newsweek*. I have eaten at Arby's, having selected it from among the many culinary delights offered on this endless stretch of New Mexico suburban strip— Wendy's, Kentucky Fried Chicken, Pizza Hut, McDonald's, Burger King, and Denny's all within a few blocks. I have watched a spectacular sundown over the rooftop of the Mini-Mart across the street. The first A-bomb exploded a few miles from this car dealer—this is Oppenheimer territory. Right now I don't care if they test a new bomb in the parking lot of the Dodge/Plymouth dealer. If it means I don't have to sit here anymore, I'm for it.

The nagging car trouble with us since Arkansas has escalated across country. We've left a paper trail of dealer stops and abortive fix-its from Austin to Carlsbad to this horrid blot on New Mexico. Mac has handled all of it until now, while I worked at the Sexton archives in Austin and played at Carlsbad. We're in a terrific mood, we are. In an effort at uplifting conversation, I just pointed out the fabulous pink-orange of the sky to Mac, and he glanced up long enough to say, "Fuck it." All the salesmen are going home to their wives. Fuck them, too, and their wives and their dogs. I have been listening to car salesmen make conversation for many hours, with the exception of the Arby's break, accompanied by one of those whining three year olds you want to either kill or stuff with an Arby's baked potato, whichever will shut her up fastest. I'll bet I was that kind of three year old.

The trouble is euphemistically called "the driveability problem." You're driving down the road at sixty plus and suddenly it starts bucking and losing gas. It has taken three dealers to think of checking the fuel pump, which is the first thing I would have checked, even though I don't know a fuel pump from a battery. Now we find out that this happens with about 5 percent of the Chrysler products that have this engine system. But that's okay. No problem. Just because we paid $16,000 for this van a few months ago so that we wouldn't be driving a clunker across country again, as we have twice before—is that any reason for us to lose our sense of humor? Just because we're now several days behind? And have had some entirely too invigorating moments on mountain roads?

This new high-tech "driveability kit" they're ostensibly installing has a few glitches to work out in an understocked New Mexico service department. Scrap of dialogue from back there:

> *Service Manger to Mechanic:* So are you okay as far as grommets and everything?
> *Mechanic:* We don't have any grommets.
> *Service Manager:* That's okay, you can use tape.

It's very reassuring to know that we'll be on the highway soon with a car held together by tape. At night. In bleeding New Goddamn Mexico in the humping desert. Someone is out in the parking lot on a motorcycle, singing "There's an Old Flame Burning in Yer Heart." I have seen the future. The future is a neon strip of New Mexico, mile after mile of fast food, showrooms, car washes, gas stations, convenience stores, motels. This makes the trailers in the Texas border villages look inviting. Also makes home look like the new Jerusalem.

Still here. It's an hour later. Have been talking to the service manager, who has about four-fifths of his face. (But hey—four-fifths is better than a half.) He must have been in a monumental car accident or a fire. I like him. He's soft-spoken, smart, careful, easy to talk to, a displaced New Yorker here for eight years. He likes it, but sometimes the isolation gets to him—that and no real restaurants, just this endless fast food and glitzy chains of steak houses. Steak—we passed our first major feedlot not far back. Feedlots should make instant vegetarians of us all. The smell of death houses is not possible to describe in any terms but its own, because not only is nothing worse; nothing is remotely comparable. It's at the top of the metaphor chain, the Ur-Smell.

John used to deliver mail on a subcontracting basis in an urban glut area near New York, and he likes this job much better. But in his quiet, accepting way, you can tell John is a disappointed man who has resigned himself to never being happy, even if not miserable. (Would you settle for a "fairly good time," John?) Dead dreams line his face—a good face, despite the scars. I wonder what those dreams were. And I also wonder: when I make up material like this about a person's life, based on a conversation, the movement of hands and feet, the manner of speaking, am I being patronizing and arrogant instead of decent and fellow human? The music just improved—"Don't Think Twice, It's All Right."

*

Last night finally ended. Maybe I'm only dreaming it did. Sometime after ten at night, they finished the van and asked us to take it for a spin. It was fine for about five minutes. As we were going to bid a fond, exhausted farewell to these good guys, it happened all over again. The van bucked and then it stalled out. They adjusted yet another item and we pulled out of Alamogordo before eleven. White Sands was only about twenty miles away, but no campsites. We decided against a motel in Alamogordo—I've seen enough of that military-base annex to last several lifetimes. We decided to just park the van in the lot at White Sands and catch some sleep. We slept straight through till morning and were ready to enter the Sands at opening time, 8:00 A.M.

But no. The road into the white gypsum dunes—miles and miles of deserted, stunning white—was closed for missile testing, army or air force. Possibly Star Wars lunacy, possibly something less lethal. Americans who came here to enter one of the great natural wonders we own as citizens have to sit on their butts while the military-industrial boys play with their toys—the toys that will certainly one day destroy this earth. Can any sane person doubt it? I am not a nuclear alarmist by any means, and I've never seen the use of apocalyptic rationales for not living a reasonable life, a life you expect to come to a natural rather than global end. But of course I think the frightened old men and psychopathic boys who run the world will one day end it all. Our weaponry cannot exist perpetually without someone having to use it someday. It's just human nature. The mountain is here, so it must be climbed. The means to destroy life on earth still exist, so they must eventually be utilized.

We were the first ones on the dunes when the testing ended. About eight miles in, it begins to get spooky. By then it's *all* white—even the road is packed white gypsum. You feel like you're at the North Pole—white sand looks much like snow—or maybe on the moon. Because we beat the tour buses, we had a lonely series of dunes to ourselves. I've never felt more out of the world than I did then. I slid down a huge dune sideways. I ran for a long time along the packed top of a long dune without my glasses on. No one who isn't extremely nearsighted will understand quite how radical an act that was. The endless sameness of the dunes was supplemented by half when I made all that uniformity as fuzzy as thick fur by changing my sight and ran through it with a sharp wind on my face. If I'd been in a different frame of mind, it would have felt almost threatening.

Then I thought, when will I ever be in a place like this, in this frame of mind, again? What else do I want to do? I wanted to take off all my clothes and run. So that I could keep trying, in my way, like a bird on a wire, to be free. Mac went along with the program happily. He was my lookout while I got naked in one of our national parks, running through the jewel-glisten of gypsum. Will I recognize myself when the pictures he took come back from Fotomat, while I'm sitting at the computer all earnest and professional? Will I have the decency, at that remove, not to patronize the naked woman on the dunes?

THE HERMIT OF OMIGOD HOTSPRINGS

Salton Sea, Sonoran Desert

I had to think a while to remember what day of the week it is, as usual. That's both a good and a disorienting feeling. Anecdote on that from a recent phone conversation with my house sitter at home in New York: I called about something and asked him what day a particular incident that I was irritated about had happened back home. (I think it had to do with which teenager had used one of my cars when they all knew I didn't want it used. Well-meaning young folks seem to have bad luck in my cars. They have accidents and raise my insurance.) What day did she take the car, I asked him. He paused—he is great at pauses—and then asked, "Well, I'm not sure—what day is *this?*" I paused, then said, "I don't know." We both paused for a while more, and then started guessing. Is it Monday? I dunno, is it? Tuesday? This went on inordinately long. Two adults, utterly unable to figure out what day of the week it is. We did seem to agree on the month. It's June. Isn't it?

A while back I was singing the praises of motels over camping. Now, after a week of motels, I am sick unto death of them and missing the rougher pleasures of camping. Unfortunately, it's too late for that now—today we will arrive in Escondido, near San Diego, for the most sedentary part of the trip. This is when we visit Mac's mom and stay in one place until the middle of June, when Bernie and his lady Mary Ellen arrive. There's good stuff ahead: the ocean and Sequoia National Park with its giant redwoods, splendid Yosemite, Joshua trees. There will be camping again, but not for well over a week. In the meantime, an experience after we left Camelback Resort, one I've been awaiting a long time, will have to hold me.

Doug Judell, who lives in a cabin he built in the woods back home, put us onto this place years ago. Doug is one of those people who suddenly disappears for months at a time. He just up and hits the road. He goes to the Farallon Islands in the Pacific off San Francisco to watch birds and count baby seals for government wildlife studies. He lives out of cars and vans or a boat on the Yukon River. He heads for Costa Rica and doesn't come back for a year. When he has adventures, he does it right. His experiences are too interesting for me to want to live them, but it's good to hear them. Several years ago, Doug told us about the Salton Sea area of the Sonoran Desert in the Imperial Valley. The Salton Sea is a weird mistake, created accidentally by railroad workers trying to irrigate the valley by digging trenches from the Colorado River. It got away from them, and all the dikes and dams in the world couldn't stop it, because the area was below sea level. The Salton Sea is the large body of saltwater that resulted from this, in the middle of nowhere.

Doug was driving around drifting, when he ambled down an obscure dirt road to what appeared to be an oasis of a few trees. Suddenly he came upon a gathering of vehicles and naked people in the middle of the desert at a natural hot spring. He got out of his car and said, "Oh my God!" Apparently that's what many travelers who come upon it say, so its casual name, not on any map for tourists, is consequently "Omigod Hotsprings." So the story goes, apocryphal or no. We've been intending to find it for years. Yesterday we did.

Coming through the Sonoran and the Mojave from Arizona, the prospect of the Imperial Valley is amazing. Everything turns screaming green. The valley is the lettuce capital of the world, fruits and vegetables growing in field after field, grape vineyards and orchards, all artificially irrigated by (mis)use of the Colorado. Massive Cal-Agriculture. Tucson and Phoenix, and all cities created by rip-off irrigation, feel like blisters in some respects, but this doesn't. If you bring "civilization" to the desert and call it a city, it's awful. If you bring it to the desert and call it agriculture, it doesn't *look* so bad. Neither the water-glutted cities nor the water-glutted fields of green "should" be here, but the uses of the Imperial Valley seem more benign. A head of lettuce is better than a leg of Kentucky Fried Chicken—until, of course, you stop to think of the exploitation of migrant laborers.

We drove down the edge of the Salton Sea, searching for the inland road that the hot spring runs near. We asked the locals, but even they are vague. We figured that since Doug told us this story several years ago, the colony of nudists might well be gone by now, but the spring must still be there. A local pointed vaguely that-a-way, so we went up the road, looking for the unmarked dirt turn-off. We followed the dirt road for almost a mile, and there it was. This was my first experience not only of a magical hot spring but also of a desert hermit, the only person there. He had made his home camped by the pools, with his pickup truck, boat, and motorcycle. His clothes hung over trees, and other signs of his established residence were clear—a lawn chair from a garbage dump, an arrangement of rocks in a rock garden. He was tan and thin and smart and weird, in his forties or fifties. His name is Brendan. He's intense, a little wild-eyed.

Brendan was very helpful. He explained the system of springs and pools and run-offs, showed us the crude wood, dirt and rock dams, and the place where the spring bubbles up, forming three pools of increasing temperature. The hottest is too hot to enter. The bottoms are sand and dirt. He showed us around very politely, said it's too hot right now and that's why no one is there (it was 112 degrees), and then he walked away and left us alone. He mentioned that some people had been there earlier today. Mac walked away toward the far pool where no one goes (too much slime and fish), and I walked around in the coolest (still warm) pool, and then I heard the damnedest thing. Brendan walked into a little area a few yards away that he had created with a sheet under the shade of a small tree and started to gasp and hyperventilate, then almost choke. He did this for a while. I thought he must be sick—and then I heard him half gasp: "Oh God. More people."

He was talking about us. This man lives here when it's too hot for lizards, and we were the second batch of people that day. He obviously wants or needs to be absolutely alone. He is okay for basic human communication, but he doesn't *want to*. I didn't feel alienated from him at all because of this. I felt ironically connected. I just wanted to get out of his way. Sometimes when I'm at work, and people have clustered too close and too much all day, I close my office door and do the same thing. I even hyperventilate. Those suffocated sounds felt familiar—they're my own. This is a strange analogy because I'm very much in the world, the opposite of hermitlike. I need people. But sometimes they're too much. The Salton Sea is a change of venue, but the situation is similar—Brendan's tolerance level is just a lot lower than mine.

When Mac came back, we soaked in the spring. Meanwhile, Brendan made preparations to move his camp. He was not offended by our nakedness, I'm sure of that, nor even by anything in particular about us. In fact, once in a while he'd walk over to give us advice about how to wash off the black sand. But he needed to be alone. Fine. It's a big desert, and it was almost evening, so he moved way off, truck and cycle and all. We waved good-bye to this desert rat walking off into the hot sands. Who is he? Where'd he come from? What's his story? How does he stand such steaming aloneness? I wanted to ask him, and of course I did not. I was quiet the whole time. He and Mac did the talking. I just listened and heard how smart he was. I did ask one thing. You been staying here a long time? He considered for a while. Then he nodded and said, *Yes. A long time.*

BRAIN-DEAD AND BIG-CHILLED
IN SOUTHERN CALIFORNIA

Escondido and Carlsbad Beach

Borrego State Park is in the Anza-Borrego Desert section of the Sonoran. Last night we found a real Mexican eatery—we're near the border again—a little hole in the wall with two booths, a couple of tables, tongue-melting hot sauce, homemade tortillas, and a little old man in tattery clothes who took our order and brought our food. It doesn't get better than this. The final note of perfection was the television blasting from the corner, with a rerun of "Three's Company." It made me feel like I was in a time/space warp.

I'm surrounded by fabulous mountains—Pinto, Chocolate, Orocopia, Chuckwalla—and dry desert again. I like Anza-Borrego. In a few hours, I'll be back in the completest, most oppressive kind of civilization and Californication: in a retirement community surrounding a golf course outside of San Diego, where nobody reads, everyone plays bridge and goes shopping and worries about what to have for lunch. The contrasts in this trip are as wildly swinging as my hormone balance. Yesterday morning a hot tub in a fancy, obscene resort—yesterday afternoon, Omigod Hotsprings. Yesterday a desert hermit—today the old widows of San Diego who hole up in their air-conditioned homes, waiting for the Millennium. I know how I'll stay sane. I'll go to the ocean, that big deep mama.

✳

I am in never-never land. California always affects me this way. Everything is suspended somewhere in the ozone, especially my mind. It's a remarkable state of the union and a remarkable, unmarkable state of mind. I know that it's probably the richest and most diverse state both geographically and culturally, with mountains and deserts and ocean, dryness and wetness and every imaginable color. It's got critters both human and otherwise animal that exist almost nowhere else—Joshua trees and Sequoias and encounter groupies and gurus with *California* stamped on their branches and their psyches. I hate southern California. I always have. I lived in suburban L.A. when I was a teenager. My soul barely survived the numb of southern California, and when I come back, I come to the child-woman who became sentient here in every way, became a reader for the first time in her life to escape the heat and the bad dreams, became desirous, learned what the minor keys in classical music can do to the inside of your ribcage. I loathed all the awakening I first did here. I'd have done it then in any case, because I was twelve. But to awaken in Babylon? To come alive in every tendon and muscle, to see with the peeled-eye madness of adolescence and find that *what you see* is country clubs glazed in neon and plastic, and you a pulsing nerve that takes it all in?

As many Californias as there are, I might have found a better one, and sometimes I did at the ocean. But I hardly saw it. Just steaming streets, everyone an immigrant from a thousand Nebraskas and Dakotas and Wisconsins, no one belonging there, including me. No real seasons—I speak here only of southern California—no snow—steady polyester and urethane—fake grass—false lushness—imported palms—stucco houses—imitation Mex—imitation everything—no rootedness in the eyes on the street, just lost and aimless energy not knowing where to light. That was my private view of California. But I should be grateful—southern California might have a lot to do with who I became. It turned me into a reader. Here I first read Dickens and Austen and Shaw. It turned me into a listener—Bach and Beethoven and Brahms and Mozart. Strange, because this was where everyone was doing rock music on the beach. In secret, even almost from myself, I did that, too.

The desire I was introduced to here was brief and tame, but significant, one of those moments you remember for a lifetime for no reason you can identify. I was twelve. I was on the beach with beautiful Greek Helen, my watchful, powerful, intellectual friend, who made my California life bearable. Full moon evening, pounding music coming from somewhere offshore, she and I walking and talking. In the other direction came two marines from Camp Pendleton. "Ignore them," Helen said, but one caught my eye, and I his, and despite Helen's power over me—she was careful to keep me from men, to keep me pure for books and the right kind of music—I left her and walked along the beach with this young marine in uniform. I don't remember his name or where he was from, I don't even really remember his face.

What I do remember was the sensation when he took my hand and we danced on the sand, looking at each other. Just hands and rhythm. Then Helen literally hauled me away from him, calling me boy crazy. I felt the injustice of that—aren't girls of twelve screwing their brains out these days?—but I also felt guilty, because she had seen desire for men in me, and she received the knowledge with contempt. That was without a doubt the first time I knew I had a sexual body. If Helen the Superego had not been there, I'd have done more. As it was, I did nothing but hold a strange man's hand. I'd still call it my introduction to sex. I thought about that young man—how old could he have been? eighteen? twenty?—for years. Decades later, I recall him now. But I don't know who he was. And decades later, I still love Helen for everything she gave to me, and everything she kept me from. I needed a keeper, and she was a good one. Her influence on my life was bigger than she knows. A neat coincidence: her last name then was George, my own name now.

Back now from a country club lunch with nice old ladies. I had a decent time by getting one of them to be silly with me. But look, I really go nuts here. I just stop functioning, my mind goes to sleep. I drive down the streets and strips and freeways, assaulted by housing developments and billboards and the smell of hot tar and dirty money, and I feel desperate all over to escape it, but since I can't yet, all my systems shut down. I go on autopilot. There's some hope of feeling human again soon. Tonight we'll be at a campsite on the ocean at Carlsbad Beach. I'm going to stay there for a few days while Mac devotes his time to his mom, whom I love dearly. But I've done all the shopping and lunch planning and napkin folding I am capable of for the moment. Unfortunately, the weather is damp and humid and cloudy, and I want sun. But I'll take the ocean on its terms, not mine, if only I can get there before all my body cells are replaced in my sleep with movable vinyl units or my blood turns into formalin or I discover that I've become a mass of computer chips. I don't know how people can live like this. There's nothing here—and such large portions of it. I think I'll stare at the shutters on Mom's windows. The shutters are always closed. The widows come here ostensibly for the great climate, then sit in their houses with the air conditioning on and the shutters closed. No wonder their minds close down, cool and shuttered.

✳

I slept with the ocean in my head, woke to it, am writing with it. I'm alone and content. Last night the beach—I'm camped on a bluff with the water just below—started to empty out because it was Sunday night, and today the place is all but empty, no one around, almost no camps in sight, the occasional Winnebago waddling by, a jogger here and there. Mac's gone. I've been for a jog around the campground area, and I've walked the beach rock hunting. There are a hundred fifteen steps built from the bluff down to the beach, and I've run up and down them as fast as I can several times. Work those quadriceps, woman. Hup, hup! Energy! It's great to feel good again after hormone zap. It's also pleasant not to hate my body and my gender—after all, it's a good and useful body, everything more or less placed correctly, functional ankles, fingers to curl around a pen.

Rock harvesting. Usually I pick up rocks just for my friend Norma Hartner, who collects them, but this time I am getting rocks for other special folks. A rock picked for one person takes much more time and love than does a commercial gift. I am matching rocks to people, hoping they won't say, "Oh—just what I always wanted—a stone." Picking a rock means you are thinking of that person's face and character, you are choosing from among thousands the one that says his or her name to you. And in this case, I am carrying them up these steps, finding hiding places for them in the van where they won't be in the way, and driving them three thousand miles. I just wish my eye would stop lighting on the big ones.

I don't ever quite know what I mean when I say it, but I have always thought—or maybe felt—that living near a major body of water would make human mortality easier to accept. I don't like the fact that we die. Who does? My struggle to come to terms with it has always been deeper than I would wish it to be. I want to stick around forever—to see how it all comes out, even, I think, if it comes out badly. "It" being? Human history (by which I really mean futurity in this case) at the least. I am endlessly curious, in every color. And if we blow ourselves out of the universe? Then I want to know what "life" will arise to replace us. I think I'll never quite get over that wanting, even when I'm checking out for good and all.

But perhaps my claim of curiosity is merely a cover for the terror I probably feel in the face of nonbeing. I'm never in direct touch with it, but I know it's back there somewhere. I don't want to be food for the worms, as I know I must be, and no sweetly cyclical stuff about rejoining nature or returning in other forms is the least bit comforting to me. Western individualism, egotism, narcissism—I am thoroughly in love with myself, even when I hate myself, and I don't want me to not be, in *this form,* forever. This much a few trusted and loved people know about me, but I have never written it down undisguised—and I suspect that most people who know me would be surprised that I'm scared of the Big Chill. I talk about death in my professional writing, but not this way. I talk about it in my poetry, but there it is the lyrical mourning for the deaths of others that my speakers speak; or the gripping, awesome fact of death in the mutable world. But now I'm talking about that selfish, frightened creature, that me who'd make any bargain with evil to gain immortality. I only regret there is no Prince of Darkness to offer me the chance to sell my soul. I take that back—there is a Prince of Darkness, and when things are bad, I have seen him on his charger ride—but he doesn't make deals.

Water. *Big* water.

This whining, niggling egotism, this desire to endure immortally that is experienced by far more people than would care to admit it—I'm not eager to admit it myself—is very, very stupid. There must be death in order for there to be life; it's that simple. The moment that generative, reproductive life came about, so did death. If growth and change and newness are definitive of anything worth calling life, there's got to be room for it. If it is right that babies are born, it is right that their parents shall die. The price of my own child's life on this planet is my death. Not only is death necessary and inevitable; it's morally and ethically right. As if that mattered.

Since it's necessary and inevitable—since, were I designing the universe, I would introduce death early and often; no perpetual hanging around in stasis in *my* universe—since all this is true, I would like to arrive at a peace with death while I still have something to say about it. All of the great paths of spiritual inquiry are about this, ultimately—though it seems regrettable to me that they usually find peace through devaluing and renunciation of life here, especially the life of the body. This is true of Christianity, of Buddhism, of Islam, of all theisms and nontheisms with which I have passing acquaintance. Minor subthemes of ancient and modern philosophies—such as carpe diem—appear to celebrate the joys attendant upon accepting the transitory nature of things here, but just beneath the surface of celebration is fear or disgust or both. Existentialism in some of its forms accepts mortality and responsibility to live, but not with delight—and when it allows for delight, it reintroduces God, and therefore projection of hope from Here to There. That's not what I'm looking for. I may

be looking for transcendence, but for my money it's also got to be immanent, because I don't believe there's a There there—or if there is, I won't
know it till I get there, and I probably won't, so I don't truck in eternal
metaphors.

What I want is simple: to feel joyful and satisfied with the generosity
that brought me here, permits me to be here now—and I want to fully
accept the fact that I won't be here long. I want to live in the body, a spirit
who is an animal, an animal who is a spirit, and then I want to let go, light
passing from my eyes in peace, without expectation that the light will
rekindle elsewhere. Because that's how I think it is, even if there is also a
spirit world, which there well might be—but not one where this form of
individuality will endure.

Water this big helps me do this. Any water does, but for the size of my
project I need the waters that cover the world, only briefly interrupted by
land masses. It's got something to do with the boundary between vast
waters and land, with the fact that we emerged from here, from water.
Ocean takes us back to sources—and knowing beginnings has to do with
knowing endings. I love the power of water like this; and I respectfully,
profoundly fear it. I love its unstoppable voice that calls out sameness,
rhythm, repetition—but that, when it comes to meet land, speaks suddenly
of change and newness. We say that waves "break" upon land, and that's
where it all once happened, broke open. I like to be humbled before this
power, much the way I like to feel small gazing through a telescope at the
stars—but it isn't the shit-eating sort of humility, and it doesn't make me
feel irrelevant. It just changes my perspective, makes me somehow less
attached to my endurance and individuality. It's strange that it has this
effect, because this ocean *is* endurance completely bodied.

I've not yet understood all of it, this business of being near water and
accepting death. It's much more a feeling than a thought. It could have
something to do with the womb? With being born, all of us individually
(as opposed to species evolution), from water to land? What Freud described as the "oceanic feeling," of original emergence from the mother's
body and our remembrance of it? No, that's not entirely it. Enough psychoanalysis—ontogeny recapitulates phylogeny, but George would rather not always recapitulate Freud.

The rapaciousness, venality, and greed that brought us Ronald Reagan
are very much here in his state, California, but so is what's left of the earthly
grace that such appetite devours. Night before last, a school of dolphins
swam right by the campsite, almost near enough to reach over the bluff

and talk to and touch. They were playing—that *is* the only word for it. Whatever we might mean by play, that is part of what dolphins do. They were swimming so near shore that you could see the shadows of their bodies under water. Then they'd leap out in that exquisite curve, arching and bending in a way that makes you arch and bend from your dry place on shore. They went by slow, almost half an hour of steady sighting. I watched and listened to the ocean while the visible world darkened. All that white foaming at the shore, bubbling and fermenting, coming at you and receding, coming hither and going away, like people do with each other.

Humans characterize the ocean and its vessels as female. Or at any rate, Western men have done so. And land—Mother Earth—is female, too. There are exceptions in some mythologies, but Poseidon notwithstanding (he's almost always standing, come to think of it), water is Woman. The great mythological matings tend to be sky and land—Father Sky, Mother Earth. But if, in the short view, "we" emerged from the sea, then there's this other mating, of sea and land, ocean and earth, that is connotatively female-female. The gendering of land and sea as female is probably a collectively male imagining, since recorded imaginings are primarily by men. Why would this be? The question is only partly ingenuous, after all these years. I know very well why and how men came to imagine both land and water as female. It creates the effect, strange for patriarchy, of Woman engendering upon Woman. In this way of thinking, that seafoam, that white-sticky-bubbly stuff, is Ocean Mama-come, and woman's greatest desire is for woman.

THE HISTORY OF THE WORLD ACCORDING

TO ANDREW JOSEPH PICARD

I just saw a squirrel roll around in the dirt like a dog. I never saw a squirrel do that before. They're very bold here at Oceanside—they come right up on the table while I'm sitting here and say, okay, lady, where's the grub? Just called my Houghton Mifflin editor from the camp pay phone. He left a message for me in Escondido. It's very strange to be on such a trip and also to be carrying on the editing of 2.5 books on the road. It both roots me to the work that keeps me sane and enslaves me to responsibility.

On the subject of strangeness, you encounter weird people when you're doing America. The other night, two young guys took the campsite next to ours and borrowed our hatchet. One is a marine from South Carolina, a beautiful man with midnight skin, savannah smooth. Nice guy, regular guy. But the other one is strange looking—you can't quite place it, he's just slightly creepy in appearance. They have no car, both hitchhiking and backpacking. The marine has been gone hiking all day, and a while ago, the other guy started packing up to hit the road. I assumed they were buddies traveling together, but it turns out they just hooked up yesterday.

The strange guy and I started talking today. He is hitchhiking through all the states in the union; he has twenty-one more to go. He got out his maps and showed me where's he's been and where he's going. "You ever heard of the *Guiness Book of World Records?*" he asked me, but he pronounced it "June-us." I said yes, and he said, "Well, it says in there that nobody ever hitchhiked all the states before the age of twenty-one, and I'm gonna be the first, and get my name in that book. I got two more years till I'm twenty-one." He checked his watch, apparently to verify this. I asked how long he'd been on the road. "Since I was twelve."

This put a new spin on it. He's been on the road for seven years. He left home—southern Louisiana—all those years ago, and ever since then he's been gone. He hadn't phoned his parents in four years until last week. (Whad your mother say when you called? I asked. "Where the hell are you?" I guess that's what I'd say, too.) His grandfather is the one who gave him the idea and the example—at ninety-five, he's still traveling America. From the ocean, Andy is heading inland to a place where his grandfather carved his initials in a post near a lake—Andy's next goal is to find that post. He travels alone. Occasionally he hooks up with someone, but after a day or two, he wants to go it alone again. In all these years, he's only had one problem. "A man tried to get funny with me, if you know what I mean." He carries an empty gun for protection. He used it that one time to threaten the man. The longest Andy has ever stayed in one place was three months in Maine. He gets odd jobs to make money and then he moves on. Once he achieves his goal, will he want to settle down? He said maybe, but maybe he'll just start hiking through Europe instead.

The thing I can't adequately communicate here is how strangely compelling this kid is. He's bright and curious, but he pronounces words oddly and he's amazingly naive. He had never heard of Yellowstone or of Rocky Mountain National Park. Odd, for someone doing the country. But he hadn't made it to those states yet, and he left school when he was a small child.

He's a writer, of course. He carries notepads and pencils as part of the shabby, stripped-down, well-organized equipment he totes on his back. He wants to write a book about what he's doing, which is a good idea, but he's only marginally literate. His writing ability—he read me some passages—is at about the level at which he dropped out of school. He writes rhymed poetry and claims he has written five plays. He was very enthusiastic to learn that I write, too. "So we're both writers," he beamed. I told him I'm keeping a journal on this trip, and he said, what's the title of it, and when I said there's no title yet, he decided to title it for me. His suggestions included "My Life and Times" and "The History of the World as I See It."

I wrote down his name—Andrew Joseph Picard Jr.—and he wrote down mine, and he said he'd put me in his book, and I promised I'd put him in mine, and I gave him ten bucks for the road. He didn't ask or even hint for it, I just figured he's doing something tough and worthwhile and I wanted to kick in. Then Andy hit the road. When he gets lonely out there, which he does, he recites one of his poems to himself. If poetry is good for anything, it ought to be for keeping a lonely kid warm on the road.

I talked to our neighbor while we broke camp this morning. He's thirty-five, from Chicago, and you could tell in a minute that he's middle class, fairly well educated—not the kind you usually find in a hiker campsite of this sort. Turns out he's trying very hard and rather late to live out his old dreams. He quit his respectable, regular job, left his wife and kid, and simply hit the road. He knew he was going to do it many months before he did it—he had started thinking about it two full years in advance and couldn't get it out of his mind. But I got the distinct feeling he's not finding what he's looking for, and he's not sure what he's after anyway. He's still determined, still has some psychic fuel left for the search. He's the first middle-class dropout I've encountered on this trip. He's worried about how late it's getting, how short his time is for—What? For figuring it all out. Maybe Andrew Joseph Picard Jr. is ahead of us both.

FROOT LOOPS IN YOSEMITE

Sequoia National Park, Yosemite
National Park, California

I'm sitting on boulders in the middle of the Marble Fork of the Kaweah River. I can't hear anything because of the power of the water, and that's fine. I've been with my son, Bernie, and his lady Mary Ellen all day, doing miles of trails and rock hiking here in Sequoia National Park. This makes the best kind of tired. I've been too cold and too hot many times today. Now I'm just right—sun and breeze and a few minutes alone.

The giant redwoods are the largest living things in the world, and I can't help but feel, in their presence, that they are conscious beings. They aren't the oldest things in the world, but they're not far from it—they live to be over 3,000 years old. (Bristlecone pines make it to four thousand plus.) They've seen so many of us come and go, and they were here before there *were* us. It's not that they seem wise to me, not exactly—more that they endure, that they're solidly here, immovably rooted. Their bark is a wondrously glowing copper red, tough and meaty, almost like skin. They hunker down and they soar, all in solitude. I admire them, and I believe they are sacred. That's why I wanted to come back here with these kids.

Who are being terrific. They're into it the same way Bernie was when he was fourteen, even though they're close to twenty. They climb everything they see. Last night after we set up camp, they wanted to hike before dinner. See you in an hour. About four hours later, they came back full of what had happened and what they'd seen—rock climbing for several miles to a meadow, wild deer, bear tracks (probably genuine—many bears here in the back country), the solitude at the meadow, the waterfall. When dark started to close in, they were too far from camp, and Mary

Ellen, who has asthma, was tired. She was on the verge of tears while Bernie, who has the endurance of a moose, coaxed her back down what passed for a trail and really wasn't.

I had been a little concerned. Bernie is too impulsive. In 1981, he was crawling around on steep rock at the rim of the Grand Canyon with his sneakers untied, while I ranted in maternal hysteria. There are many Ways to Hurt Yourself in Our National Parks, and something could indeed have happened to them last night. I have a tendency to expect bad things, and they usually don't happen. I acquired my tendency years ago in honest ways—bad things really happened, so I learned to expect them. The past fifteen years have been calmer, so I would like to stop expecting trouble before I reach the stage of life at which it will undoubtedly be time for trouble again. Last night when I felt the maternal worry machine start to gear up, I kept stopping the motor. I refused to give it gas. Sure enough, they showed up, no worse for their brush with adventure and suffused with the stuff of permanent and marvelous memory.

Today I was ready for sweating, so I went along with their program. Bernie decided to climb the face of the roots of a fallen Sequoia. That doesn't sound like much, but it is—about twenty feet straight up, holding on to pieces of smooth root jutting out. These buggers are big. My fear of heights is only mild; Mary Ellen's is worse. Bernie has no fear of anything. That's the problem. He's not afraid of things he should be afraid of, and try as I have, I've never been able to teach him fear or communicate mine to him. About three-quarters of the way up, I got the creeps and started to laugh. I couldn't stop laughing, couldn't move up or down. Bernie's on top, M.E. is at the bottom, I'm mostly up, we're laughing like idiots. Bernie hauled me up, and then Mary Ellen, we all laughed some more, ha, ha—and then it was time to get down. Up had been easy by comparison. Bernie got down and then began heckling me and M.E., who were both right-proper helpless females. We couldn't stop laughing and we certainly couldn't get down. We figured we could find a way if Bernie would let us alone, but of course he would not, accusing us of wimpdom and false feminism. He said he'd catch us if we'd jump from halfway, and we both said no, at which he simply reached up and pulled us down. He's bigger than we are.

We walked the entire length of another fallen one, 250 feet of dead tree 15 feet off the ground. Later we climbed a large rock (or small mountain) called Moro Rock—a quarter mile up, strenuous, with views of the surrounding mountains and valleys dropping away on either side. Railings line the way up, and some spots have stone stairs, but sometimes the willies sweep your innards anyway. It's strange, that feeling, because even the most normal people are probably experiencing not only the fear of falling but also the perverse desire to jump and get it over with, as I experienced at Devil Canyon. How is it that we think of suicides as cowards? To *do that*—make that leap, pull that trigger—may be awful, but it takes resolute courage I can hardly imagine. I still think of my father when I look down from heights. But mostly I enjoy the view.

Bernie wants me to go on another trail tonight. I'm tired. On balance, I won't choose to. But he wants his mom to play with him. It's hard to say no to this large, muscular man with a neck the size of my waist. It's hard to say no, not because he's so big, but because he's still my boy, my darling, and he wants me to play with him. Things like this can't happen in the safety of home. No sufficiently large tree roots and rock formations there. I'd think Bernie would want to have some separate time with Mary Ellen alone, but what he wants is to drag his mother on every trail in Sequoia until she drops. He wants to argue with me. He wants me to listen to his music. It will be decades before our tastes converge.

✳

The approach into Yosemite from the south amazes me. You drive through a rock tunnel blasted through a mountain, and when you emerge on the other side, you are confronted without preparation by one of the most spectacular views in the world—El Capitan and Half Dome with the valley in between. We camped on the valley floor at Yosemite Village, smack on the Merced River. We rafted the river two by two, went to breakfast at the Ahwahnee Hotel (where we were by happenstance seated at what they call "the Queen's Table," because Queen Elizabeth sat there when she came to Yosemite), hiked to Yosemite Falls, saw Bridal Veil, hit all the major clichés. Yosemite Valley is so beautiful that there's something almost ridiculous about it, as if it were designed by God in collusion with John Muir and Walt Disney. At Disneyland three years ago, I realized that Disney must have had the national parks in mind, and particularly Yosemite, when he designed Disneyland. The valley floor is crowded, and during the season, the village has the population density of a major city, but even traffic jams can't spoil it. When you get on the river or in a meadow or on a trail, people disappear or don't matter.

Rafting the Merced in our silly rubber boat, Mac and I figured there must be a shorter way back instead of carrying the boat along the same curving path we rafted. We checked the map and found that because of the curves of the river, it should work to cut overland and make the trip back about a quarter as long. Bernie and I tried it. We took out the boat at the right spot—Half Dome staring at us—and had to make a tough choice at one juncture. Wrong. What should have been a five-minute walk turned into an hour of meandering, Bernie in bare feet, me in a for-God's-sake bikini, cutting through what amounts to shopping centers. Bernie's feet boiled on the pavement, then got torn up by pine needles on the forest floor. I felt sorry for him because he was having it worse than I was. Then the score evened. My flip-flops both broke.

I wanted to ask directions, typical female behavior. Bernie was determined to find our way back on our own. Typical male behavior. We compromised. The first half of the trip we didn't ask. The second half I was ready to ask the nearest dog. Asking a dog would have been just as helpful as asking the well-meaning bozos I did, all of whom were wrong. When we finally made it back to the river, we were way upstream and had to float back down. Mac and M.E. wondered if we'd gotten lost, and we said, oh no, everything was fine. We kept up the ruse. Bernie said he felt so embarrassed he was going to zip up his tent and stay there. He made Indian jokes about natural abilities to tell directions in the woods. He'd disgraced his Seneca heritage. I never had one to begin with, so I wasn't disgraced.

Last night we made a campfire, sang songs, played cribbage and backgammon. Our campsite area is so crowded that we call it the slum, but we *like* this slum. The pines are high and tall, so that lying in the hammock you can watch them weave and bend in the wind in a way that makes you feel that maybe you, too, could deal with whatever happens to you and to people you love without breaking apart. Maybe you could. Maybe you will. Pieces of conversation from nearby camps waft over on the wind. A little boy turns around and around in circles after dinner. A group of Christian couples sing around their own fire about Jesus and victory, and their sounds are lovely, even though every song sounds the same, except one: "How sweet to dream by the river alone." I love to be here with my family, cooking dinner and rafting the river and playing games and scrapping with each other.

Mac and I had a fine moment today on the beach. I asked him if I have changed lately, and what do my changes look like to the companion who knows me so well. He said that yes, I'm still me, but I'm acting and moving and thinking more like a third baseman. A third baseman's job is to keep the ball in front of him, and it's hard, because the majority of batters are right-handed, and a well-hit ball comes from ninety feet in about half a second at over one hundred miles per hour. No matter how fast it comes at you, you try to keep everything in front of you. It's seldom that Mac's passion for baseball and my essential indifference toward it meet each other, but it worked this time. He is of the opinion that life is a complex metaphor for baseball.

We left Yosemite the long way, driving up to the Alpine Meadows above the tree line in the Tuolumne area. Very few people, cold, pristine lakes, mountain peaks covered with snow, open meadows of short, hunker-down grass covered with wildflowers during the alpine spring. It's rock climbers' paradise, and clearly the practice area—several mountaineering schools—for the crazy folks who climb El Capitan. The latest thing is free-form with no pitons. Climbers sleep in the crevices. I don't get it. I know that mountain climbing is one of those fundamental human urges, but you couldn't get me to do any serious stuff if you offered me endless riches, immortality contingent upon surviving the climb, and perfect natural eyesight without glasses.*

We also saw someone hang gliding from Glacier Point. He (or she?) crossed the moon while we watched in the early morning from the valley floor. The shadow looked like a giant bird. I understand this urge better than I do mountain climbing because it's the perfect expression of the desire to cross boundaries between one species and another—to become a bird. Flight is probably the most pervasive metaphor for freedom and escape. Run away, fly away, fly away home, fly away *from* home. I could not do it. One reason I feel friendlier toward hang gliding than toward mountain climbing is that so much of the language associated with climbing is the language of conquering, of getting one over on nature, of laying claim. Recently I have heard some mountain climbers try to disconnect their passion from the language of imperialism. Are these the same people who do encounter groups or have been through consciousness raising or what? They speak of cooperating with the mountain, of working through it and with it. I'll buy this ecofeminist rhetoric.

Now let me speak of Froot Loops. One measure of the distance between adults and kids is food. They eat eleven times a day. They buy Froot Loops and Spaghettios and Gatorade. Next to the Froot Loops that will not quite die are my yogurt trail mix and dried banana chips, which the kids find as appetizing as a drain plunger. I tried to eat a few Froot Loops, just to

*Wrong. See part 4.

prove I'm a regular guy instead of a sixties retro earth biscuit. I can deal with an occasional Whopper. But Froot Loops must be made entirely of unpronounceable multisyllabics that bear no relationship to anything that could remotely be called food. America, where are your values? America, where are your complex carbohydrates? The birds and squirrels got what was left on the picnic table. I expected to find them dead on their backs in the morning with their little legs sticking up in the air. Even the Froot Loops box is indestructible. I tried to burn it, but the wax and multicolored dyes killed the fire. Ah youth.

After Yosemite, the kids and I went to the beach at Oceanside for an afternoon of sun and water. Bernie surfed for hours with one of those blow-up boards, again dragging the mother and the girlfriend out to play. The power takes you and throws you all over, and even if you can dive into a wave, the ocean does with you what it will. Then we had another family squabble—this one over whether we should lie there with rock music in our ears or the sound of the waves reaching for us. I have nothing against blaring music in other places—like on Southern California freeways at seventy miles per hour, all the way to the beach and back. But the ocean? That song? Next he'll want to feed Froot Loops to the dolphins.

In a few hours I will be immersed in Georgia O'Keeffe's high desertscape, visiting Abiqui and Ghost Ranch where she lived austerely, alone, in a lush inner and outer world for some forty years. America has fallen in love with O'Keeffe, that life divided between Manhattan with Stieglitz and New Mexico without him. Six months in New York, then six north of Santa Fe each year until his death, when she packed up everything to live in the desert for the rest of her life.

It is peculiar that I am drawn to her. I am a people person and she was emphatically not. She rarely painted the human face or form, barely painted animals. She was essentially a still-life artist, and still-life has always bored me. Yet I love her work more each year, despite rather than because it's now an American cliché to like her or dislike her. O'Keeffe is to painting what Emily Dickinson was to poetry. She was a formal revolutionary, an early cubist-abstractionist in Picasso's own time, but not taken seriously by the boys until they had no choice. Her vision was private, idiosyncratic, spacious within the confines of a world of small objects minutely observed and described. Her painting avoided personality in favor of depicting what she saw as essence, as did Dickinson in her poetry. The flower paintings are flamboyantly "outward," but you can see at a glance that the real gaze, hers and her direction of ours, is toward interior space, genital and mental.

I think of the differences between her two lifelong landscapes, Manhattan and the high desert—one essentially vertical (she saw the first great skyscrapers dominate her New York skyline and lived on the thirtieth floor

in order to free herself from the ground and see the sky), the other hori-
zontal. There is nothing wider and flatter than desert, even high desert
such as this. In New York her major subject was flowers, in New Mexico
dry bones in the sand. The flowers are lush, erotic, purple in every respect,
wet, throbbing—and the bones are spare, dry, white, stolid. Yet they are
very much connected, and I make no simple Freudian interpretations of
them as representative respectively of eros and thanatos. The interpenetration is complete. The flowers are so overripe that they could, even must,
drop away into death any moment; and the bones are oddly life filled,
shimmering with potential, so that you expect them to jump up and dance
or procreate like the inhabitants of Ezekiel's valley of dry bones. She was
as clear as she could possibly be about death in life, life in death, almost
making it a joke by sticking lush flowers into the eye sockets of cattle
skulls and painting them.

I'm much absorbed by her life and her work, her solitude, her tough
and uncompromising oddity, and especially by her relationship with Stieglitz—unpredictable, energetic, gentle, overpowering, monumental life
force that he was. He ranted constantly, held forth for hours about art and
photography, imposed his brilliant and erratic vision on the entire generation of American modernism, surrounded by admirers and detractors.
He was twenty-five years her senior, her mentor. She outgrew that to his
great dismay, yet they endured. But she needed her independence and won
it from him over a period of years in a pitched and firm battle of wills.
Some said he was a raving egotist, but he was also generous, spirited,
magnanimous. His thinking seemed to many people to be full of contradictions, but Georgia understood it and translated: he'd often announce
an opinion on a subject firmly in the morning, change it 180 degrees by
noon, and arrive at a completely different thesis by evening. But why did
he make these firm pronouncements? To confuse everyone? Did he or
didn't he know whereof he spoke? Of course he did, Georgia said—he's
thinking out loud, and thought can and should evolve over time, even a
day. He reminds me of a combination of two men in my life. That's probably the source of my personal interest in how she negotiated with him,
how they endured, how she won through to meet her own definitive ends.
Will I and my Stieglitz endure?

The Rockies rising all around me as I travel toward her—Big Sky, vast
expanse. I'd like to learn to take the long view in life, and the big one. I
think O'Keeffe's desert helps me with that continuing quest, much as the
ocean does at Cape Cod. Her desert shimmers like water—and what's a

seashell but an ocean-going bone? Bones on the inside under flesh, or flesh on the inside under bone, ecto or endo, it's all one.

A lucid dream last night, the kind that comes seldom, speaks its meanings clearly enough that if you just pay attention, you can see what it's saying to you. A message, a vision. Here is what I remember: I am trying, with difficulty and frustration caused by family and business obligations, to get to a place that I think is going to be a museum exhibiting O'Keeffe. I have to disentangle myself from loved ones and from hangers-on, catch several buses, then get in a private small commuter plane to get to this place. When I finally arrive it's a museum, but it consists of a very large cemetery entirely enclosed inside a building, complete with garden-cemetery style streets and sections. I find the O'Keeffe area after going through many rooms, recognize her work immediately, and fall to my knees in both relief and revelation—for they are not paintings, they are gravestone carvings. She has done relief carving on stone, and the designs look somehow like living forms but are not representational, not identifiable objects or people. She has carved completely in harmony with the striations of the stone, so you can hardly discern where "natural" carving or quarrying ends and "artful" human work begins. I take all this in at a glance. One exception to the rule of nonrepresentation, though: a high relief, almost freestanding figure, a round rough fieldstone form that is both human (unusual for an O'Keeffe) and female. No, not just female, but mother, and not just mother, but mother and child. This is the largest stone, dominating the others, and it alone is encased in glass. I am contemplating it when suddenly a group of girls appears and begins wandering among the stones, chattering aimlessly, paying little attention to the carvings except as oddities. I'm annoyed. End of dream.

Even during the dream, I realized that this was a dream and that it was telling me something that had so far escaped my conscious attention. A formulation of part of it was there for me when I awoke, and it took this simple form: Georgia O'Keeffe would have loved early New England gravestones. That message was an invitation to think about it more. O'Keeffe was unimpressed by the Great Tradition of western European art. She didn't participate in the expatriate exodus to Paris, or even make the obligatory gesture of a visit there until she was an old woman—and when she finally went, she didn't much like what she saw, not even the Cézannes that had so influenced Stieglitz's circle and the modernist movement of which she herself was a part. She liked Asian and Chinese art far more than European.

I think she would have liked early American gravestone carving because it was a vigorous folk tradition that grew naturally from life in the harsh environment of the early years in America. Like her own work, gravestone carving lived at the intersection between representational and abstract art, often taking the form of designs and patterns suggesting the body—frequently the body as bone, and bone representative of spirit. A single image often filled the frame, as was also true of her work, so that a detail—a skull, a geometric abstraction—became the whole world, and in those stones the "faraway" was always implied in the "nearby"—eternity in the stark image, for instance, of a skull. This art was about the intersection between, the interrelatedness of life and death, and so was hers.

A barely suppressed eroticism is also characteristic of gravestone carving—an eroticism its makers would have denied, as O'Keeffe did. And, perhaps most importantly, eighteenth-century stonework was about the struggles of spirit and flesh, the yearning of flesh for eternal form, but ironically the representational human form was muted on the stones in favor either of its essence in bone or its representation as "soul," with the minor and brief exception of portrait stones. The same is again true of O'Keeffe, whose art is about human consciousness represented more through the absence or essence of body than through its ordinary presence. Gravestone carving repeatedly looks to natural form for meaning, is about the human connection to the earth—literally, since its cause is the burial of the dead—evidenced in its frequent decoration with gourds, flowers, vegetation. Death and fertility, the natural cycles of rhythms and returns—all of it essential to O'Keeffe's vision.

More personally, what this dream tells me is that my work on O'Keeffe is linked with work I've done for years. In a conscious state I might never have connected my interest in eighteenth-century stonework for the dead with my new arousal by Georgia O'Keeffe, a twentieth-century artist who painted flowers. Now I see that my own themes are played out against this new backdrop. Everything old is new again. There's nothing new under the sun, but nothing is used up. I continue to explore the connections between mutability and essence, mortality and eternity. This time, though, my mediator is not dead men's stones, not a suicidal poet like Anne Sexton who died when she was little older than I, but rather a woman who believed in survival, stubbornly hung on to health, and lived to be almost a hundred.

My dreams loop back upon themselves, snakes with tails in their mouths, bats with human faces emerging from caves. Fifteen years ago I

wrote poems for another survivor, my friend Nancy's sister, Susan Espersen, for whom breast cancer was the nightmare. Finding a poem I wrote
for her as I write about Georgia, I realize that I have been dreaming about
women and stone all my adult life—the igneous privacies of a woman
whose rocky surfaces must crack.

DREAMING THE BREASTS

I am in a museum.
I wander out the back door into a phantom
town of dust, its streets peopled
by echo and empty houses.
Backhoes and earth-moving machinery
lie scattered over the landscape.

A wind calls me down the street.
In the space between two tall buildings,
I see a woman carved of granite,
three stories high, massively bellied and breasted.
Her stone arm cradles her breast, her finger and thumb
wrap around the nipple, her pieta-bent face
is frozen in this granite pose.
I stare up, mouth open.

Moving around her hulk, I am on a plain
of sagebrush where hundreds of her
hard sisters rise from the earth,
a silent mass.
She duplicates herself on the receding plain,
hundreds of stone women, stone breasts.
Wind sings down the plain, sagebrush rolls past me
in tangled clumps, dust works into my eyes.
I look up at their impassive faces. Nothing.

Turning to leave, I see something move
from the corner of my eye, almost imperceptible.
I face the first one, shift my balance, ready.
I see that her thumb and forefinger
are moving slightly, lovingly, along her nipple.
I have seen this movement before.
Women feeding babies.
Women caressing themselves on a rainy night.
I have seen this before.
I have done this before.

—For Susan Espersen

PART 4

BLOWING IN THE WIND

WOUNDED KNEE AT BONDCLIFF

Franconia Notch and Pemigewasett Wilderness,
the White Mountains, New Hampshire

I leave the book upon a pillowed chair
And walk from window to closed window, watching
Boughs strain against the sky

And think again, as often when the air
Moves inward toward a silent core of waiting,
How with a single purpose time has traveled
By secret currents of the undiscerned
Into this polar realm. Weather abroad
And weather in the heart alike come on
Regardless of prediction.

Between foreseeing and averting change
Lies all the mastery of elements
Which clocks and weatherglasses cannot alter.
Time in the hand is not control of time,
Nor shattered fragments of an instrument
A proof against the wind; the wind will rise,
We can only close the shutters.
—Adrienne Rich, "Storm Warnings"

Like a novelist in charge of her characters and their fate, I planned how this section of my book would turn out. As always, the best-laid plans of men and women go astray in the wind that will rise, no shutters to close it out, to seal you in. I set out on a two-week backpacking trip in the Fran-

conia and Pemigewasett Wilderness Areas of the White Mountains with
a clear purpose in mind: to write a moving story of a woman's confrontation with her fears about physical challenge, heights, endurance, and
childhood demons, an adventure from which she would emerge strong,
unbent, fearless. Or something like that. It was particularly important that
my book, and my life, meet the elements more closely than from the safe
remove of car windows or even day hiking and camping. I'd tried once
before to plan a travel essay to this degree. With two other women, I went
to a hunting camp in the Allegheny Mountains for quiet creatureliness.
We know how that turned out.

This time I would construct carefully, with weeks of planning ahead for
every contingency—and the safety of a male hiking partner. One makes
these compromises. It's prudent, given the violence against women that
is not a mere statistic for me but an aspect of my life that has recurred at
barely decent intervals—marriage to a man who committed a serious
crime, two relationships that have ended in varying degrees of bodily harm
from men I would not have thought capable of it, random threats such as
the night of terror from the men in the woods. I'm slow, but I'm not stupid. Women need men of goodwill on our side, and sometimes by our side.

I would also make this a symbolic statement of my healing from a shattered partnership of twenty years' standing, whose end had broken both
woman and man. I would be standing on a mountaintop in the clear air
of my life's afternoon at the very moment when the man I'd had to leave
was beginning his marriage to someone else. And how shapely it would
all be—my book begins with the tale of traveling to Wounded Knee to
confront my distant past and America's cultural genocide of its indigenous
people, an oppressed group with whom I had lived, from whom I had been
born into awareness, in whose midst I had given birth to my son, now a
man. It would near its end with me as a representative of another group
of Americans, women, whose lives have also been truncated, their possibilities limited, rights denied, me inspiring others to travel widely not only
in the mind but also in the vast American places that belong to all of us.

All wrong, down to the last detail. Although I'd planned well enough
to protect myself against two-legged marauders this time by having a man
with me, no plan could be proof against the wind, a hundred miles an hour
of obliterating force that smashed me into the top of the mountain on
which I'd hope to stand. The legs that bore me to the peak were injured.
The hand that was to write the triumphant narrative was broken. And the
man who might have been my lonely other? We quarreled at the foot of

the mountain over what happened up there, and within a few months, I asked him to leave.

Yet my story does "make my circle just, and make me end where I begun," as John Donne, who wrote "My America, my newfoundland," and "No man is an island" said in "A Valediction, Forbidding Mourning." I did face my fears in the White Mountains. My childhood griefs did not leave me, but rather returned to me, mightily transformed, so that I might better understand them. Ten years of psychoanalysis could not accomplish more than the confrontation with my father's suicide, his leap from a high window ledge to the ground, embodied in my injured crawl along a sheer cliff in the high wind, fighting hypothermia. Like the Native Americans I have lived with, I had to encounter defeat where I had hoped for victory, or at least vindication, and learn how to keep renewing my sense of struggle. Limping through the long summer, I became my own wounded knee.

For our two weeks in the White Mountains, Dirk had ordered topographical maps from the New Hampshire state parks and supplies from the Campmor catalogue. We went to the local outfitters, preparing for conditions we could expect in summer mountain circumstances. Dirk's hiking experience was limited in the White Mountains, but he was familiar, from month-long treks, with both the Green Mountains in Vermont—similar in most respects to the terrain we'd encounter—and the Adirondacks, where we'd both been the previous year. I broke in my new hiking boots for weeks before we left, noting with amusement and pleasure the way they made me walk different and feel different from the way my day-tripper hightops did. All of my old gear was too color coordinated anyway.

Our goal was the horseshoe-shaped loop of the Franconia Notch ranges, starting at the Lincoln Trailhead. The central region of the White Mountains is a "vast wooded area studded with beautiful peaks," according to the Appalachian Mountain Club guide. No highways interfere with the wilderness, and only gravel roads score the edges. Most of our hike would be in the Pemigewasett Wilderness, of which the Franconia area is a part. A bit more than a century ago, this region was untracked and pristine, but between 1890 and 1940, it was logged and burned. This is once again genuine wilderness, among the victories of restoration projects.

Our plan was to start on the Wilderness Trail, specifically the segment now popularly known as Lincoln Woods Trail. Following the old railroad bed, this trail begins as a comparative thoroughfare. We'd cut off to Bondcliff after about five miles, beginning a steep and narrowing climb toward the cliffs, almost ten miles in and up from the Lincoln Trailhead. Bond-cliff Trail connects the Pemigewasett Wilderness with the summits of the Twin Range.

✳

Bondcliff hazards: small cairns above treeline . . . not easy to follow in strong weather; cliffs west of trail.—Philip Preston, *White Mountains West*

Long section above treeline, with great exposure to the weather. The views from this trail are unsurpassed in the White Mountains. Caution: the trail runs above treeline for about a mile and is dangerous in bad weather. . . . . Stay well to the west of the precipices.—Appalachian Mountain Club, *AMC White Mountain Guide*

Day four. Two fingers on my left hand are taped in a makeshift splint. I have swollen kneecaps and a bruised rib cage and a sprained left ankle. Since I already have a bad right ankle, now I have two weak ankles, but they'll get me out of here. A similar economy of balance applies to my knees. My right one is most injured, but that's comparatively good since the ligaments of my left knee are already damaged from repeated disloca-tions. If the major impact had been to my left knee, I'd have to be carried out of here on a litter.

One finger of my left hand is, I'm convinced, broken. My partner says it's just badly sprained, but he's putting on a brave face for me. It's bro-ken. My neck and shoulder hurt where I made intimate contact with rock. I started my period a few hours after the accident, so I'm bleeding, which seems strangely comic right now. I have black fly bites everywhere—they've even burrowed underneath my splint. But I'm reasonably happy. I've been flying.

✳

Starting at the Lincoln Wood Trailhead, we cut off onto Bondcliff. On day one, we hiked about six miles, much of it on the old railroad logging trail. The first night we stopped in the early evening and set up camp. We were breaking in our minds and bodies, enjoying getting sweaty and being away from traffic and people and sounds, just far enough into the wilderness that we could feel alone and remote. That evening the rain started and continued all night. We had just bushwhacked off the trail when the storm came. We have excellent equipment with one exception. The tent is ser-viceable, but it's not built to withstand heavy rain. The first night was manageable, but we had to pack damp. Hikers try to avoid that, but we didn't have any choice. We waited until afternoon but finally had to move on. We weren't on a strict schedule but we wanted to log a few miles before night set in. So we kept going, the trail becoming narrow and rocky and the altitude rising sharply. We got close to five thousand feet.

Late afternoon the rain started again. The temperature dropped fast because of the altitude and the storm system. It's not as though we were stupidly unprepared for what we were likely to deal with. We packed adequate clothing for this time of year under normal conditions. But these weren't normal conditions. Neither of us had sweaters or multilayers of pants. We had one sleeved shirt and a T-shirt apiece, and a sweatshirt between us, in addition to our ponchos. It seemed good enough, but none of our gear is Gortex. We put on our ponchos when it started to rain and just kept climbing.

At dusk, judging from the quick sundown the night before, we knew we had to stop soon. We hadn't eaten since morning and we were tired from the steady climb. We looked for a place to pitch the tent. I was getting colder, soaked clean through despite my new poncho, which didn't cover my lower arms and legs and boots. The boots were waterproofed, but leaks began to run rivulets into my socks. We kept thinking, just a few more minutes and we'll come to some place that's obviously right. We climbed from birch to pine, from deciduous to coniferous, from inclines to densely forested slopes. Finally Dirk said, we must stop. But I said, not quite yet, let's keep going, the landscape will change soon. It didn't.

In the end we bushwhacked straight in from the trail and made ourselves, in the nearly dark, a makeshift site I hoped the trail workers couldn't see when they next passed by; we couldn't get in as far as the rules request. Very dense forest—Dirk had to kill a small tree to make enough room even for our small tent. We got inside, but without enough space to get it pitched completely, the fit was tight. It was still raining hard so we turned on the weather radio. That's when we heard this was an unusually strong weather system for June. The rain was forecasted to continue through the night and into the next day. Very strong winds accompanied this front. It blew so hard over the next hours that the sound and impact peeled our eyeballs open from restless sleep—we thought the tent pole might snap. This went on all night. Water seeped into the tent and the temperature was dropping and one sleeping bag was getting wet inch by inch. We generated as much body heat as we could, ate cereal, and moved around to keep from getting too cold.

Are we in any danger of getting *too* cold? I asked. He said, No, we're just in danger of getting very miserable. Dirk doesn't use intensifiers like *very*. This would be like somebody else saying, We're going to want to die. It wasn't quite frightening—we knew we'd get through it. We didn't know that the genuinely dangerous experience was still on its way. Breaking camp in the morning, we heard that the winds on Mount Washington were 143 miles per hour during the storm. The wind would continue, though the rain was to clear out. We figured we probably wouldn't get across two mountains that day, but we wanted to cross at least Bondcliff. It was actually a nice morning. We dried out as best we could and began hiking toward the cliffs. Up in the trees it was windy, but not bad on the trail. The trees provide such dense cover that you can't tell how strong the winds really are.

Near the tree line we encountered a rock ledge steep enough that we had to take off our packs and use handholds in the rock. I passed my pack up to Dirk and pulled myself up into the most spectacular view I've ever seen. Above the tree line is an almost full-circle panorama of the Franconia Notch. I had to cling to the rock surface and acclimate slowly. Because falling from a great height is how my father died, I pack some extra psychic weight near pinnacles. Heights have been among the determinants and shapers of my life. I clung to the rock face and breathed deeply—then slowly turned around. The peaks were pristine, worth every moment of the climb, more stunning than anything I've seen east of the Grand Canyon. We sat quietly, enjoying the great wind as it blew.

Hiking across the cliff tops an hour later, we were well above the tree line. The cliffs were not sheer, but close enough to vertical to make you suck in your breath when you first see them from around a bend. While they dropped to one side of us, to the other an incline of jagged rock face cragged across the mountaintop. The trail itself runs right along the cliff, marked by stone cairns. At some points the trail was only a few feet from the edge of the cliff, so it was the sort of landscape you want to move through briskly and safely. The wind picked up again and began to stagger me sideways. Even Dirk was unsteady. My pack was light and I had a very wide ground pad, which may have been important to what next happened.

We encountered a flume of stone, a curved, broad avenue perhaps forty feet wide that formed a concave area through which the wind whipped. We had to decide whether to go on or to turn back. Dirk threw rocks over the cliff into the wind. They blew back our way or eddied wildly before disappearing down the cliff. The gusts that moved us sideways grew spooky, dangerous. We were now into the middle of this open area. I had already hit the ground several times, figuring that if I stayed low I'd be okay. The gusts were so high we couldn't hear each other well. I remember thinking that the only really safe way to do this, in such a high wind, would be to tie ropes to each other. You wouldn't need pitons for the angle, but you could use protection from the wind itself.

Just as I was thinking, *I need to turn back now,* a huge gust seized my entire body and I flew through the air. We weren't far from the cliff edge, but the wind was blowing in the other direction. I was completely airborn, and then—I never thought I'd have occasion to use this expression—I was dashed to the rocks. I tumbled side-to-side, smashing up against an outcropping, knees first.

Dirk had said earlier that he wondered when would be the first time on this trip that I'd say, *What am I doing here?* Now. What am I doing here? My life didn't flash before my eyes, but I remember thinking, you're in trouble, girlie-girl, maybe big trouble. I instantly entered a timeless realm. Dirk was beside me. "Oh my lover," he spoke into my ear over the wind. Even at the time I thought this was a fine thing to say, and no matter what's happened since, I will always remember it. He asked how badly hurt I was, but I didn't know. I needed to see if anything was broken, so I twisted my legs out from under me and tested my knees to see if they worked, especially the left, which cannot be repaired with arthroscopic surgery.

But the left knee worked. Then I realized the right knee was injured, though I literally felt almost nothing. Dirk was sheltering me with his body while pulling my backpack off me, and the wind still screamed obscenities. We called to each other over its blank roar. Dirk asked me if I thought I could get to a place he was pointing toward, one that might offer some shelter. I said, *yes, I can.* Later he said it was obvious I was stunned. Since I thought I was answering him quite normally, how could he tell? He said there was something egoless about my voice, resignation expressed in a flat, emotionless, humorless tone. I was an automaton with a single, simple focus: to get some place before—before what? I could navigate, since nothing was actually broken. I half crawled, half staggered to that place of relative safety. Dirk dragged my pack over to a windbreak formed by two large rocks, where I could be assured of not flying again. Once is enough. I felt utterly weightless in that wind.

While Dirk scouted ahead, trying to figure out what we should do—go forward? go back? down the side of the mountain opposite the cliff? too rocky?—I lay there with my pack up against me. Then his pack sailed into me, nearly knocking me out, but when I recovered from the impact I realized that was a good place for it. I made a triangle with the two packs behind me and watched Dirk run from rock to rock, hunkering down behind large outcrops when the fiercest gusts came. Eventually he disappeared altogether from my sight.

There was something fringy, off-the-wall about the entire experience, but especially about this seemingly eternal time alone. I don't know how long it was—fifteen minutes, twenty. In my essentially timeless state, I felt forever alone. I took stock of my situation: I was in a severe windstorm on the top of a mountain and I was injured and I didn't know how I was going to get out of there. I had confidence in Dirk's abilities to help me out of this situation, but his help depended on his return, and something could happen to him. I remember thinking, *my dad died this way on purpose. I don't want to die this way by accident.*

I now realize that while waiting for Dirk to return, I was beginning to experience the first stages of hypothermia. It was late afternoon, the temperature was dropping, I'd just sustained a shock to my entire system, I had not eaten in several hours, and my clothes were too thin and still damp from the night before. While Dirk scouted ahead, I sat still in one place with the cold wind blowing on me. The *AMC White Mountain Guide* specifies that hypothermia is the most serious danger to mountain hikers and is caused by an inability to preserve body heat because of "injury, exhaustion, lack of sufficient food, and inadequate or wet clothing." In my case, most of these conditions applied.

Contrary to popular opinion, it's not cold that kills a person in these circumstances, since death can occur at an air temperature of eighty degrees. Temperatures below fifty are ideal for hypothermia to develop, and the temperatures on Bondcliff were in the forties that day. I was shivering, but I assumed it was from lack of movement in the cold and the shock of impact to my system. The AMC guide states that in the circumstances outlined above, shivering "should be regarded as absolute evidence of hypothermia," which, in mild cases such as mine fortunately was, ceases on its own. The crucial thing about hypothermia is that the person experiencing it usually does not know it and is likely to behave in strangely reckless ways—nor will others with him or her necessarily know the cause. When Dirk returned, we made the decision to go back along the cliff trail to the place below the tree line where we'd seen a possible campsite on our way up. What Dirk later described as my state of shock during our descent back down the trail along the cliffs, and the behavior he indeed called "reckless," was undoubtedly due to hypothermia. In memory, I have been able to reconstruct what was going through my mind—or what passed for a mind in those moments.

As we had negotiated the trail along the cliffs on the way up, I was somewhat fearful but resolved to do it and was greatly comforted by knowing that I would only have to do it once—our planned loop would have taken us along the ridge linking Bond, Guyot, South Twin, Galehad, Garfield, Lafayette, Lincoln, Little Haystack, and Mount Liberty. In fact, as I later learned, none of these mountains would include rock formations as steep as the one that brought us above the tree line that day or cliffs of the height and relative sheerness of Bondcliff. Now I was traversing them again. Inching back along the trail that ran as close as a few feet from the cliff edge, trying to stay low and keep my balance against the rising wind, I reassured myself further with the knowledge that, as Dirk later put it, the "physics of the thing" was with us—the wind came up over the peaks, blowing in the direction of the craggy but rounded mountaintop. Yet eddies formed at the edge, buffeting me in every direction, so that surefootedness was important. I did not think of my father's fall to death as we traversed the trail the first time, but it cannot have been far below the surface of my consciousness. When we made the decision to return along the same path, that long-buried death broke through my thought lines, reminding me that legacy and inheritance sometimes work in ironic ways.

Dirk coaxed me forward along the quarter mile we had to make to reach the rocks where we would climb down to get below the tree line, but there was no way we could hold hands—the rocks were too craggy, and we each needed both our hands to maintain our balance. When the huge gusts blew over the steady winds that would have been gale force had we been on water, I hit the ground on my knees, now bleeding through my leggings from the cuts. It was the absolute necessity of rising from each fall that felt more nearly impossible each time—clinging to the cold rock, nearly every inch of my front body in contact with terra firma, I felt relative safety. Every rise against that wind, closer and closer to the cliffs as we traveled back from where we'd come, was more terrifying. I began to fear that I would not be able to move at all.

So that when I'd rise part way, crouched low to make as much ground as possible while I could, I began, as Dirk said, to be slightly reckless, moving too fast, too far, with each foray. I knew that I could do it, if only the eddies did not stagger me sideways toward the cliff—but I also knew

I could not do it for much longer. A sense of immobility was beginning to clutch, not my body, but my spirit. Beating back the sense that panic could overtake me at any moment was not easy. And in this time, I began to think, woodenly, robotically, of my father.

I had escaped the family curse of depression that extends through four generations, that led my father to his suicide—or so the story I had told myself had gone, for most of my life. Until I was almost forty, I was usually happy, seldom downcast, never what I'd call depressed (even in depressing circumstances or crises), always seeking to understand depression from outside of its grip, studying poets such as Anne Sexton and Sylvia Plath who had lost their struggle with self-hatred or with the inability to live their lives, as my father had lost his.

Then, nearing forty, a hormonal imbalance that signaled the onset of early menopause, though I did not know it at the time, threw me into deep, cyclical depressions. Depression—I hate the word, often say it with sarcasm verging on a sneer, both loving and missing the friends in my life whom it has in one respect or another claimed, and also, tight-assed, work-ethic Protestant that I am, fighting the urge to judge those it has crippled, who, I have sometimes felt, can use its litanies and privileges as a crutch to avoid living their lives, taking existential responsibility for what they do, who they become, how they act upon their world. You want to be a victim? Be a victim. Shut up and leave me alone and get out of my way, because I'm here to live. And if you die, I'll step over your body and get on with it.

Depression, familiar, hated family friend, destroyer of eros, of delight, of life well lived. I am not always so mean about it, have indeed spent a large part of my professional life trying to promote understanding and compassionate responses to its ravages. "And I alone have escaped to tell you, I shall tell you all . . ." I thought I would always be the messenger, translator of the language of depression, never to speak it as native tongue. Because they were cyclical, my depressions always allowed me to imagine my way out; I knew that however I felt, I would not feel this way next week or, at most, in a month. But as the depressions deepened, I began to imagine this, too: what if it didn't lift? What if this black, clammy mist remained shrouded over me always? What if you woke up every morning, instead of just a few, feeling that you couldn't live? For that is what my father and millions of other sufferers have experienced. For him, and him alone, I always saved complete compassion, never judging him. He is dead. My impatience is only with the living, of whom I am one.

Even at my lowest ebb, I never considered suicide. There were times I did not care very much about life, didn't care whether or not, in particular, I lived—but that is not the same as an active desire to die, as I have been well taught by my father and the poets. The suicides are, as Anne Sexton wrote, "stillborn." Like carpenters, their building is the destruction of the self.

Yet knowing the unconscious as I do, both theoretically and actually, what validity could I really attribute to my conviction that I never wanted to die, that I am, on the contrary, committed to living? Only opposites are true. A cigar is seldom only a cigar. With Freud, I believe in what psychoanalytic theory calls the "death instinct," fell enemy of the pleasure principle. The aim of all life is death; we just go about getting there in various ways. Looking at myself and at most of the people I know, I see how self-destructive patterns give a degree of lie to our lively struggles to live, always to live. The enemy has outposts in our heads.

Had I come to this height, like the white moth devoured by the spider in Robert Frost's "Design," to die? Was there a dark plan for me? Was it the universe's or merely my own? Years before, at Big Bend in Texas, I'd watched dung beetles on the trail and corrected Frost's "What but design of darkness to appall— / if design govern in a thing so small"; for me, it would be, "What but design of lightness to delight— / if design govern in a thing so bright." Now those lines of Frost's came to me again, turned back toward their dark and original plan:

> What brought the white moth thither in the night?
> What brought the kindred spider to that height?

Unsure whether there is a plan for darkness or for light, I have always opted in favor of no plan. And yet? And yet? No inflated sense of personal significance need attach to me or to my life for Frost's nightmare vision to come true—I am indeed a "thing so small." Does some malign force in the universe, or in me, take delight in such infinitesimal, vicious ironies? If so, what a fine one this'd be, I thought, face against rock, raised eye occasionally commanding the stunning view of the peaks from which I could fall and die. After all, I'd come here pridefully planning to master my fear.

And a further, final, tidy irony came to me in the form of my last words to my father as he left that morning to kill himself. I was upset that he'd tied my shoe too loose. He tied it tighter. It was too tight. I cried. He tied it looser. Nothing would please me. "I hate you, I hate you, go away!" I screamed it at him, over and over, sitting on the top step, looking down at him where he stood on the stairway landing, gazing a final time at his daughter wild with stupid rage, shrieking imprecations at him.

It hardly takes a rocket psychoanalyst to know that when, just hours later, the news of his bloody death came, I blamed myself for it. For years I told no one what I'd done that day, successfully repressing my guilt. Later, as an adult, I exhumed my tirade for examination, forgiving myself, knowing that the child was not to blame, could not have known. Then I banished it—healthy, healthy me—from consciousness, never bothered by it or feeling any terrible attachment to it even when I spoke of it. But probably no priest in the world, even were I Catholic instead of a Presbyterian minister's daughter, could offer absolution to my unconscious.

There on the mountaintop, beside the cliff, injured, in shock, affected by hypothermia, with night coming on, feeling as if I might be fighting for my life, clipped phrases came to me:

Like father, like daughter.
It serves you right. You killed him and now you will die in the same way.
An eye for an eye. A life for a life.
Dust to dust, corpse on the sidewalk to corpse on the ground.
Ashes, ashes, we all fall down.

✳

But I didn't fall. Not all of my poets and parents are dead. My mother, Janice Hume, still lives, a strong and determined and independent person, alone in her seventies. I am her inheritor as well as my father's. Adrienne Rich continues among my poetic mothers, speaking to me after the fact, though she wrote "Turning" long before my trip:

My foot drags in the foothills of two lands;
At the turn the spirit pauses
and faces the high passes:
bloodred granite, sandstone steeped in blood.
At the turn the spirit turns,
looks back—if any follow—
squints ahead—if any lead—
What would you bring along on a trek like this?
What is bringing you along?

At the turn my spirit paused, faced the high passes. At the turn my spirit turned and looked back—at my father. And then I looked ahead to survival. My recklessness I attribute to hypothermia. The calm beneath it, the steady steps that finally brought me back, arose authentic, simple, whole, from my desire to live. What I brought along on this trek was my fear. The question Rich does not ask, I ask now: What did I leave behind there? My answer is the same: my fear. I did not fall. My father is still dead, and I am still alive.

ATTITUDE MATTERS: A WOMAN

ALONE WITH LIGHT

Lincoln Woods Trail and Lincoln, New Hampshire

For three days we stayed in our bushwhacked campsite, where Dirk cared for me and helped me to be well enough to walk. He hiked half a mile each way twice and three times a day, placing a fresh bag of icy mountain water on my knees to bring down the swelling. He cooked for me and made me eat and splinted my fingers and sat me in patches of sunlight, propped up with a gift from my friend Richard, John Crowley's *Little, Big*. He whittled for me a fine walking stick. He is tender and capable. On the fourth day, we broke camp and started down the mountain toward the valley, hiking as long as my legs held out.

Two days later, Dirk and I parted company. He has stayed on the mountains at my urging, committed to finishing the hike. It was nice to part quietly on the trail with someone with whom I live and make love and eat dinner and sleep. I'm on the last leg of my own part of the hike, within a mile of the van. There's a stream right next to the path here. Some people just passed by and I asked them to get my tape recorder out of my pack. I have the trail to myself now. I'm almost sorry to leave but I'd have to be a masochist to go on with Dirk. I can't sleep well. My legs hurt too much—I begin to hurt all over. Shifting my weight to my stronger leg has made my hip sore. I'm worried about how fat my knees look from way up here above them. I don't have leggings on anymore, so I can see the swelling all the time. It seems wrong to walk on them, yet it's my only way out. I want out.

But something is strange—before I came here into the wilderness area, I considered this place unknown, unsafe. Now, even with the accident, as I'm leaving to go back to cars, cities, and people, it seems almost the opposite. I will be emerging from the woods after many days away from people, traffic, cars, tourists, stores, road signs. I'm not altogether ready for the pace of civilization. I'm looking at the stream here now, realizing it's my last gaze into the depths of quietness for a long time.

Earlier I passed a troop of city kids up here to backpack. I just encountered another group of people because this part of the trail is used by the day-trippers. Women look at me with respect and curiosity. I probably look like someone who's been on the trail for a while, and I'm alone. They may assume I'm a woman backpacking in wilderness by myself. In these ten days Dirk and I have passed quite a number of men alone, but women appear only with men. Dirk said that last year he saw a few women with women, but never alone. For the moment, I'm content to appear to be what I am not, but what I hope one day that I may become—a woman emerging from the wilderness completely on her own, unafraid of the wild animals outside herself or in herself, a creature at home in her body and in the body of the natural world, a woman able to be alone with darkness, and with light.

❊

I'm in a wonderful resort lodge in Lincoln called the Mill House Inn at the end of one of the most difficult days of my life. I came off the trail with my backpack and as soon as my feet hit the concrete I became unsteady. I hiked to the ranger station where I found my car unmolested. But on concrete I could feel my injuries more. I felt a strangeness I can compare only to what it must be like to be involuntarily, unpleasantly drugged. I couldn't find my land legs. This aspect of coming out of a wilderness area after many days must be common. There must be a name for it among packers. Because it was my first time, I was a hazard to myself. If I had been hiking into town with a pack and a walking stick, perhaps people would have expected me to act a bit odd, but not behind the wheel, wielding thousands of pounds of powerful machinery.

I couldn't keep a handle on where I was or what I was doing. I would say out loud, *find a money machine, get ice, Ace bandages, a hotel.* But I couldn't manage a whole series like that in one chunk. I had to break it down into simpler tasks. *Turn here. Park car. Get out. Put keys in hand. Walk across street.* I couldn't focus or concentrate, couldn't keep my mind on what I was doing. I just sat in parking lots and stood outside my van for long periods of time. I consulted my hands often to see what, if anything, was in them. I would be suddenly convinced that I had left my bags some-where or hadn't locked the van. Sometimes it was a good thing I did check. This is a mountain town where I suppose people must stagger in from the woods a lot, vulnerable and slightly crazed. I could feel the impact of every step on the pavement. It took a couple of hours to get to the money ma-chine, buy ice, bandages, a splint. I started trying to find a motel. I would get in the van and say, *Okay, you've just done this. Now do that.* Then I'd stare ahead at nothing.

My injuries hurt more throughout the day—and I had thought they'd hurt less when I'd ceased maneuvering over tree roots and rocks. I stopped at three motels, all with rates higher than I wanted to pay, especially since I would be staying for two nights before picking up Dirk at a trailhead. After the third motel I headed to the highway south of Lincoln for cheaper rates, but that's when I realized I was not safe on the road. So I turned around and went back to this resort with off-season rates—sixty-five dol-lars a night—and saunas and pools and anonymity. I wanted that. I didn't want a bed and breakfast or a Mom and Pop place where you have to ask Pop for ice. But most important, I couldn't deal with just a shower—I had to have a bathtub to soak my injured legs. Most of these mountain places have only showers and I finally realized I'd have to pay more for a bath-tub. So I stumbled to the desk and got out my credit card and said some-thing really cogent, like *Here.* My hands were filthy and my bandages were splitting and dirty and my kneecaps were crusted with blood.

The manager behind the counter seemed to recognize this situation. I told him I just came off the mountain. He said, *You want a room and a bath. Where's your car? If you have any trouble, let me know.* He was accommo-dating, but not in that looking-for-a-tip way. Then I stood near my van thinking: *I don't know what I need in the room. Some of it is in my backpack, some in the van.* I was standing at the open doors, dazed, when the man-ager appeared at my side. He helped me sort through things. He told me how he had gone up the same mountain last year alone, had an accident, fallen and cracked some ribs and injured his legs. He wasn't sure if he could get down. This explained his sympathy. He directed me to the clinic where they handle a lot of people who come down injured. He advised me to have someone look at my hand and my legs right away. My cloth tape was falling off and I was limping. I wasn't trying to look pathetic; by this time, I just *was* pathetic. Whereas I'd felt strong just hours before in the woods, I now felt suddenly weakened. I believe this must be how Dirk often feels when he needs to be reclusive—normal, everyday encounters can drain you deep if you're in a certain state of body and of mind.

The process of getting into my room, eating bread and cheese and Mounds Bars (my first purchase was chocolate), wandering around assembling things the way one does in a motel room took me literally hours. I checked in at three o'clock and it was somehow eight o'clock before I climbed out of the bathtub. But I got myself some ice, though I had to walk clear to the other end of this big hotel and avoid being stampeded in the hall by a busload of old folks. They saw a woman grunting and limping— but my hair was clean, my wounds were rebound, I put vitamin E on my knee, and I made an appointment at the clinic for the next morning. I turned on the TV and watched "Murphy Brown" and "Sherlock Holmes Mysteries" and the news. It's raining now, and there are thunderstorms up in the mountains. From the window in my room I can see them. Dirk is somewhere up there.

Garbage. I brought out a full eight days' worth from the woods, and parts of two more days. It doesn't even fill a big freezer bag. A few crushed cans and Tampax, some wrappers, toilet paper. We created very little garbage, burned most of our refuse in the fires. Extraordinary, the difference between the garbage you make at home and while backpacking. Bare bones, no garbage cans, and you haul out whatever you take in. The way Dirk cooked on the trail creates almost no refuse.

I should try to sleep. I have a bed now and ice packs on my knees. No, I can't sleep. Black flies. When I unsplinted my finger today, there were, as I knew, many black fly bites between the two fingers bound in the splint, including three red swollen areas on my ring finger. These pests are adept at getting into the places no other creature can go—scalp, hairline, fingers. How did I get seventy-three bites when I was covered with musk at all times? Just now I was lying here and I felt something on my hand and instantly I swatted it as though it were a black fly. This is a hotel with Jacuzzies. There are no black flies here. But I was back up there swatting at the outside of the tent where a bear is sniffing at the flap.

When Dirk and I were on the last part of the trail together, he said, *What might be important enough in the outside world that people coming up the trail would stop you and tell you about it?* You could gear the importance of something that way. Did you hear southern California fell into the sea? Did you hear there's been a nuclear war? Did you hear everyone is dead? What's the magnitude of an event that people would inform each other of up there? Tonight when I went to buy a newspaper I ended up with one of those local mountain weeklies with a kid holding up his fish on page one. Later I flipped through the TV channels and on CNN the big news was of blasting Iraq. While we were in the mountains, America bombed Iraq again. President Clinton's approval rate went up 50 percent because he did something decisive and military. I'm hearing this news alone, which reminds me that *nobody* in the world knows where I am—not my mother, not my kids, not my employers, not my friends, not my loves, not my dog, not even Dirk knows where I am. This gives me the solitude I need to continue the work of thinking my way through this situation.

Dirk said to me in a fight a year ago that he didn't regret anything that he had done during our relationship. Since what he had done to me at the time seemed to me to be cruel, I said, "How can you never regret?" He repeated it: "I never regret anything. To regret is to permit self-hatred. Not to regret is my religion." I thought that was strange—lack of regret as a fundamental religious tenet? Over the past year I've come to see some of what he intended. He meant that you must challenge yourself to learn from that for which you might merely have said, "I'm sorry." I still believe that if one commits an act of violence, not regretting is inflexible and cruel. But Dirk meant it as William Blake meant his Proverbs of Hell: *Sooner murder an infant in its cradle than nurse unacted desire.* Take that literally and it's homicidal tyranny. If read more radically, it's useful. I am learning how rejecting regret can be creative, and how much it hurts.

Since I usually go to Cape Cod at this time each year, I'd normally be on the cape right now, sitting still, recharging my batteries, reading books, relaxing, looking at the bay, my creature comforts well met. This trip was the substitute, and it hasn't been anything like that, nor did I expect that it would be. I let go of the need for the cape this year. I couldn't go there because my ex-mate got married in our cottage of twenty years' standing, to which we returned every season as veteran renters. He asked if he could use the place for part of the time this year, and I said sure. He had left it to me—even though we don't own it, I got the right to rent it when we broke up and that division was his idea. When he asked if he could go there, he didn't say why. He didn't say he was getting married there. He didn't say he was going to use it as his honeymoon cottage. Had I done such a thing without a word to him, he would have regarded it as yet another of my betrayals of trust and love. Whatever he did was justified, he felt, by the fact that I left him. This is painful stuff that I'm working through. When it's there, it's just there. I wouldn't feel at home on the cape now.

When Dirk suggested backpacking with him, I thought about it carefully and long and finally said yes. Part of what I'm doing is a voyage of healing, a final journey during which I am letting go of Mac as he let go of me. It's difficult, filled with pain and love and his belief that I nearly destroyed him, as he put it. He takes little responsibility. It's difficult to have designated this a healing journey and to end up at the top of mountain cliffs, hurting myself physically and mentally.

Many times a day since it happened a week ago, I see myself heading for those rocks. Thinking it through, I encounter more symbolic levels at which it occurred. Every night since then I have dreamed about Mac—a man nearly old enough to be my father, who has been at times as convinced that I set out to destroy him as I am internally convinced I destroyed my father. When I told Mac I was going backpacking, he said with a dry laugh, "Right. When I asked you to go with me, you never would." That's not really accurate—I devoted my summers to traveling with him for fifteen years and would have gone almost anywhere. For a woman so hellbent on destroying men—Mac is not the first to accuse me of it—I've loved mine pretty well. They don't accuse me of hating men until I display a will of my own that cannot always bend to theirs. Then they see me as a malicious destroyer, a fatal attraction that nearly broke them down. The pattern is amazingly consistent.

Now, several interpretations are possible here. Might they be right? I know I have to resist mental overgeneralizing about men, but I *do* resist it; and while I potentially fear men, that's not the same as hatred. In my relationships with men, I have often felt my own needs nearly obliterated by meeting *their* needs, an internal perception supported not only by others close to me but also, ironically, by each of my lovers in his turn. Observing that same pattern in my relationship with his predecessor, each one says that although he's seen The One Before Him doing that, and doesn't understand why I don't stand up for myself, it will be different with him. So far it hasn't been. Another possible reading is that I am a woman who unconsciously seeks out men who will try to control her, against whose supposed tyrannies she will always have to rise to function as an individual. This possibility is not unlikely, though I hate it. Or perhaps the construction of masculinity in our patriarchy creates a surfeit of such men, such that no neurosis on my part is necessary. This is the possibility often mentioned to me by both women and by men of goodwill. I hesitate to believe it because then it's back to square one, where I'm able to be cast as man-hater by the very men who come to hate me. I suspect a lethal combination of the latter two hypotheses—I'm sick and so are they.

In any case, feeling strong without Mac at the time of his marriage was important to me. Instead I'm in bed with bloody kneecaps, swollen ankles, a broken finger. What do I do with that? I've got to do *something* creative with it, and it's got to be mental. Coming down off of the mountain, hurting, the matter of attitude has been crucial. I have had an adventure I'll never forget. I will tell this to my grandchildren: I was once picked up by a hundred-mile-an-hour wind on the top of a mountain. I learned about turning back as well as going forward. Talking that way, thinking that way, was important to getting down from the mountain. If I had looked at it only as a terrible accident, I might have had to be carried out on a litter. Attitude matters.

Now that I'm on the ground, I'm recovering. This morning I'll go to the walk-in clinic. I'll be okay. But this lost time isn't retrievable. I needed it desperately. I can't work eighty and more hours a week without a rest to gather my forces. I would, I believe, simply break down if this pace were to go on. How do I now keep the experience and the memory fundamentally positive? How to keep thinking the same way I did on the mountain? I need to find the right metaphor to place it into an eternity within time, make a way to keep it sacred. And that brings me back to understanding what Dirk meant by *Never regret*.

I must speak as if in some way I don't regret what happened, until I really believe it. I have to keep speaking that way and thinking that way as much as I can, taking into consideration this challenge I've faced and learned from. I have to say, This is what happened here and this is what I did to contribute to this and this is what I newly know. And I've got to do this fiercely or I will lose myself in the muck of self-pity. I must rethink what this trip came to be about, symbolically, regarding Mac as well as my father. It was about being strong without Mac, my twenty-year base camp. It was about having experiences I never had with him. The years since I've left him have been filled with fine ways of being that I would never have known in our life together. I permitted them to myself—myself, not half of a Platonic soul egg whose embryo was desires and needs that came to feel destructive to me. I could not have remained half of that whole and still have come to know myself this way or grown to become the me that I am.

I wish Mac had been able to change with me and not have been afraid. I loved him, and our parting wrenched me. I'd rather have grown old with him. But he didn't or couldn't change and more, and I had to leave. What I have found out about struggle, achievement, knowledge, and my own dearly individual joy for many moments at a time, I could not have had with him. Though we were supposed to be about all those things, we had come to be about repression and good behavior—mine, not his. That double standard was what I would always have known in the home of my dear old love, not mountains and edges and cliffs and wild wind. I do not regret. I will say it until I believe it is true.

*

I went for morning coffee in the Mountain Room. I brought it back here to my room because I really don't feel like talking to anybody or being in any room connected, even titularly, to mountains. I walked in there completely forgetful that last night I put a sanitary napkin folded in half on my knee because I had run out of gauze pads and my new Ace bandage was too tight. I came hobbling into the lounge with my Kotex on my knee, my splinted fingers, and probably a stark, rabid look in my eye. The senior citizens milled about, speaking of someone in their group who was limping. A woman pointed to me and said, "Oh look there, she's just a girl and she's hobbling, too. What happened to you?" She almost shrieked it.

The whole room looked at me. People pointed to my kneepad, also constructed of other intimate wear—a pair of panties tied creatively around the Kotex. The woman who pointed said, "What did you do, play soccer?" I told them the short form of what happened up there, which sounded lunatic to them. It was, but not in the way their perceptions processed it. "I'm not a girl, I'm a grandmother like you." She replied, wry, "You're still a girl to me, dear." She had white hair, walked with a cane, and was traveling alone, probably having outlived her husband. A lot more women than men were there, as always with groups of seniors. The widows travel in herds. As I left the lounge they were talking about the crazy things young people do. I'm not feeling young at all right now. I'm creaking.

All right then. How not to regret *that?* Easy: this is good rehearsal time for empathizing with the stringencies of old age, when women must so often be alone for the last years of their lives. The younger woman I looked like, emerging from the woods, is the foremother and foreshadow, the daughter and the inheritor of the woman who emerges from the Trailways bus. They have much in common. One uses a walking stick, the other a cane. One still looks primarily to the future and the other to the past, but this difference determines their continuity: if remembering the past is part of the old woman's present, if her past constitutes, shapes, builds up moment by moment to that always emergent present, then let her be always active, immanent, embodied, and tough enough to walk that lonesome valley by herself.

BLOWING IN THE WIND

Lincoln, New Hampshire

Dirk and I have been close and loving since I picked him up at the trailhead, so I thought he understood that right now the web of peace I'm trying to weave around myself is a bit fragile. My optimism and my constructive frame for this experience are genuine, but also new and delicate. He is indeed a fine man, but something familiar is happening here. He needs me to respect his emotional and physical limits and boundaries, but like many people in my life, he seems unable to respect mine—or even to understand that there *are* limits to my capacities and tolerances. It's my rock problem in more ways than one, as I have long known. Many people see me as a rock, and I'm often not permitted cracks or fissures by those who depend on me—family members, partners in love, friends, even students who work closely with me. "If you're weak," asked one student friend for whom I was a role model, surprised to find me human, frail, imperfect, "then what hope is there for the rest of us?"

The question stunned me, both in its unreasonableness and in its accurate accounting for why she grew to loathe me when she discovered I had feet of clay, not rock. I never asked to be made a goddess and hadn't understood the height from which I fell in her regard. This issue has plagued my relationships for years, and it is only in the past several that I've begun to insist that my intimates not expect me to be their rock. With this accident, the metaphor became reality. I proved I was not made of rock physically by smashing into that very substance. Dirk knew and accepted my physical limitations, but within a day of our reunion, still far from home, with me fighting feelings of defeat and trying to hang onto my newly created perceptions, he decided it was time for me to face harder facts.

Dirk said, *One thing I have to admit to myself is that I overestimated your abilities.* I swallowed hard. I said, *Okay, maybe that's true, if you think so.* He took it one step further. *You have to admit that your experience and abilities have something to do with what happened, because otherwise no lesson is really learned.* I would like to have believed that almost anybody in that position would have been blown away—not to wish it on anyone, but to see myself as a competent person caught in extreme circumstances where my competence couldn't save me from damage. It was upsetting that Dirk didn't believe I was adequate, but I admitted it anyway. I'd been comfortable not subjecting the experience to any such analysis at all, at least not yet. When I'd caught myself beginning to ask internal questions that touched on the issue of competence, I'd been uncomfortable. But I made room for his conviction that we needed to analyze, even if the results were not pleasant to my ego.

If we were going to engage in tough analysis, though, it didn't feel right to leave his role in this unexamined, taking in his perspective to the exclusion of my own. There was another issue here. If he were going to press me to such an admission, he might well make an analogous one. He should see that *nobody* should be climbing in that part of the White Mountains when a storm front has lasted for two days and high winds are forecasted. Nobody. I was there because I had trusted his judgment. I hadn't said anything about this, despite having browsed the guidebooks in the bookstore by now, finding specific warnings against exactly what had happened. So I voiced my concern. He hikes alone a lot. This is about the future as well as the past.

When you tell the story at home, I asked, leave out the part about my abilities and experience? The part about Diana the inexperienced female backpacker? I needed him not to say to our friends, in his weary, knowing, quiet voice, that, yes, when it came down to it, I overestimated Diana's abilities. She was in over her head. I wanted that to stay between us. I can deal in private with matters I'd rather not make public property, except if I make them so, as I do now. The more I have thought about it, the more I have realized that by doing this I was also protecting him, as I often do, from facing his own responsibilities. His mistake in judgment wasn't so much overestimating me as it was underestimating the danger level. Part of my own error was in trusting the judgment of the one who said he'd take full responsibility for our preparations—the one who insisted that I leave it all to him and got impatient with my questions, as if my curiosity and desire for more knowledge constituted an invasion of his territory and a mistrust of his expertise. We should have consulted the AMC guidebooks.

Every hiker knows that in the mountains storms come up quickly and are sometimes of great and unpredictable force. That is part of what causes my concern for him as a lone hiker—you have to make conservative judgment calls about things that are potentially hazardous, especially in terrain that's not deeply familiar, not your own. In the past several days, while he's been climbing on his own, I've repeatedly received admonishment from the locals: *You shouldn't have been up there. You should have known better.* Yesterday in the antique store I encountered an old-boy local who has done many of the same things Dirk does on his trips. Even he said, *An experienced hiker wouldn't have been up there.* I said, Well, that's not true, I am not very experienced, but my hiking partner is. *Well,* he said, *he's not experienced in the White Mountains then, because nobody who knows the White Mountains would have been up there that day. It was one of the worst summer storms in recent history.* Telling me harrowing stories of the power of the mountain winds, in loving detail—trees uprooted, trucks blown many yards from where they were parked, cabins shredded—seemed to be the local version of ragging the greenhorn. Gimping along in my many Ace bandages, I had no choice but to capitulate.

As I heard these admonitions, I felt a pang of resentment, not for myself but for my man, who has a lot invested in his experience and knowledge of backpacking. He hikes alone in remote areas for weeks at a time. The chances were good that we both could have made it across that ridge intact but the risk was significant. I fantasized about how different it could have been: if it hadn't been for that one moment when the wind picked me up, we would have made it across and our adventure would have been full of risk, but not of injury. But I did get injured. The odds were perhaps with us, but not by much. If he would have seen that we shouldn't have been up there, if he would merely have said, *Yes I know,* that would have been the end of it. But he wanted to preserve the notion that while it was indeed foolhardy to have brought incompetent me up there, it wouldn't have posed any significant risk for him alone—less than driving drunk, as he put it, which he's done. I don't buy that.

He says, *Truths don't have to be symmetrical. Just because you have to admit that you shouldn't have been up there due to lack of experience and ability doesn't mean that I should have to admit the same thing.* That's too much for me to accept in silent capitulation. Usually I would say not another word about it all my life—I've silenced myself for years at a time to keep delicate peace with my lovers, and I know how to do it. No lack of ability or experience there. But lately that stance feels compromising, patronizing, inauthentic. I'd frankly thought we were going to protect each other for a while on this one, but apparently not—it soon became clear that while I was called upon to face unpleasant possibilities, he had no intention of joining me. He was going to stick to his story, which made me responsible for attempting this hazardous range and him responsible only for taking me seriously as a hiking partner. He added that if I hadn't admitted I was out of my depth, I'd be full of false pride about my abilities and would have learned no necessary lesson. He couldn't have trusted me as a hiking partner again. What I said was, Yes, and there's a lesson here for you, too.

He got so defensive that I haven't told him what the locals or the guidebooks said. At the injury clinic I was told that more accidents happen in summer than in winter here, because the winter people are generally seasoned alpine hikers who know what to do and what not to do, while summer hikers, lulled into the certainty they can handle it, are more likely to get into trouble, particularly with hypothermia, but also with winds. I don't see what the big deal is about admitting that when you're in the mountains in a windstorm, you should sit it out. He couldn't give me anything back and I finally gave up trying to get him to hear during this tape-recorded exchange. This is one man and woman talking, but the issues are larger than we are.

Diana: My fear is more significant than your knowledge? I don't think so.

Dirk: I've been in that situation I don't know how many times.

Diana: On a cliff? 4,500 feet above sea level in an 80–100 mile-per-hour windstorm? No, I don't think you've been in that situation much.

Dirk: The "situation" is when you get knocked over into a certain grade of slope. With a certain force on a certain terrain—that's the analogous circumstance.

Diana: The nature of that "certain force" is more than incidental. Look, all I'm saying is a few days ago you asked me to admit something. You didn't really ask, you demanded. You said, *Babe, you haven't learned your lesson here. You need to admit that part of this had to do with your inexperience and your inability. If you don't admit that, you haven't learned anything.* That truth hurt and you were indeed right and I conceded that, and it was hard because I'm already injured and fighting feelings of defeat. I'm asking you to do the same thing you asked of me—only a lot less of it.

Dirk: I have done that. I *will* do that—in a situation I know to be dangerous, I will not risk serious injury.

Diana: But you're saying that the situation we were in was not dangerous.

Dirk: Yes. For me, that situation posed no threat.

Diana: A storm that made East Coast news because it was so strong? One-hundred-mile-per-hour gusts of wind?

Dirk: I've been in them before.

Diana: Posed no real danger?

Dirk: No.

Diana: Near a cliff?

Dirk: I wasn't near the cliff because the wind was blowing away from the cliff.

Diana: But the gusts were swirling and we were *very* near the cliff.

Dirk: The gusts were not capable of going against the physics of it. If you got near it, you would have been blown back.

Diana: Okay, so you're blown back. So what happened to me—getting blown back into the rocks—could happen to you if you were alone, too. And you could be injured without help or a partner. Right?

Dirk: I get blown off my feet and I start to fall . . .

Diana: You get blown off your feet and are airborn.

Dirk: With a forty-pound backpack? No. And it's my experience that allows me to situate myself so that I won't be injured.

Diana: I did that.

Dirk: No, you didn't.

Diana: I did do that to a great extent, and you don't give me credit for it. I didn't break anything except a finger.

Dirk: I saw you fall, though, and you were not doing it in the way of someone who had been knocked to the ground a couple hundred times.

Diana: You have not been knocked to the ground a couple of hundred times.

Dirk: I have.

Diana: When?

Dirk: Over the period of my life. Whether it was in football or wrestling or . . . I've fallen by a cliff before and I've dropped close to forty feet. I've also fallen another time which was close to twenty feet. And the slope was much more close to vertical. I've been in your situation. I've fallen fifteen feet to concrete. These are just hard lessons. Like what just happened to you. If that happened to you . . . you don't live in that world . . .

Diana: What world's that?

Dirk: The one where your body mechanics and strength is—when—well, you said you had a lot of time to think before you hit the ground.

Diana: Yes. In a way. And I know what world you're talking about . . .

Dirk: Okay, now, experience means that in that period of time . . .

Diana: Which is about a second . . .

Dirk: Yes, but the mind works in the situation like stunt people's would. They fall on a pile of rocks and it looks like pillows to them, know what I mean? Sure they get banged up, but they know what to do to minimize the damage.

Diana: You're telling me that if you had been in my situation, you wouldn't have been blown away, and if you were, you would have known where to place yourself to not be hurt.

Dirk: Almost 100 percent.

Diana: I'm sorry, but that strikes me as humorous. When a hundred-mile-an-hour wind picks me up and throws me into the rocks, I hate to have a guy who played a couple of seasons of football look down on me so patronizingly. I think you need to be on equal terms with me on this lesson in judiciousness.

Dirk: I'm sorry that this situation was so far out of your experience and scared you into worrying about me in the same situation. But remember that I always did this kind of thing alone, and why should I tell you about it?

Diana: And why should I tell you that the overwhelming majority of people who get injured or killed in risky adventures alone are guys with an attitude like yours? Have you forgotten that you broke your neck once and were expected to die? All along here it seems like you're telling me that my experience is female and yours is male, without using the terms. That's okay. But it's no good reason to justify *dumb* risks, you know?

Dirk: We learn to not do those again. But this was different.

Diana: You're saying this wasn't dumb? Being up there in those high winds in a storm front into its third day? You're still maintaining that would not be dumb if you had been alone?

Dirk: Well, there are some situations when I *did* risk my life and I'm scared to death to get into those again.

Diana: Like when you broke your neck.

Dirk: Yes. I won't fall asleep at the wheel again. I won't get drunk and hang from steel grates fifty feet up again. I won't speed through suburban streets at one hundred miles per hour anymore.

Diana: I believe you won't. You're more grown up than that now. But when confronted with a circumstance similar to the one we were in, and alone, you would have gone on rather than stop.

Dirk: I would have probed farther than I was able to, because I had to tend to you. And if during my probing I would have found something that was above my limits, I would have stopped.

Diana: But just before that gust caught me, in the push of those steady winds, I was still doing fine—and just like you I did not really think I was above my limit until nearly the moment it occurred. That's the whole point. It happens fast in conditions like this. The panic you saw in my eyes wasn't until after this had happened, when I finally understood that my previous sense of control was illusory—the wind was in charge, not me.

Dirk: Remember, I had concerns *before* you fell down.

Diana: Like what?

Dirk: That after a gust of wind, you would stand up straight again. And I repeated, *Stay down.* You say you did, but not as much as I wanted.

Diana: You're making this up, Dirk. When I stood up, it was to test standing up between gusts, just as you did. I saw you doing it too, and I said to you, Dirk, I'm going to hit the deck a lot getting across here. Do you remember me saying that?

Dirk: Yes. But you didn't . . .

Diana: I was in the crouch position a lot more than you—appropriately because of your weight, in spite of your pack.

Dirk: First of all, the *wind* did not pick you up like you think. You're going to have to let go of that idea.

Diana: It didn't? What do *you* think happened?

Dirk: The wind pushed you in the back and your first reaction was to put your foot out to stop yourself, and that acted like a pole vault, which acted with the wind to push you off instead of hitting the dirt.

Diana: That may be partly true, but if you think I should have prevented it, then you don't understand the power of the wind at a certain force and angle. It didn't happen to you—it happened to me, and I know what happened. I was there.

Dirk: *You* don't understand the power to learn to control your body at that moment. I'm not talking about the wind. I'm talking about the power of your own leg. I'm saying that the only thing you need to worry about is to catch your balance.

Diana: Honey-man, it was a gust that *instantly* lifted me. There was no time for balance.

Dirk: Yes, there was. With experience you would have bent your knee and lifted it off the ground instead of merely pushing it out or straightening your back, which is another thing you did.

Diana: There was a lot more time between when I was picked up and when I crashed, time to make those intelligent decisions, than when I was initially fighting the gust.

Dirk: Sure. But part of that problem was your orientation to the wind. And it worried me. I'm not making that up.

Diana: My orientation to the wind worried you? Then why hadn't you said anything about that?

Dirk: Because as I've already said, I was too worried about my own safety and I had my fingers crossed when I thought of yours.

Diana: Now you're contradicting yourself about your not being at risk. Look, it was hazardous for me and it would have been hazardous for you to have gone up there on your own. Hikers alone die as a result of pride like yours. They can get a small injury but don't have help and get stuck above the tree line and become disoriented from hypothermia and they can just die. I've been told about this the last few days by people who've lived here for years, who know these things. You say that if I were to learn anything from this, it would come after I admitted my lack of experience and lack of ability in these kinds of situations—otherwise no lesson here. All I am saying is that in addition to what *I* need to do, *you* need to do something, too. God, you're laughing.

Dirk: No, no I'm not.

Diana: Instead of hearing me genuinely. . . you're . . .

Dirk: But I have heard you. And I've done this myself.

Diana: No you haven't, you haven't gone through exactly what happened to me the other day.

Dirk: Why is it so important for you to believe that? When I'm relating this, you don't want it to sound like you were just a wimpy female and my main mistake was my overestimation of your abilities. That's fine as long as you admitted it to me in private, so that would give me confidence to lead you into some similar situation in the future. That's all.

Diana: That's not all. *No one* should have been there under those conditions. *That's* all.

Dirk: What you really asked me to say was to acknowledge that when you're in a dangerous situation, don't pursue it.

Diana: Yes. So are you saying that yes, it was a dangerous and hazardous situation? If you are, then great, we're done, argument over.

Dirk: No, I'm not saying that. Diana, your perspective in situations like this is so—this situation to you looks like everything right now.

Diana: Well, at the moment, it looks large. I might have to have surgery on my hand. My knees and ankles are going to be hobbled up for weeks.

Dirk: Well, to me it's like this: Diana, you've burned your finger on a stove, don't do it again. I learned my lesson, I grabbed the stove, I don't want you to do that. That's how I approach it. Whereas you're sitting here telling me, Dirk, don't ever use the stove again. I'm not speaking from a rationalization, I'm speaking from having been scared to death a number of times. Because I *was* stupid.

Diana: So you know the difference between the kind of stupidity that results in your possible death and this situation, which poses no risk? There's nothing analogous to that kind of danger up there?

Dirk: That situation to me would have probably been—well, it *all* sounds stupid to me. It sounds like a twelve year old—*I gotta go to the hospital because I broke my finger.* You know?

Diana: I see what you're saying, but I don't accept it. And it's insulting. Look. If you're going to be hiking alone in rough terrain when nobody knows where you are, which is by all reasonable measures stupid in and of itself, then you need to make judgment calls that are conservative. You did exercise prudence about me and my recovery.

Dirk: It's easy to do it for someone else rather than having learned about it on your own.

Diana: Well, yes. I was aware that some of your own experiences played into that, but there are different principles at work here. You've done lone hiking in your life, you probably always will. You should make sensible judgment calls all the time on stuff this big, if you're asking me to.

Dirk: Didn't I do that the last two days when I continued hiking alone?

Diana: I'm sure you did. But why won't you admit our mutual mistake that day? You asked me to take a lesson—how come you won't take a lesser one?

Dirk: Because to admit it—the hard lesson I would have to admit is that I have to let somebody else determine what my limits are and have someone else say, *I think you aren't as good as you think you are.*

Diana: Well, damn it, man, that's what you were asking me to do, and I did it. It's not like it was easy for me to admit. I have done day hiking for over twenty years. I'm not somebody who's never hiked before. I've hiked in Texas, Colorado, California, Utah, Arizona, New Mexico, Nevada . . .

Dirk: I did make a confession earlier.

Diana: But what you "confessed" to was overestimating my abilities—thank you so much.

Dirk: That's how you're hearing it.

Diana: That's what you *said*.

Dirk: Now let me interpret what I said in a way that maybe you will learn something.

Diana: We're going to have Diana learning something again, are we?

Dirk: You seem to have no problem doing it to *me*.

Diana: I'm having a considerable problem, actually.

Dirk: Okay. Why can't you just accept that there doesn't always have to be a symmetry between the kinds of lessons learned from the same perception? You learned one kind of lesson. I admitted to another kind of lesson. It had to do not so much with whether or not I had brought an inexperienced person along—it had to do with whether or not I was going to attend to humanity and reason in a dangerous situation and not risk someone else's life. Like having a passenger when you're driving drunk or something.

Diana: Well, now you're changing your story a bit. But don't you see that in this case, if it doesn't apply to you and your own personal thinking, it's not much of a lesson at all? It's just about caretaking the greenhorn—or the poor little girlfriend.

Dirk: But admitting anything else would be a lie.

Diana: If you were to admit what I'm saying, it would be a lie?

Dirk: It would be to say that climbing that mountain would be as dangerous as driving drunk.

Diana: Excuse me? Are you saying that climbing that mountain under those circumstances was not even as dangerous as driving drunk?

Dirk: Yes.

Diana: That's it. I give up.

✳

By the time the summer wore into fall I gave up entirely on Dirk. As others who might keep our separate souls from being lonely, we ultimately failed each other. We helped each other on our journeys for a few years—we could say we walked together, conversing and lending support, for many mutual miles. But then we needed to part at a predetermined place. Neither of us could know that our parting on a literal trail would soon be echoed by the parting paths of our lives—nor that the very issues encoded in this adventure would be among those that tore us from our companionship: the wrangle of gender, subtextual constructions of masculine and feminine, the inability to compromise further, the mutual exclusivity of our perceptions if not of our goals, issues of personal pride and responsibility. When I told him I wanted him to move out of my house, I was angry in much the same way I have been here, and for some of the same reasons. I could see his point of view, even if I didn't agree with it completely, but he rejected mine completely, reducing it to "stupid" or "irrelevant." Finally he decided I was cruel to him, even "malicious" and "inhuman." And of course, he now sees me as a man-hating feminist.

Backing up from the intimate intentions of my single point of view, I think of the most famous American poem that symbolically parallels paths in the forest and life choices, Robert Frost's "The Road Not Taken":

Two roads diverged in a yellow wood,
And sorry I could not travel both
And be one traveler, long I stood
And looked down one as far as I could
To where it bent in the undergrowth;

Then took the other, as just as fair,
And having perhaps the better claim,
Because it was grassy and wanted wear;
Though as for that the passing there
Had worn them really about the same,

And both that morning equally lay
In leaves no step had trodden black.
Oh, I kept the first for another day!
Yet knowing how way leads on to way,
I doubted if I should ever come back.

I shall be telling this with a sigh
Somewhere ages and ages hence:
Two roads diverged in a wood, and I—
I took the one less traveled by,
And that has made all the difference.

This beloved poem is well known to the American heart. It's not the exclusive property of the academy, the critics, the poets. America owns few poems in common, for this is not a country in which poets are held in great esteem, as they are in Latin America and Eastern Europe. We seldom send our poets as ambassadors of culture and goodwill to other countries, Carolyn Forché notwithstanding. Poetry doesn't make much difference here. While in many countries, poets are imprisoned for their writings, all poets may speak freely here—except that no one really listens. Only occasionally do we take to our collective heart a poet's words.

Robert Frost was one of the great exceptions, and of his works, none is better known than this simple verse that functions simultaneously at two levels. Our fathers and mothers and grandparents knew its cadences, or at least those of the last three and most quoted lines. It appeals unfailingly to American audiences because it seems to be about individuality, independence, difficult choices, the rewards of choosing the road less traveled, of doing things one's own way. The implication that individual choice will raise one above the common herd appeals deeply to the American need to see ourselves as rugged loners whose life decisions shape and determine our fates. We're in control: "I took the one less traveled by, / And that has made all the difference."

The wish to see ourselves in this fearless light must be strong indeed, because this universally accepted reading of the poem is dead wrong from my perspective. Frost is far too cynical and ironic to throw us such a sentimental and self-aggrandizing sop. He knew his audience would simplify its ambiguously encoded message as a sign of individual hegemony, which *is* the poem's point: "The Road Not Taken" is about mythologizing self-deceptions and lies, our uses and misuses of memory, our need to see ourselves as the heroes of our own life stories. Frost does not condemn this human and possibly inexorable need, but merely exposes it for our examination, challenging us to engage in self-reflection that leaves us looking at our lies, or our myths, in newly constructed ways.

The dramatic situation is simple: a speaker walking in the woods comes to a divergence marked by two roads and must choose one to follow. In the traditional reading of the poem, he takes the one less traveled by. But in stanzas two and three, the actuality is clearly explained. The speaker *tells himself* that one is less traveled than the other, then immediately admits that this conviction is simply not true: "Though as for that the passing there / Had worn them really about the same." He takes the one he has earlier told himself is the less traveled, keeping the first for "another day." Yet even then, "knowing how way leads on to way," he knows it is doubtful that he will ever return to be presented with the option of reliving that decision and selecting the other road. The traditional reading literally blocks out, fully represses, four lines of the poem that could not be more clearly or simply written, and about which there can be no mistake. Yet, having taught this poem for twenty years, I have never encountered a single group of readers who did not perform precisely this misprision. To read the text on the page, instead of the one desired, would be anti-American. We wipe it out, ignore it, erase it, obliterate it by the end of the poem, creating our own collective, edited, fantasized text.

At the end, the speaker projects himself into an imagined future, "ages and ages hence," where he would "be telling this with a sigh." When the present has become the past, we rewrite our personal and collective histories to accord with our sense of who we are, what we have become, who we wish to have been, where we wish to have gone. The story the speaker will tell, possibly propped in a rocking chair on a future porch, speaking to a rapt listener, a grandchild, perhaps, will be heroic in significance and design. The implication that the speaker made the best decision, opting for the high road, is sufficiently seductive that every group I've ever discussed it with has felt this conviction. Yet nowhere does the speaker actually say that the "difference" was for the best—only that the process of choosing, in and of itself, is determinant of one's future course.

That is perhaps the poem's core "truth," though it is interpreted by a speaker who has already confessed to being thoroughly unreliable. He also admits to that tendency toward mythologizing, inevitably attended by self-deceiving and self-serving lies. We need to be the heroes of our stories. We need to justify our choices, and we do it by storytelling, by narration, by creating a personal history that permits us to pretend control over our material—the material of potentially chaotic experience onto which we must impose a sense of order, pattern, sense. Our lives are rendered whole only by ourselves, by our manipulations of memory.

That is the process in which I am here engaged, in which we all engage daily, hourly, moment by moment, in one direction on our time lines—and then annually, and by decades, over a lifetime, in the other direction. We try to bring it whole. How I perceive myself, and the consequences of my choices, is vital to me individually. How I am perceived by those with whom I live, those from whom I part, members of my family, my widening, concentric circles of family, friends, readers, is a matter over which I have less control, since each reader of my experience, in person or in print, brings to my extended life-poem her or his own experiences, textual subtleties, interpretive strategies.

I know some of my own subtexts; of some, I am sure, I remain completely unaware, constructing this mythos of an American traveler, gazing through a culturally female eye, late in the century, moving among others yet essentially alone, and searching always for the lonely other who is my twin, my doppelganger, my fellow-sister celebrant—that one who must always remain my self-reflection, and my fiction.

PART 5

LITTLE DARLING, DON'T

THINK TOO MUCH

San Antonio and West Texas

The San Antonio *Express-News* is under my Amtrak compartment door—Easter Sunday, now I realize, looking out my window at God's country, George Bush's country, Lyndon Johnson's, Texas eternal. The rebels are riding in southern Mexico. The pope is meeting with rabbis and declaring Jews "our elders in the faith." The Waco investigations are covered in official silence and gag rules. A U.S. soldier is "sorry" he killed his wife's lover, kicked off his head, and brought it to her in her hospital bed. Whitewater is straining ties between Treasury and the White House.

The rich farm land and cow country near San Antonio is giving way to the western Texas desert. We're traveling along the Rio Grande, with Mexico right across the border. Desert now, lechiguilla and ocatillo and mesquite—then some sudden red-rock country, sheep out the window. Dry, dry, dry, barren beauty. A while back, the Pecos River Bridge, highest railroad bridge in this part of the country, then Eagle's Nest Canyon near Longford, home of Judge Roy Bean. A few yellow wildflowers among the sage and cactus and sand and desert hills, bent-over telephone poles. No one lives here. The wooden crosses of the hill country disappear.

When I was growing up, Easter Sunday meant church all day—Sunday school, then the lily-laden Easter service with its talk of the resurrected Christ, then coffee hour, a later service, evening youth group. Daughter in a ministerial family, I chafed in my Easter dress, impatient, irritated, bored. Yet this morning, when the newspaper informed me it's Easter, as did the train conductor's announcement, slices of old hymns began to sing themselves inside me—

> Easter Bells are ringing,
> This Easter Day,
> All the birds are singing,
> They seem to say:
> Hallelujah, He is risen,
> He is risen, Christ the King.
> Let us all our songs and praises bring.

And

> Oh God our help in ages past,
> Our hope for years to come,
> Our shelter from the stormy blast,
> And our Eternal Home.

Then "A mighty fortress is our God."

Perhaps I will some day discern what valuable aspects of my character were forged by my early Christianity, but I've no idea what they might be. I reject that God. He is dead, as I told a loud jerk in the lounge car yesterday when he tried to convert me, and it took me years to kill him off. I do not dislike Christians (some of my closest loved ones would, I think, still call themselves that), I just dislike the institutions of Christianity, equally with all other organized religions, whose major contributions to human history have been alienation, murder, guilt, greed, imperialism, exclusivity, fear, and loathing. I know that the human animal has always had to believe in transcendence, to seek meaning, to create it by creating the gods. There is no culture that has not done this, bless our fearful hearts. More sheep out the window, to whom the shepherd is God. Christianity's major metaphors—the Lord as shepherd, Christ as sacrificial Lamb of God.

The Law of the Father be damned. My Christ, when I have one, is William Blake's:

> Bring me my bow of burning gold
> Bring me my arrows of desire
> I will not cease from mental fight
> Til we have built Jerusalem
> In England's green and pleasant land.

Or America's. It is only the past few years that I've been able to amputate the leftover limbs of God the Father from my soul. My litmus test: in immediate extremity, with loss of life immanent, would I in my last moments call upon him? Let me commit my reply to paper as my celebration of Easter, and not altogether ironic—No, I would not call upon the Christian God in *any* extremity. And I thank whatever strengths of heart in me have come to know this, because otherwise the tentacles of original sin, of woman-hating, of body-hating, would reach too deep for me to uproot them *in me* in this lifetime. I have some forms of the internalized oppressor, the specter, left in me—to declare myself completely free of this would be to pridefully regard myself not a member of my own culture, not in part a product of my time and place. But the God of the Patriarchs does not get my worship—his ragged body parts are all that's left.

Our obsession with the slaughtered, risen, resurrected Son King, however muted in the daily lives of most Christians, is yet a powerful unconscious force, keeping most of the nominally Christian world from living Here, making us focus on future and past rather than present, on external rather than internal agency, on elusive essence at the expense of embodied, known, felt existence. Bless that martyred boy as he represents rebellion, imagination, creative urge, grace, mercy, love—and damn him as he represents the sword, the right hand of God the Father, judging the quick and the dead, rejecting Mary the Mother and the sexuality of Magdalene, resisting temptation, fulfilling the Law. I do believe in resurrections. I'm having a few of my own. Here end my Easter thoughts.

THROUGH PURGATORY TO THE SILENCE

OF THE LAMBS

Spring Creek Canyon, Colorado

I spat the testicles, the blood-salt pleasing my mouth.
Each man turned from my mixed embarrassment.

We were at once connected in that blood luxury,
raising heads
while the tribe circle waits,
turns away from the hungry self,
begins to guard.
—Jesse Loren, "Sheep Production: 101"

Bobby rose from a lamb's body, blood on his mouth. He said, "Pardon me, I usually don't spit in front of ladies." Bobby Wheeler is castrating the lambs the old Basque way. He sucks the testicles into his mouth and pulls the cord, snapping it from the lamb's body, using his teeth if the cord won't break. Later I sat and shared a cup of coffee with Bobby, a retired Colorado state trooper. We talked about public hostility toward police, an interesting subject to me since my son had become a policeman. Bobby has been retired for fifteen years. He's in his sixties, weathered and worn and vigorous, good-looking, comfortable in his body. I just saw a man suck testicles out of lambs and at the time it didn't even seem too strange. How is that possible?

✳

I'm in Durango, recording my drive on Route 550 through Ridgeway to Montrose to visit my old friends Tom and Marilyn in their new life on a

Colorado ranch. Mississippi chiggers and racism finally got to them, so they moved their dream another leap across the continent. These are the highest mountain passes in the country. I've heard stories from locals about people turning back on this road, unable to deal with the drop-offs. No guardrails. I'm not comfortable at these heights. I've been on this road before. Someone else was driving and I could hide my face. The alternative route would take me by Mesa Verde, but it's two hundred miles around the mountains. I very nearly opted for that, since I could be at Arches National Park in time for sundown at Delicate Arch, but I'm trying the more challenging road to see how I manage.

Few women on the road alone—I'm still watching after all these years, waiting to see if the pattern available to ordinary observation will change. With the exception of Amanda, whom I met on a train at the beginning of this month-long journey through Arizona, New Mexico, and Colorado, I have encountered no other women traveling alone. It's started to rain. I'll be driving through high mountain passes in stormy weather. I told my friend Richard Lehnert that I was almost fearful about leaving Santa Fe and the warmth of being with him. The fear took the form of fantasy. "He left her in Albuquerque and she was never heard from again." Time to face the fear, first of leaving the comfort of a soul mate, next of driving into mountain storms visible from here, dark and spooky.

Later. This is getting mighty too interesting. Even in the rain, the sky is so big that you can see where it's not raining. Mountain peaks to the east, red rock. I chose this route because it's in the direct neighborhood of land I own, but have not seen, overlooking the Uncompahgre Plateau near Montrose. The distances are so huge here that your neighborhood is a hundred-mile radius. You don't think like that in the East. In Erie, it would be like saying that Cleveland is in your neighborhood. They're sister cities on Lake Erie, but not in the same way that distances became intimate out here. I'm only a little over a hundred miles from my land. If I want to check out my backyard, this is it.

A waterfall pours out of red-rock cliffs. The Rockies are beginning their friendly loom. Back in Durango, people said, "I've been up that road, but I don't like to drive it often" or "I only drive south or west of here." Perhaps the Continental Divide, which splits the country geographically, also functions as a kind of sociocultural marker. Teenagers test their drunken adulthood on these roads. I'd feel better in my own car. But this is a '94, so I'm sure the brakes are just fine.

I am looking forward to passing through Ouray. Though I've been there only once, that town had an influence on my life. When Mac and I were still together, but on the rocks—the metaphor becoming literal here—he called me on the phone from Ouray. We had an argument about what constituted "betrayal," one human of another. His definition was narrow, mine broader, objectionably so to him. From his point of view, I was betraying him. From my point of view, he was betraying me. I was willing to buy his definition, but he wasn't willing to entertain the notion that he was betraying me, too. This allowed almost any behavior on his part to be excused, because it wasn't technically betrayal. The conversation from Ouray was a watershed in our relationship, and Ouray is on the watershed of the continent. Now the wind is blowing harder, of course. Rain, thunder, lightning. Am I having fun yet?

I'm in a hailstorm in the Rockies alone, blowing sideways in the wind. Now see here. On the phone with my mother last night, I assured her everything is safe. Oh, yes, I'm quite safe on this mountain pass with no guardrails in the wind and hail. How could she doubt it? Conditions like these scare everyone, men as well as women. No, I'm *not* having fun. But I want to see how I handle this. The thunder is hammering. All cars are suddenly gone from the road. I've found the lights and the defroster. Hail is changing to snow. I'm pulling off here into this little fish-and-tackle gas station, but everything seems to be closed. I need to talk to locals to find out if this kind of storm passes over fast or if I should be heading back to Durango. Where am I on the map? Here. I'm here.

The area I'm in is called Purgatory. I am not making this up.

Heading south now from Purgatory on the advice of locals who say there's a serious snowstorm up north. They asked me four questions: Do you have four-wheel drive? (No.) Snow tires? (No.) Chains? (No.) Are you with anyone? (No.) Then turn back. They talked about a car accident last night. They told me to go back to Durango and cut through the lower mountain passes to the west. So I'm just barreling down the mountain here, happy to get out of that storm. Mother, you would be proud. When I was talking to a man in the store, the storm seemed to be letting up, but he told me that two miles down the road and ten minutes later I could be back in white hell. And *he* wouldn't do it without four-wheel drive. When you hear that from a local who's describing a bad accident, it seems sensible to turn around. Highway 145 is relatively tame, mountainous, but nothing like this.

It looks like I have learned something from my misadventure in the White Mountains. Less than two years ago I was both too reckless and too trusting, too eager to establish my jock-feminist credentials about how hard a woman must work to face her fears head-on regardless of the danger, so I did something ill-advised and stupid. At the same time that I trusted another person to make my decision for me, I also failed to consult the people who really knew the local score, the ones I should have listened to. Now I don't feel like I have to prove to myself or to anyone else that I can do it. Of course I wanted to confront some of my fears here, and challenge myself, too—but not if it's stupid to do so, which it is. I'm glad I had the sense to make this decision myself, based on good advice.

The higher mountains are north of me now. When I look back, I can see storms and lightning in the distance. I'm in bright sunlight again in the foothills, and I'll be in desert soon. All the reassuring cultural landmarks are here. This country is amazing in its diversity, but Americans are also so recognizable, speaking the same vast language even within our dialects. Country and western music on the radio now. As Richard says, country and western is a misnomer. First there was country, then there was western. "Country" is Eastern and Appalachian and Southern. Tacking them together created a hippogriff, this strange new genre of broken hearts and moldy romance.

Romance. In Santa Fe, Richard and I talked for days about what I said in "Love Lost on the Road." We are trying to get rid of that destructive mythos in our lives—waiting for the "one," making someone into your myth, the driving power of the urge to do that, the ways in which it doesn't serve people well. Lies, lies, and a grief, expense of spirit and waste of shame. Yet Richard and I have watched each other reconstruct our romantic myths from their ruins, phoenixlike, for years. We both have come to the point where we've had enough of our tendencies to mythologize and fantasize about the "one," always thinking that the person we were with at the time was that "one." As we see it, it's not bitterness or cynicism to part with that myth, but an absolute necessity for humanizing relationships, for experiencing confident awareness in the moment, being with who you are with, yet knowing that you may later be with someone else, or alone.

You're with somebody and you believe this person *has* to be the one. Hope is ruinous when it takes that form. Richard just finished a relationship in which he refused to romanticize, and the woman thought he didn't care about her because he wasn't feeling hopeless desire. He didn't commit himself to romantic language or behavior. He enjoyed being with her, but he didn't long for her when they were apart. She needed him to do that in order to feel she was cared for. His other relationships were destroyed by such myths. I haven't indulged in that for a good while now, though I'm just as much a repeat offender as Richard. I intend to keep avoiding the trap at all costs. I intend to keep traveling alone. It's not *that* scary. You just get off the road when a storm comes.

I'm coming back up into mountains again, red-rock country. The moon is up. I'm going by a river. Pine-littered cliffs up ahead, San Juan National Forest. It's going to get more mountainous as I go up Blizzard Pass toward Telluride, though I won't go through the town. I must stop and call Tom and Marilyn. I'm hours late. Snow on the side of the road and on the peaks. I can't find a telephone booth. I've been looking for seventy-five miles. There should be signs saying: No Amenities, No Phones, No Gas, No Potties, Go Ahead and Wet Your Pants. I'm between nine thousand and ten thousand feet. There. There it is. I've found the only phone booth in the whole of western Colorado, here in Sawpit.

✱

Marilyn says, "She's healthy, she's branded, she's dehorned, she'll be a big cow."

"She's beautiful," I say.

Marilyn smiles. "Isn't she? It's like the doc was saying, it's not a personable breed, but break her to the bottle and she'll be just fine."

Bobby says, "Ever think of using longhorns just for easier calving?"

I got to Tom and Marilyn's down Spring Creek Canyon Road in the dark. Two days later I'm sitting in the guest cabin of their ranch, looking out the window at land that belongs to me—forty acres of mesa top high up a road called Old Paradox. That's appropriate, given that this land is jointly owned by me and Mac. We're both English professors as well as people who've made each other miserable when we meant to stay happy, so we know a bit about paradoxes.

I am meeting wonderful people, all of them living below the radar near Montrose as carpenters, artists, or politicos of one sort or another, such as the animal rights activist from Texas who established Texas's first Amnesty International chapter. John and Kay are committed vegan vegetarians, yet they are friends of Tom and Marilyn, who milk, raise, and slaughter animals and live on animal products. There seems to be mutual respect between them. Another friend, Pete, plans trails in parks. I met Karen, who runs a speech therapy clinic. Her husband, John, is a carpenter building a house with walls made of tires. Tire houses are the new thing here. Tires provide good insulation because they're heat conductors. Linda and Tom live just down the road in the canyon. For eight years Linda was in charge of an environmental action group. She's just had a baby, so she's taking time off from activism. Leif and Liza have a ten month old named Wheeler. Leif and Liza lived for two and a half years on their bikes, traveling around the world. They built their own house. Susan and Ed are in their forties. She has been both a psychologist and an English professor, and she ran women's services in Montrose for fifteen years. Montrose just recently got a safe house for battered women. This serves as a dose of reality because here I have been talking with people whose activism is environmental. Susan said it's redneck country through and through, beaten women everywhere, same old story. Ed does town surveying and grows fields of shallots, fulfilling his passion to sell yuppie onions. There's a critical mass of fine and thoughtful people here, living differently from the middle-class norm.

Most of these folks don't have nine-to-five jobs. They are part of the mountain subculture. I talked with the men outside smoking their hand-rolled cigarettes. When I joined them, the subject was someone who ate a car to get into the book of world records. That led to the story about the deer who ate an entire patch of cayenne peppers, the way that bears will eat soap left out. One man spoke of a steer who was fond of eating rope. They peeled yards of it out of his throat. Rope talk led to building materials and new methods to cut styrofoam. I heard about hanging upside down with chainsaws to cut doorways in log cabins. I offered that if I were going to eat a car, it would be a '57 Chevy.

We've been to my land on Old Paradox Road. Until today I had only seen it from the canyon floor, like last night under a full moon. My land is juniper trees, pinion pine, sagebrush, cactus, sand, rock, cliffs, a 360-degree view of the Cimeron Mountains, the San Juan Mountains, the plateau, and Grand Mesa, the largest flat-top mountain in the world. To "own" land is an absurd proposition. I'm its caretaker, protector, and I have the privilege of being here. Nobody can kick me off when I come to this land that's been here millions of years, and for the few years of its life that coincides with mine, I get to look out for it. When Mac and I bought these forty acres, we thought in terms of never doing anything with them, leaving them pristine. That's what Tom and Marilyn thought, too. They wanted insulation so people couldn't buy and develop near them, so they got friends and relatives to buy the land. We purchased the rim, arguably the best piece on the mesa.

Tom, Sami, and I hiked from the valley floor to my land, three hundred to four hundred feet up from the valley floor at seven thousand feet elevation. When you finish a climb like that, you're winded. I thought I was being wimpy, but Tom said, No, we wouldn't even try this with most people, everybody's winded when you get up here. I put my hand down on a cactus on my way up, and I picked the needles out while my hand burned for the next hour. Then I smacked my head while scrambling up rocks. We walked below the cliffs at the mesa edge, looking for a good place to get up to the top. Sami had spotted some deer, so we followed deer paths, those of least resistance. We found a mountain lion den. Apparently you don't actually see mountain lions, you just see your sheep dead by the creek. The game and wildlife man who's been working in this area for thirty years has never seen one in the wild, though he's tracked them down with dogs to shoot them when they were preying on herds of sheep. Our friends Glenn and Linda actually saw a mountain lion that had killed a lamb here, returning for another meal.

Circumstances have changed for Tom and Marilyn. They would like to build a "speculation house" on my land and turn over a profit. Tom is pushing against his limits, building houses into his middle years, living on ibuprofen. His body can't take this much longer, and he's the father of two young children. It may become important to make some money so Tom doesn't have to work off-ranch like that. Tom says, meaning it, *It's killing me, living like this.* He hasn't been able to get back to his writing, which he's put on hold for years while building other people's houses as well as his own. He's built houses in three places across the country—Martha's Vineyard, Mississippi, Colorado. Even his plaster seems almost like a signature, his name on the walls in invisible ink. His poem. But he can't continue this, and I need to clarify whether my commitment and dedication to people I love is bigger than my dedication to the land. The view from there is the view from heaven, valleys and lush green and snow-capped peaks and rolling hills. I can see pitching a tent, when I have my nervous breakdown, and staying for months.

Since the three of us have been speaking together of ultimate matters—what to do with land that's in your care, how to plan for the far end of life, the suicides of friends—we came to the question of whether or not people's value systems should be challenged, by those who love them, at the very end of their lives. Tom said he thought that the moment before death is a perfect time to advance yourself. Right up to their dying breaths, Tom believes it is right to challenge people on what Wallace Stevens would have called their supreme fictions. I took the other side with Marilyn. Why send people to eternity wondering if they'd failed or wasted their lives? Yet I really agree with Tom. My sense is that we were both playing devil's advocate, that Tom's ultimate position would be that deathbeds *are* places to let people alone, and that my true desire would be to say, *Talk to me now*. I don't know why he was taking that position and I the other one, because there's something much more live-and-let-live about Tom than there is about me. Marilyn is not seriously troubled about this. She works it out functionally. One of the surest signs of human health I've seen is her lack of need to confront her parents, or anyone else, because she knows who she is so essentially. Hers is not a life without commitment or passion. It may instead be a life so attuned to natural rhythms that include beauty and gentleness on one hand, and brutality on the other, that she just accepts both. I don't.

I aspire to a stance as integrated as Marilyn's, assuming that Marilyn's is authentic. That's not to say Tom and I are not authentic—he's one of the realest people I know. But he's in continuous struggle in some of the ways that I am, so that I recognize him. I could be romanticizing Marilyn the goat woman, the person who moves from dawn to dark in the rhythms of other creatures. She's had to work hard to come to this intricate balance she embodies. Marilyn's life is almost entirely about feeding—goats and sheep and cows and kids and men. She nurses her daughter Rhea. Her body is a constant source of food. She gives milk and she milks other female creatures. Past ten o'clock, she starts separating the milk and cream, as she does every night. It's a life of virtually endless work, but in many respects she's the happiest and most confident person I know. She says she milks the moon for thoughts. She just needs to do a little less of what she loves, like me.

This morning I said my good-byes to the animals and Sami and Rhea and Marilyn. Tom and I rolled down the canyon road in the truck listening to Crash Test Dummies. Tom always gives me music I get hooked on—Greg Brown, Leonard Cohen. On our way to the train we talked about Tom and Marilyn and Mac and me. He knew that I would listen. In the division of parts when Mac and I split, I didn't lose Tom or Marilyn after all. I used to feel in an unspoken way that I would get Marilyn and Mac would get Tom. I felt as though I wouldn't be able to be real with Tom again. Wrong. I have spent time with Marilyn, precious children and animal time, but because she's so busy, Tom and I have done more big talking. We didn't lose each other. The dynamics between him and Marilyn are similar to those between me and Mac. It's good to see the view from the other side of the valley.

*

My patient editor calls to check on my progress. She asks, "How's the sheep castration piece going?" Well, yes, *that*, I'm working on it, I lie, but I haven't got it quite right yet. I've written all around it in so many directions that I have a hundred pages about this trip. I have read everything in print in the United States on Basque sheepherding, the source of the method of castration still employed in the West, looking for discussion rather than parenthetical mention of the custom, of which there's also precious little. I've found nothing that could help me get a grip on it, though I am now a font of trivia on Basque culture, including theorized connections between Basque notions of conception and of cheese making. (Pregnant women are said to have been "curdled.") The closest I've come to help is a photograph of the procedure, sans sucking, in William A. Douglas's *Basque Sheepherders of the American West*. No discussion in text.

Synchronicity works in strange ways. Combing library collections, I come up empty, and consulting a Spanish colleague said to know about Basque culture, I find he is not familiar with sheep castration. Attempts to contact someone I hear was once married to a Basque rancher never materialize. No one can quite remember which famous rock singer is said to have done this. At last Richard brings sudden news from a far less likely source: in the MFA program at Warren Wilson College, one of his classmates, Jesse Loren, submits a poem titled "Sheep Production: 101" to their group. One of two women in a group learning to "emasculate rams the shepherd's way, with our teeth," she begins, "with eyes open, bending with hands behind my back," hearing the "nervous breath of men all around."

Her poem provides my epigraph, but now I am on my own. I have been politically correct, mentioning it only among other ranch facts. Why be ethnocentric when you encounter cultural customs different from your own? I teach about diversity and multiculturalism in my classrooms. I was privileged to witness something far outside my ken. The people who own the lambs are my dear friends. They trusted me not to lose my cookies or pass out. They even let me take pictures. It's not my job to pass judgment on a custom that's been around as long as the people out west.

Yet when I returned from this lengthy trip and mentioned the highlights—the Grand Canyon, Anasazi ruins, Georgia O'Keeffe's mountains, lamb castration in Colorado—it was predictable to gear the complete shock and disbelief on people's faces, if they could be persuaded that I was serious. I knew what they'd say next. Never mind the earth's biggest hole or holding shards of pottery made by human hands thousands of years ago or the genesis of great art—*you saw what?* And when I'd say, *yes, and this is how they do it,* I always had a rapt audience. The trouble was, I couldn't answer questions like Why? Perhaps the most interesting aspect of this is that to people in the West who own small herds of sheep, it's normal, a given, hardly worth mentioning. To anyone else, it might as well take place on Mars.

The spectacle has not left my memory, and it's time to see what insights nine months of rumination have produced—an appropriate gestation period, even though I, too, am now an animal who's been fixed and will bear no more young except books. The human/animal parallel is at the heart of my thoughts about this. Although the fact that humans are just animals is commonplace, I do not think we believe it or often use that knowledge when it might help us or our fellow creatures. I was in my thirties before that knowledge hit home, with the help, ironically, of Tom. We were walking on some remote road at one of his isolated compounds, on Martha's Vineyard or Cape Cod or in Mississippi, when he said, laconically, in his displaced Floridian drawl, that it was a great relief to him to remember that we're just complex biological beings, just critters. He was speaking about how this came to him sometimes when he fed his animals. I'd never seriously thought of Tom, much less myself, as belonging to the same order as his pigs or Marilyn's goats.

Like all important, simple truths you've always known but hadn't considered, this hit me with the force of revelation and has often since sustained me in moments of self-importance. So when I had my tubes tied not long after that, I said I'd been spayed. It's an inverted form of antianthropomorphism I find useful. I'm an animal, and so are the other animals, and if I believe that humans should be treated decently, then that courtesy should extend to other creatures, too. Such courtesies require no Wordsworthian excesses, no pathetic fallacies, none of what Blake called, detesting it, Natural Religion. My language about myself—which I would never use to describe human females who are forced into sterilization, except ironically, to make a case against that practice—helps to keep me in a happy kind of humility about my stature in the universe. It also assists me in a stance I want to keep, the "in-betweenness" I have spoken of that vibrates on the edge of contradiction, of paradox, so that I won't settle into complacencies on any side of either/or—like the body/mind split of post-Cartesian thought or those intricate dualities conceptualized as any form of *us* and *them,* like male and female. It's not productive to project human motivation onto other animals or the earth itself; nor is it useful to behave as if the earth has no intention. We do not know.

One thing I do know: those lambs, corralled and chased down and held in Marilyn's hands while Bobby applied the knife that cut the sac and revealed their fragile testicles, were in pain, at least briefly. So was their owner. Marilyn has dedicated her life to her young, both human and otherwise. There is no thoughtlessness in her. She is not capable of it. She loves those lambs and their bleating mothers and the rowdy kids and goats who depend on her for their life, and whom she depends on for hers. Of this there is no doubt. She sees the castration procedure as absolutely necessary. Any romantic twaddle to the contrary can arise from nothing but ignorance. Without birth control, the sheep would multiply beyond this limited land's ability to sustain them and they would starve. Perhaps at some future date, technologies will make less painful methods of management possible. But these people, and those who came before them in the western Rockies, are living on the edge of another dichotomy, that between past and future. Anesthetics and pills are still in the future. This method of castration inherited from the past is very much a fact of the present.

To anyone who witnesses this procedure and thinks about its genesis in a culture marked by poverty, and by lack of ample resources and people, it makes perfect sense. Basque sheepherding populations were small. Labor had to be efficient. It's a two-person operation. One person has two hands fully occupied by holding the lamb still so that it will not be injured, and the other must employ both thumbs to press on either side of the testicles, which naturally retract when the sac is cut, so that the testicles protrude enough to be removed. Without the intervention of a third person, this leaves only one logical alternative, probably rendered further necessary by the slipperiness of the organs surrounded by juices, which would not in any case easily yield to large human fingers. Suction is, if not absolutely necessary, at least the fastest and most painless way to get it done.

I watched close up. Marilyn sat on the pickup truck's tailgate, holding her lambs one by one, eventually covered with spurting blood from the tail docking done at the same time. She was in pain because her animals were in pain, but there was nothing sentimental about her demeanor. She's as tough as hide, though not the least jaded. She and Bobby exchanged ranchers' small talk as five-year-old Sami brought the lambs, one by one, isolating them from the mothers who bawled and bleated in maternal distress. Sami had my camera and it was she who did much of my photo documentation, backing up and wiping her face when blood spurted in our direction. It never occurred to me to decline when I was asked to bring another lamb. A family of Amish ranchers drove up with their own lambs for Bobby to attend to. Marilyn spoke with the woman, who stayed in the truck with the young children. I nodded hello, much less certain how to converse with an Amish woman in a truck than with this man sucking the balls out of lambs. Bobby was cordial as well as methodical. This is just what you do on a ranch.

But I am not a ranch girl, nor are the hearers who want to comprehend this custom back East. In my circles, such an act inevitably elicits an eyebrow raised toward psychosexual interpretations. My own predilections tend in that direction. It is natural to suppose that if I have seen a grown man leaning over the helpless bodies of lambs, sucking the testicles from them, I will have an analysis that is at least metaphorically sexual, about patriarchy, victimization, and the symbolic Law of the Father. The custom arose in a sheepherding culture about which jokes regarding animal-human sexual joining are commonplace; Basque beliefs include rich ambiguities about "human" and "animal" conception; Bobby, for the love of God, is a retired state trooper, veteran of a profession rife with liberals' assumptions about macho masculinity; how, then, could I not produce a psychosexual reading of this "text?"

I don't know. Just stupid, I guess. Where is Freud when I need him? Right here: Sometimes a cigar is only a cigar. There was nothing "sexual" about this scene. I cannot dredge up a single perception of prurience about these matters, any more than about human midwifing of cow and horse births. All I am left with is the silence of the lambs. That is what I remember most. The mother sheep fussed nonstop, knowing something was happening to their young. The lambs cried out when we caught them up and when Marilyn held them. But after an initial cry when the sac was cut, a great silence. Their eyes went blank with fear and shock. After the initial drama of watching a man's head descend between their legs, my own focus shifted to their eyes, in which I could read nothing but vacancy.

I would rather be a poet than a critic. Instead of sexual or feminist analysis, then, I offer another image from another canyon. Sometimes you have to back up a long way to see connections emerge. In my life there is one other association with missing testicles.

Yesterday I was hiking along a creek canyon in northwestern Pennsylvania. At Howard Falls, I entered the ravine by Falk Creek, a stunning wonder just miles from the dirt road in Edinboro on which I have often stayed this past year. Here I can walk for three or four miles, hiking into the canyon or remaining on its rim. I have been thinking about the lambs. While hiking, I acknowledge thoughts that come into my head. I nod at them, let them go. At last I am thinking, gratefully, of nothing. Suddenly an image, which the poet in me trusts will tell me something. The image is of my friend Chip Susol showing me red and blue snow. Two weeks ago Chip and I hiked down into the canyon, wandered there for hours, crossing and recrossing the creek, scrambling up the hillside, stopping to listen to the wind in the trees and wonder at the cliffs of ice. As we hiked back out at dusk, Chip pointed to the snow and said it was purple. Red. Blue. Sparks of color shot off the backs of our boots.

Chip was my student ten years ago. He wandered into my poetry class fresh out of high school, looking more or less exactly like the young Bob Dylan. That's what we called him around the halls of the English department. It was not an affectation that he wore a Bob Dylan T-shirt or that he was, like so many of his generation, discovering Dylan. Terrifically bright and a bit dreamy, he was a natural at writing. He promptly fell in love both with poetry and with the best writer in the class. His closest friends in college were Dirk, the man in these pages with whom I later lived for three years; and Ken Sonnenberg, who died of lymphoma in 1989 in Arizona, turning in six weeks from a healthy young writer into a dying man. Two years later, Chip's love affair was over. He came to my house for a few days to recover. I couldn't think of anything wise to say, so we sat in the hammock and I taught him how to weave a basket out of sea grass. Then he went on a long journey to Germany, working his way from one place to another, washing dishes for a living. At some point he noticed a hard spot on one of his testicles. After ignoring it as long as he could, he went to a German doctor, who told him it was a common condition among men his age. Although he felt reassured, he later cut short his trip and returned home.

It was cancer. Chip's testicle was removed in a swift operation—he had little more mental preparation time than did the lambs snatched up in our arms. Chip read the runes of his life, looking for and finding signs of life's vast capacity to amuse as well as to terrify us mortals. He was more interested in the amusement, as always, but now he had a way of putting the two together in deeply playful images. Walking through a cemetery, he said he'd decided that instead of being buried, he'd prefer at his death that his body be dropped from an airplane into dense tree cover, to land in whatever position it might, tangled in the treetops. We proceeded through a fantasy about what such a graveyard might look like, with all those folks hanging from trees in various stages of decomposition. After his cancer, from which he is now fully recovered, Chip could not be persuaded to live by anyone's lights except his own. His long-term resistance to "getting a life"—a career, credit cards, middle-class goals—solidified. He'd looked death in the face and knew that he had no time to waste on other people's ideas of what he should do with the life he had.

Always an idealist, he became the resolute dreamer in my group of young friends and found a fine woman to dream with him. Perhaps he and Patty would raise organically grown vegetables and sell them. Maybe chickens. Yes, they'd move to the country and raise chickens and children. (Unlike the lambs, reproduction may still be possible for Chip.) They'd build their house by hand. They saved up their money and hit the road for months, driving, backpacking, hiking across America. When they ran out of money, they worked in order to keep going. When the chance came to run an inboard tour boat, Chip claimed he had experience, which he did not, and got the job. Chip and Patty journeyed to my land in Colorado before I even saw it. Eventually they landed back home and at work, Chip in a master's degree program for high school teaching. But he wearied of the bureaucracy and the bad education courses and quit that, too, to attend carpentry school. Now he's a carpenter. He's also still a dreamer. He dreams while he's building things. Since Chip is my other experience with the removal of testicles and since he has been on this very land where I saw the lambs lose theirs, they come together in my mind.

I was at first silent about those lambs, although my initial response to seeing animals undergoing castration was keen, visceral, moralistic. But sometimes things are not what they first seem. These two incidents together—now entwined with my land, my journey, my life, my death—gave me a new angle on each. Chip would be dead if a man hadn't leaned over his body and knifed out his testicle. The lambs would die if they reproduced. Sometimes the very mechanism of life is the mechanism of death.

SEEING MINDFULNESS:

A WALKING MEDITATION

Elk Valley, Edinboro, Pennsylvania

When the pupil is ready, the teacher appears.—Chinese saying

In Buddhist mythology, the term "hungry ghost" is used to describe a wandering soul who is extremely hungry and thirsty but whose throat is too narrow for food or drink to pass through. On the full moon day of the seventh lunar month in Vietnam, we offer food and drink to the hungry ghosts. We know that it is difficult for them to receive our offerings, so we chant a Mantra to Expand Hungry Ghosts' Throats.—Thich Nhat Hanh, *Touching Peace*

Too many people too soon
you know they're gonna wake up dead
to find they spent their whole lives
just knockin around in their head
oh oh oh little darling
where we're going there ain't no rush.
Little darling, don't you think too much
—Greg Brown, "Don't You Think Too Much"

I listen to a letter tape from my Buddhist friend Pat Lee in Missouri, a recording of a Dharma retreat on the nature of emptiness. Pat's tapes remind me of what matters. He is one of my life's teachers, and I haven't even known until recently. The bells of awakening clang, and the teacher speaks of the illusory nature of reality—we're dreaming, and if we don't know we're dreaming, our sense of the real induces suffering. Suddenly in front of me a bright, cylindrical silver semi wheels across the road, and the sun reflects from it a blinding light while I'm being instructed on the nature of awakening, of seeing the light. I laugh. It's fun, it's funny, it's simple. The semi backs up across the road, revealing railroad tracks and a train coming through. Stunning silver yields to the flashing red lights of the rail crossing at the same time bells ring on the tape. Then I realize I'm not just hearing bells on the tape, but also the clang of the railroad bell, unharmoniously lovely. I almost fall into a meditative state there behind the wheel and am called back by what called me here—flashing red lights.

Ever since I can remember, I've been complaining how busy I am, how I need some peace, that I have to center my life in a coherent way and listen to the quiet within me. At the same time that a Buddhist master is telling me to cease living in an illusion, the red light in front of me on the road declares "Stop now." Sometimes I believe the only thing that will stop the freight train of my life is disaster—an accident, disease, death. I have many ways of slowing down, but since those strategies seem to work only briefly, I wonder if I can create a disjunctive break in the way that events seem inexorably to lead to other events, until there is no time for sleep, for love, even for bathing. I wonder if the disaster need only be illusory, imagined, or created, not actual, in order to stop living disastrously. If I change fundamental things in my life, and then let whatever "disaster" that causes for other people around me to occur—parents, students, colleagues, friends, kids, grandkids—perhaps it will be enough. I could say *no* to many more things than I do.

I know I'm not the only person who has these problems. The best people I know are in the process of trying to save their spirit-lives. Short of quitting your job and going to live in the rain forest, there's got to be some way to do that, to make deep alterations in established life rhythms. Just about all the people I care about—not only in their forties and fifties but also in their twenties—are fundamentally not happy with the way they are living. Their lives do not correspond with what they thought they wanted to do, nor have they been able to radically change their expectations. Most people find it very difficult to alter their exterior or internal experiences in a crucial way. You have to change perception, because perception is all you have to work with, to learn to love the life you live rather than the one you wish you had.

We all have the seed of a hungry ghost in us. I am trying to feed mine, but I think too much, and she cannot be fed on mere thought. Something else must intervene. I am learning "mindfulness" slowly, haltingly, as it leaks down my narrow throat. It has nothing to do with what usually passes for thought. As Jon Kabat-Zinn has written, "Meditation does not involve trying to change your thinking by thinking some more. It involves watching thought itself. The watching is the holding. By watching your thoughts without being drawn into them, you can learn something profoundly liberating about thinking itself, which may help you to be less of a prisoner of those thought patterns—often so strong in us—which are narrow, inaccurate, self-involved, habitual to the point of being imprisoning, and also just plain wrong."* Eastern and Western laziness take different forms—Eastern is sitting around, sipping tea, listening to the radio, whiling away the time with no "productive activity." Western laziness—by which I mean lack of awareness—often takes the form of so much productive activity that there's no time to confront your life or the issues that might really matter. I am Western lazy, hurtling, rushing, spending time on senseless, useless stuff in this, the only life I know I have. I don't fight hard enough against that obliterating, thoughtless force of Western busyness. I am trying to wake to the world around me.

October morning, shortly after dawn, walking down a dirt road outside of Edinboro, Pennsylvania, I see three deer on Silverthorn Road. It's not deer season yet, but gunfire blasts birdsong throughout the short days and into the dusk, reporting these facts of Pennsylvania hill life into the far folds of every animal brain, my own included. The morning mists are heavy, but the does clarify on the road before me, breath heaving from their mouths, mine catching in my throat as if stilling myself will make them stay. But they have seen me. They leap into the field. I watch them go. Two keep running, but one stops, looks back toward me, alert. We stare at each other. Finally she walks away, looking back and back again, not afraid.

Returning to my car, I drive into town for an appointment with a healer, a woman of great gifts named Sandra Barnard, who helps me to know myself, perhaps to save myself. For two years after my life heaved itself out my own front door in 1989—the end of a love and an era of my life—I did co-counseling with Deanna Ferraino, who helped me keep my skin on my bones and my bones inside my body. The talking cure did all it could, and for three years I did well. But now I know it is time to work with my body (I don't mean aerobics) and my spirit (I don't mean God). This work is what Sandra helps people do.

Sandra has studied Eastern philosophical traditions, including Hindu,

---

*Jon Kabat-Zinn, *Wherever You Go, There You Are* (New York: Hyperion, 1994), 94.

Buddhist, and Sufi ways of knowing as well as Kashmir Shaiviism and Taoism. She also has a background in diverse forms of Western esoteric knowledge. But Sandra does not like labels and resists my attempts to plaster them on her work. When I ask her what it is that she does, how she works, she writes to me: "The real thrust of my healing work is about transformation, about transforming one's limited sense of self. As Richard Moss, in *The Black Butterfly: An Invitation to Radical Aliveness*, puts it: only real transformation (i.e., healing) can happen when we create a fundamental change in the energy or 'note' of our consciousness. What I do is help to make that shift—or to use another metaphor, help to open a door that the person may not even know exists or help to open a door that s/he may know exists, but is unable to open on her or his own. When the door is open, then it is up to the person to make the choice to walk through, or not."*

I ask her about her spirit guides, since I know that she has always walked with them; but again, I had the wrong idea for a while. She says, "When I work with non-physical beings they aren't usually someone who has recently passed on, but are highly evolved energies or consciousnesses who may never have had physical incarnation, or if so, then they incarnated so long ago that their reason to contact us now is about unconditional love, compassion, and service to humanity, rather than about any interest in the daily goings-on of planet Earth. My Beings have yet to give me the inside scoop on the Lotto or to reassure me that my Aunt Bessie says 'heh.'" Talk and touch inform her method, but she works primarily with silence. The labor that body and spirit do, with Sandra as witness, guide, and mediator, is often very difficult, perhaps the hardest internal work of which I am capable. Other times it's easy, like a gift from the universe.

What I'm doing with Sandra is coming together with other movements in my life, new and old. The old: for twenty years I have been exchanging letters, tapes, and visits with my friend Pat. A serious and dedicated practitioner of Vajrayana meditation, he has shared his Way with me, and I have listened, but I have not pursued my own. Now synchronicity, surely the only god I believe in, takes me to the edge of a path. This book leads me to it, though not through it. Reading myself, I feel the readiness that is always all, ripening toward what could become dedication. Everything that rises may yet converge.

*Personal letter, Sandra Barnard to the author, April 1, 1995; Richard Moss, *The Black Butterfly: An Invitation to Radical Aliveness* (Berkeley: Celestial Arts, 1986).

The new: in the spring of 1994, I first encountered the writings of Thich Nhat Hanh, Vietnamese poet and Zen master, chairman of the Vietnamese Buddhist Peace delegation during the Vietnam War. Nhat Hanh was nominated by Martin Luther King Jr. for the Nobel Peace Prize and has lived in exile in France for many years, in a meditation community called Plum Village. He travels and lectures in the United States every two years. Vietnamese Buddhism blends Theravada and Mahayana traditions and is particularly well adapted to the needs of American Buddhism. Nhat Hanh calls his own tradition "engaged Buddhism," in part a result of his own and his fellow monks' activism against the war. One does not withdraw from the world in Nhat Hanh's meditative tradition. I believe, with writer bell hooks, that he is among the finest teachers in the global village.

The Miracle of Mindfulness came to me through a route that has affected, paradoxically, both my relationships to nature and travel and my sense of home. Susan Daley, a psychologist who lives with carpenter and sailor Jim McEnery in a remote cottage built on the cliffs of Lake Erie, introduced me to her extraordinary friends. Dave Bennett and Donna Douglas live here in the hills outside of Edinboro, next to a waterfall, where Dave operates Falls Run Woodcarving studio. Donna works in town as an arts administrator. Through them I met Michael Richardson, a sailmaker who lives clearly, quietly, intentionally, in touch with both life and death. He grieved for his parents' deaths by building their coffins by hand. He celebrates his life with equally resonant rituals. He walks down a dirt path to work at the Bierig sailmaking loft overlooking Presque Isle Bay on Lake Erie; and again at the end of the day, he travels dirt roads to his old farmhouse. He clears and maintains trails in the woods, establishing a firm relationship with terra firma. His favorite mode of transport, when feet are not possible, is a mountain bicycle. Like the rest of these water people, he is also at home in canoes and sailboats.

With Sue, Jim, Michael, Dave, and Donna, I had my first experience of sailing Lake Erie in the summer of 1994. On Jim's twenty-two-foot *Starshine,* we sailed from Erie to Longpoint, and from Longpoint to Port Dover, Canada, a hundred miles round trip, over a three-day period. I can barely swim and have always been terrified of deep water. Fear of water has followed me all my life, seemingly unroutable. I could never have pictured myself in a small boat with no land in sight in any direction. With these sailors, I faced that fear, much as I confronted my fear of heights in the White Mountains. On the way we had clear, fine sailing all night through a mist that lifted by midnight to reveal a sky scattered with smashingly bright stars. But on the way back we had tough wind and big waves, the boat pitching and rocking for twelve hours. I jammed my feet against whatever I could find, poised most of the time at a forty-five-degree angle, holding on and idly wondering, as waves of nausea snaked through my trunk, if I was going to live through the day. I did. I never got fully seasick, keeping my eyes firmly fixed to the horizon. It was among the best journeys of my life. It marks the moment of a sea-change in me.

Water people see the world differently from land people. They speak more deliberately, think more mindfully, perhaps more comprehensively, than people do on land. They speak another language even though it's English, barely recognizable to one who does not know it. They live more in the present moment, experiencing a subtly altered relationship to time and space. On water one must Be Here Now, to use the title of Ram Dass's famous book, more than on land. Weather over water changes suddenly. Wind can shift direction and speed in moments. Darkness descends rapidly. Temperatures fall fast. It's always important, sometimes vital, to be attentive to what's going on in the here and now. Getting to know water people—not power boaters, but those who depend on wind and oars, who love sailboats and canoes—seems to be more connected to my growing sense of questing toward a path, a way of being and knowing, than I would have guessed.

So that when I found Thich Nhat Hanh through Michael and encountered "breathing meditation," a standard Buddhist practice geared toward mindful living, I sensed I might be reading something important to me, despite my own defenses. Some of it seemed nearly comic. "There are two ways to wash the dishes. The first is to wash the dishes in order to have clean dishes and the second is to wash the dishes in order to wash the dishes." Then there's tangerine wisdom: "A tangerine has sections. If you can eat just one section [in mindfulness] you can probably eat the entire tangerine. But if you can't eat a single section, you cannot eat the tangerine."* I smiled. Sweet dharma twaddle.

But those two examples haunted me. I came to see that they summed up the way I lived my life. "If while washing dishes, we think only of the cup of tea that awaits us . . . we are not alive during the time we are washing the dishes. . . . If we can't wash the dishes, the chances are we won't be able to drink our tea either. While drinking the cup of tea, we will only

---

*Thich Nhat Hanh, *The Miracle of Mindfulness*, trans. Mobi Ho (Boston: Beacon Press, 1976), 4–6. Subsequent citations to this work will be given in the text.

be thinking of other things, barely aware of the cup in our hands. Thus we are sucked away into the future—and we are incapable of actually living one minute of life" (*Mindfulness* 5). Had I ever eaten oranges or tangerines without popping the sections rapidly into my mouth, barely finishing one before beginning the other? Not once. The implications are enormous. They have to do with finding the lonely other inside oneself, becoming mindful, living in contact with your own consciousness and that of the sentient world, and perceiving these as continuous. This new angle on a philosophy that had been near my life through Pat for twenty years was revelatory.

Thich Nhat Nanh reminds me of that other monk whose contemplative life was "engaged." My trip to Thomas Merton's monastery at Gethsemani conceptually began the journeys recorded here. I have come to see parallels to Merton throughout Buddhist philosophy, as Merton himself did. It is inaccurate to perceive Buddhism as religion, though it certainly is spiritual practice; it is more a science of the mind or, as Pat calls it, a "technology of compassion." Most people form inverted ideas about who comes to Buddhism and why. If we envision Buddhists as peaceful souls filled with grace and the immanence of enlightenment, we ignore the root of such paths: disgust with the whole vain and paltry and greedy world, and with oneself as a reflection of it.

Disgust brought Merton, writer and English professor, to Gethsemani: "Everything I had reached out for had turned to ashes in my hands. . . . I myself, into the bargain, had turned out to be an extremely unpleasant sort of a person—vain, self-centered, dissolute, weak, irresolute, undisciplined, sensual, obscene, and proud. I was a mess."* Like me, his first glimpses of spiritual life came through the "tremendously genuine and spiritual fire" of the visionary poet and mystic William Blake. "He has done his work for me: and he did it very thoroughly. I hope that I will see him in heaven" (190). I had lived my adult life just a few miles from the place where Merton discovered his calling, a slow dawning that came to him near St. Bonaventure, in the hills behind Olean, New York. My daily view of the hills of New York and Pennsylvania when I was a child was his own view.

Even now, rereading his autobiography in Erie, I am touched by his spirit. From his first journey to Gethsemani: "The train had hardly stopped

---

*Thomas Merton, *Seven Story Mountain* (San Diego: Harcourt, Brace, Jovanovich, 1986), 132. Subsequent citations to this work will be given in the text.

to let me off, and immediately gathered its ponderous momentum once again and was gone around the bend with the flash of a red tail light, leaving me in the middle of the silence" (319–20). The same train route that brought him there passes half a mile from my door. As I read, the train whistle sounded, and I understood, for a goosefleshed moment, how synchronicity might create conversion in the longing human heart. Entering the monastery permanently months later, Merton again described his journey through my world: "Then the Buffalo train came in through the freezing, sleety rain, and I got on, and my last tie with the world I had known snapped and broke. It was nothing less than a civil, moral death. . . . The last city I remembered was Erie" (369). And at the very moment that I read this in Erie, the train spoke outside my door again, shuddering the very tracks onto which I boarded for many of the trips recorded here, the same tracks I have walked with my housemate, Susan Lavrey, speaking of how to live our lives, smuggling moments of clarity from the vague and blinding mess of mall-infested life in the nineties. And these are the same tracks, this the same train, that stopped me months back with its lights, its bells.

But if I imagine the contemplative life as an antidote, Merton corrects me, and connects to me yet again: "For it seems to me that our monasteries produce very few pure contemplatives. The life is too active. There is too much movement, too much to do. That is especially true of Gethsemani. It is a powerhouse, and not merely a powerhouse of prayer. . . . It goes by the name of 'active contemplation.' The word active is well chosen. About the second half of the compound, I am not so sure. It is not without a touch of poetic license" (389). Poetic license is precisely what Merton brought to Gethsemani. He knew that art is a form of contemplation, and that writing was "the one activity that was born in me and is in my blood. . . . I brought all the instincts of a writer with me into the monastery, and I knew that I was bringing them, too" (389). In the most powerful moment of Merton's wrenching autobiography, he curses his gift:

> Then there was this shadow, this double, this writer who had followed me into the cloister. He is still on my track. He rides my shoulders, sometimes, like the old man of the sea. I cannot lose him. He still wears the name of Thomas Merton. Is it the name of an enemy? He is supposed to be dead. But he stands and meets me in the doorway of all my prayers, and follows me into church. . . . He generates books in the silence that ought to be sweet with the infinitely productive

darkness of contemplation. . . . Nobody seems to understand that one of us has got to die." (410)

The writer Thomas Merton lived on and did not die until the monk himself did, years after he wrote this. I appreciate his concern with what seemed to him a life-and-death struggle with the writer. Art is contemplation. Writing is art. May not writing be the way one contemplates? That should be possible, but Merton seems not to have come to terms with it. Thich Nhat Hanh, who entered upon the writing life and the life of contemplation at the age of sixteen, seems to have integrated the artist and the contemplative within himself with great equanimity.

I cannot enter with Merton into the "everlasting movement of that gravitation which is the very life and spirit of God," a God "Who is everywhere, and whose circumference is nowhere," a God who "called out to me from His own immense depths" (225). That God does not exist for me, nor do I long for him or miss him. But I do seem able to follow Thich Nhat Hanh's teaching, which seems to me close to Blake's, in which the Eucharist is the practice of awareness and of imaginative living, a way I would call mythopoetic.

> Jesus knew that if his disciples could eat one piece of bread in mindfulness, they would have real life. In their daily lives, they may have eaten their bread in forgetfulness, so the bread was not bread at all; it was a ghost. In our daily lives, we may see the people around us, but if we lack mindfulness, they are just phantoms, not real people, and we ourselves are also ghosts."*

The dishes, the tangerines. In mindful living, the demarcation between action and contemplation disappears, and you find yourself able to meditate while driving, writing, walking, working. "Each thought, each action in the sunlight of awareness becomes sacred. In this light, no boundary exists between the sacred and the profane" (*Peace Is Every Step* 27). He speaks of "wishlessness" or "aimlessness," both words for ways to let go of constantly goal-oriented activity.

The insights of mindful living are often simple, and they tend to hit home with force in direct proportion to that simplicity. In the West we strike a bell. In Nhat Hanh's tradition, the bell is invited to sound. There-

---

*Thich Nhat Hanh, *Peace Is Every Step*, ed. Arnold Kotter (New York: Bantam Books, 1991), 22. Subsequent citations to this work will be given in the text.

on hangs a universe of difference. Serious though it is, practicing Buddhism is a "clever way to enjoy life."* The nontoothache is an example. When you have a toothache, you think that not having it will make you happy. Celebrate your nontoothache. Having had recent toothaches and root canals, I know that this can work. You don't empty yourself of fear or anger in Buddhist practice simply by ignoring it. Instead you greet it, acknowledge it rather than repressing it, on the one hand, or merely indulging it, on the other. If you wake up depressed, says Nhat Hanh, there is an appropriate greeting. "Good morning, my little depression." The same with fear. "Fear, my old friend, I recognize you."†

Practicing the technology of compassion is not always easy or simple. This is especially true when the practice asks compassion for the suffering of our personal enemies, those who have most deeply injured us. For women, especially feminists, getting out of the nurture-and-compassion mode and into a robust bit of pissed-offness often feels like a lifeline thrown into the seas where we were drowning in our own maternal milk. This has certainly been the case for me, and I like my goddamned anger. (Hello, my little anger. How are you this morning? Eat, you're too skinny. Have a big muffin. Mama loves you.) Yet this philosophy urges me, ultimately, to spend time contemplating the roots of the suffering of my ex-lovers. Just thinking of it makes me tired. Yet I believe that this practice is right, that the global form of such compassion is probably the only way life on this planet will survive.

Reading Nhat Hanh, I realize that "engaged Buddhism" names not a new way of knowing for me but one that intersects who I have been for as long as I can remember. It names the way I have been trying to move through these journeys, thoughtfully, in the present moment. But its ideals are also a measure of how far I have to go—I am still, as Greg Brown says, thinking too much. I am working on ways to stop that. They take place on tables and in the woods.

※

I parted my gaze from that of the deer on the road and drove to my appointment with my healer. I lay on a table, Sandra next to me. Last spring, she midwifed a kind of rebirth in me. It had nothing to do with words or

*Thich Nhat Hanh, *Being Peace* (Berkeley: Parallax Press, 1987), 33. Subsequent citations to this work will be given in the text.

†Thich Nhat Hanh, *Touching Peace* (Berkeley: Parallax Press, 1992), 30.

writing, nor with the welter of emotions that emerge in psychotherapeutic situations. Miserable and martyred when I arrived that day (I forget what about), I knew something was up and expected a sniveling wave of tears. But lying in meditation, following Sandra's gentle lead, what emerged was a laugh. I wasn't laughing at or about anything—I was just laughing. Sandra later called it the "Buddha laugh," something that comes at moments of mental and spiritual breakthroughs. This was a freebie, given through no good offices or sustained practice of my own, and therefore most like Merton's Christian grace. When the laughter subsided I traveled deeply into my core and began to hear my blood in my veins. Behind closed eyes I saw—there are no other words for this—my own mind. This experience was not brief. I was gone from normal consciousness, in some sense, for almost two hours. I had to rise from the table carefully and could not immediately drive a car. Sandra and I had been planning dinner with our friend Pam, but I couldn't deal with the restaurant. Sandra sent me home. Go and be with your dog, she said.

I spent the evening with Boofer, my aged collie/lab, visiting me from the homestead where she lived with my ex-partner, Mac. I have not been with an animal in that way since I was a small child. We lay together on the floor. I petted her and looked into her eyes until we slept together. Woman and dog had a fine time. Boofer died just months later. Half a year past her death, fresh from the deer on the road and reading Nhat Hanh, I reach for Nothing in Particular with Sandra. Laughter comes, but briefly, and then as quickly a sadness that feels comprehensive. In both the laughter and the sadness, the deer on the road is behind my eyes, incomparable beauty that may die. Deer season starts soon. The beer distributor's sign near home says, "Hunters—Beer Season Is Open." Some hunters will do it right, if there is a right way to do this; perhaps there is. But some will mix beer and shots with their shots, ensuring that many deer and a few people will die all wrong, the way it happens every year.

The deer eyes behind my own eyes change into Boofer's, and I am once again in my own en(light)enment moment, like that last laughing time. Boofer's dear eyes were deer eyes, yet she, all gentleness to people, brought down a deer once in the grape fields, dragging home sections of its stinking carcass for weeks. Boofer makes me feel Mac, and now I am breathing deep gulping grief that he did not call me so that I could say goodbye when Boofer was dying, and then I let that pain and anger go somewhere else—he meant no harm. I feel sadness for his own pain. Since his prostate cancer, he and Boofer bound through my dreams, chasing each other down the halls of the psyche's past. Mac has survived, he is okay, but the scare has gripped my memories.

"Sex is such a pounding," said another lover, who collects guns and a deepening depression, who has not visited his father's grave these twenty years he's been lying in it, the son never done with loss, learning guilt better than he learned love. Dead fathers. My own. His hungry ghost and I are doing fine these days. I think of me when he died, five years old. Then the five year old in my mind changes genders, and I see my father at the same age, my pattern a photograph now nearly a century old. What happened to him, I wonder? What ancestral wounds passed from generation to generation that he could not heal in himself, that I am trying to heal now? Hungry ghost. Take, eat. It's all right. The deer is here again, alert, unafraid, walking away slow. Sandra is beside me, bringing me back to the present moment in which I dwell.

*

Months later, nearly March, almost another spring, Michael Richardson and I amble along the creek at Elk Valley. Walking meditation, Thich Nhat Hanh calls it: you speak little, and what you do say is about what's in front of you, ground, twigs, trees, water, snow, sky. You breathe consciously, deliberately, slowly, as you walk. Sights worthy of every sort of contemplation present themselves—meditations on life, on death. We see a deer carcass, head, backbone, and fur remaining, flesh torn away, twisted around a small tree. I brush snow from its eyes, bland and blank, no longer here, and think of my October deer guide, and of all the deer, dead and alive, running through fields or slung over trucks, that I have seen since then. I will return here again and again to see this deer disappear into the earth. Turkey tracks wind crazily around the trees. We follow the trail Michael made here years ago, clearing as we go, to the mink tree, its root system an intricate home. The mink must still be here—we track her along the ice-jammed creek, then up the hill where the logging has decimated this splendid new-growth forest, compounding natural deaths caused by the stranglehold of the beautiful and lethal wild grapevines, before losing her tracks in the felled tops of trees. Coming back, we see the flock of wild turkeys move with stealth and speed through the woods, quickened by the smell of us. Past the deer carcass we stop, sit, stay quiet, breathe in and out, know that we are alive in the present moment. The wind rings in our ears like a bell.

The Bell of Mindfulness is the voice of the Buddha calling us back to ourselves. We have to respect that sound, stop our thinking and talking, and go back to ourselves, with a smile and breathing. It is not a Buddha from the outside. It is our own Buddha calling us. If we cannot hear the sound of the bell, then we cannot hear other sounds which also come from the Buddha, like the sound of the wind, the sound of the bird. . . . They are all calls from the Buddha to return to ourselves. (*Being Peace* 43)

Two red-tailed hawks, perhaps a nesting pair, fly overhead, lighting high in the trees. Walking here with Michael is almost as good as walking alone. Perhaps it is *just* as good. His otherness is genuine. He does not want to merge with me. His affection feels different from any I have known with a man. I was not lonely when I met him, and I am not lonely now, with him nor without him. But I like to be with him. Although I have left Thomas Merton behind in my journeying, he comes back to me now, ruminating on love. He always resisted "possessive affection on the part of any other human being—there has always been this profound instinct to keep clear, to keep free." This is the love of two people he knew: "It did not burn you, it did not hold you, it did not try to impress you in demonstrations, or trap your feet in the snares of its interest" (57). And so he could love in return.

Mindful loving without a particular and human object, without demonstrations or snares, or perhaps with the totalized form of sentient world as object, seems increasingly possible to me: world as beloved, world as self. Such open, exploratory affection is most often blocked by human fear. In my most recent session with Sandra, I encountered two of my enduring constellations of wish and fear—watery depths, careening heights. I have explored both water-depth and mountain-height fears in these pages, from oceans to cliffs, but I would not say I have overcome them. Until recently, I have thought more in terms of confrontation than of embrace. With Sandra, I gave myself another opportunity, though I did not know what I sought when I went to her this time. It works best when I have no goal.

Deep in a meditational moment, I felt myself reaching outward instead of within—or I felt the movement inward, toward a kind of spiritual atmosphere available at the core of me, as if it were a reaching out. I experienced this movement as a journey that took place in a deep sea and a night sky at once, where I was both swimming and flying. Yet when I would get far from shore or far from land, I became afraid, and instantly I was back near shore, or down toward land. Sandra knew this and chided me for chiding myself, which she also knew I was doing. *Set out again, and again, and again,* she said. I thought of being on Lake Erie with my friends, no land in sight, and how safe it could feel. I thought of returning to the White Mountains, without that conquering determination. I set out again, and again.

And at last I floated somehow free of the need to touch normal mental ground. I saw nothing out there—no tunnels or blinding bright lights. No being, spiritual or physical, spoke to me. I was in no location I knew. I just floated, weightless in an amiable depth, a darkness strangely and vaguely illumined. I was shapeless sight in an airy expanse. My feeling was of simple, mere openness. Nothing at all happened. Yet I knew that something sweetly momentous had occurred in that openness to nothing, a way of being that, cultivated with attentiveness, can enable me to make my way a little less attached to my precious and fearful ego. I heard Sandra's voice while I was in here, out there: *Now go beyond the You that you know.*

To My Faraway Son
1988

Dear Bernie,

Many grown children feel that their mothers and fathers are disappointed in them. Some people carry through their lives a certainty that they'll never measure up to parental expectations. Each generation vows it will be different with their children—but somehow it turns out much the same. This generation handles its disappointment with shelves of self-help books, sad and necessary. When you were born twenty-three years ago, I told myself determinedly, predictably, that it was going to be different between you and me, that you were always going to know how much I loved you, that you were not ever going to feel that you didn't live up to some unreasonable, vague, perhaps unstated expectation. I was certain you would always know that what I wanted for you was internal peace and accepting affection for yourself, whoever you grew up to be. You would always be able to talk to me about your feelings, tell me what was on your mind, be real with me. There wouldn't be any unreasonable rules, I wouldn't try to control you, I wouldn't withhold my time or my love. We would be happy together and we would escape that generational curse. But of course we didn't.

I succeeded in a few of those things I was determined about. You always knew that I didn't think there was something wrong with enjoying life, with finding delight where you could. I always liked being with you. And I still think there have been many times that you felt you could really talk to me and tell me what was on your mind. But that's about as far as I can go toward claiming any major difference from the norm. You and

I are not free of the mother-child curses. There has been tension between us over the years. I suspect that you do indeed feel you have not lived up to some undefined thing that you think I expected of you. Many times you felt I was trying to control you—certainly that was true about school. And as much time as I felt I spent with you, that is not how it felt to you, or how you remember it. You remember at least as clearly the times I was at my typewriter or with Mac, instead of you, in those days when you and he competed for my attention.

Once, several years ago, after I'd prided myself for so long on how openly you and I could talk to each other, you said—I remember it well—that I never talked to you, that you could never tell me anything, that I didn't listen. The "didn't listen" part was more than once—you have said a number of times that I don't hear you. So apparently I failed there, too. Just like my mother, I accused you of being a liar. In truth I *was* a liar. She accused me of it when it was true and when it wasn't, because she couldn't be sure of the difference anymore. And neither could I with you.

This had been one of the major goals of my life, to be a differently loving and giving mother. Such an old and predictable story. It didn't work out the way I wanted it to, and I wonder why that is. I would like to talk with you about it to get your points of view. I don't mean that I just want you to make me feel better by telling me it wasn't that way. If I am being too hard on myself, on us both, then sure, tell me that. But about the sadder parts of our pattern, what do you think? How is it that parents and children, this mother, this son, began to grow apart? Why did I become, like most parents do, some kind of enemy?

I have at least thought that certainly you know how deeply unconditional my love is. So I was surprised and sad when you opened a recent phone call about needing to borrow money with these words: "I know you hate me, Mom . . ." I realize that partly it was a figure of speech, an apology before the fact for needing to borrow money, but still it shocked me. Does some part of you think I hate you? Is that possible? If it is, what is it, in what I have said or done, that has made you feel this way, even a little? This isn't just a rhetorical question. I have always thought that I am capable of deep love and incapable of hatred. Yet my truth isn't your truth, any more than my truth is my mother's. How negative do you think or feel or fear I am toward you? If I have projected negative feeling toward you in some fundamental way that I am not aware of, I would like to know about it.

Because this is a letter about the sad way that people in families can't tell each other how they feel and what they feel, I want to say how much I love you. I know I say it already, maybe too much, embarrassing you on the phone when people can hear. But that's different. I want to say to you, not in the formula of a phone call or a good-bye at the door of a house or a car, that I love you very much. I love you the way parents love their children—it's solid as a mountain, just as immovable, it doesn't change, and no argument or problem between us alters it one bit. You are the person in the world for whom I know I would give my own life. I know that sounds absurd, too extreme, but it's true, and I've always known it. It's not necessary that people have that kind of built-in sacrificial love for the generation before them, but perhaps it is necessary that many of us have it for the generation following us.

This kind of love is not dependent on the individual qualities of the person; I love you because you are my son. But I also love you because of who you are. I love the ways your mind works, how funny you are, your particular and individual intelligence. I love the circuitous and graceful pathways of your thought. I love the way you have always watched the world, the people and events around you, taking them in and keeping your own counsel, mulling things over and forming your own opinions. I admire your willingness to work hard. I love the way you walk.

I can disagree with some of your opinions and decisions, and it doesn't do anything to alter or lessen this love. I have never wanted you to be some version of myself—or at least no more than is inevitable in parents regarding their children. Of course I hope you're not going to suddenly become a person whose convictions I do not recognize, and I want some of the basic values I've given you to remain useful to you. But I want you to have a life that satisfies you, and that life won't be like my own.

Love,

Mom

✳

Dear Mom,

I really don't know exactly what to tell you. The troubles we had are normal parent and child ones. There's no such thing as a perfect relationship between children and parents. All kids go through bad times with parents in one way or another. There were some things that you were ridiculous about when I was growing up, while at the same time you were fine about other things. It all evens out. As long as we are being honest with each other, I can tell you that I resented certain things. Before I mention them, understand that I don't expect you to agree with me, but I don't want you to tell me that I am *wrong* or that "that isn't the way it was," the way parents usually do. Just understand it's the way I felt and saw things.

Old stuff stays in people's heads for years. I don't think it was right for you to keep me grounded a whole school year in high school because I couldn't or wouldn't get my grades up far enough. I know you think it was right because you wanted me to know I had to respect your word and your rules—but there is a line. It doesn't seem important to me anymore, but at the time it was *very* important. It's not a big deal now. It's just something to be able to tell your friends about after they've told you something ridiculous about their parents, like everyone does.

[paragraph deleted to respect both parties' privacy]

One thing I think you should understand is that you are no different from all normal parents—and maybe you won't like that. You used to say to me, "You don't know how lucky you are, you don't know how reasonable I am. How many of your friends' parents would let their kids do this or that?" True, there were some things you were extra cool about, but other things you were extra uncool about. Like I said, it balances out. You're an excellent mother and I love you very much.

I say the same things you may have said before you had me. I say that there are certain things you did that I won't do to my child. Some of those things I probably won't do, and others I will do without even realizing it. Being a parent is something you can't really understand until you *are* one. I may have been jealous of your work or of Mac at some times, but if it wasn't that it would have been something else. I was basically independent and I could handle myself. So that's how I feel about things. But who am I to say anything about parenting? I'm not a parent yet, and I'm not a psychologist, I'm the manager of a beach bar.

I love you, Mom. I wouldn't trade you for any other mother.

Love,
Bernie

✱

Dear Bernie,

Your letter to me ends with that disclaimer about not being a parent—and now a few short months later, you're going to be a father, and I a grandmother. Krissy has always felt like my daughter and your sister, so Ayron feels like my granddaughter. But you're my blood, so it's different this time.

We're both kind of young for these weighty roles, but I know we can handle it. I am delighted at the prospect of this new and distant being with whom my own future will be wonderfully tangled.

Thanks for your response to my letter. It was loving, and it was straight. You pointed out some of my blind spots, and when your truth rankled a little, I tried to remember that it was, after all, your truth I asked for and got. I suppose I wanted partly to be vindicated, to have you tell me I have been the best mother in the universe in spite of it all—and I really do thank you for not giving me that Hallmark junk. But just one thing, even though you told me not to say it—I never ever grounded you for a year. A *year?* Did not. (Did.) Did not. (Did.) Did not.

We'll have to agree to disagree on that bit of history. Your memory that I did, your absolute conviction about it, has made me think again about my own mother, and about the human need to make ourselves the heroes and the martyrs of our own stories. When you and your friends sit around swapping horror stories about the difficulties of your childhoods and the impossible things your parents did, this is one of your biggies. It makes me wonder about some of the crowd-pleasers I've depended on in similar conversations all of my adult life. One of my stories is about how Mom always used to get me out of bed in the middle of the night to clean the bathtub if I had forgotten it. In my memory, that happened dozens of times, maybe hundreds, geez, a person couldn't get any sleep what with this person waking her up at 3:00 A.M. and shoving cleanser in her hand.

Did that really happen many times, or did it happen once or twice and I magnified it out of my resentments? Or, speaking of being grounded, how about the way I remember that once when my curfew was 9:00 P.M. and I got in at 9:01, she grounded me for months? Was it for months, or only a couple of weeks? I used to think I knew these things. But if I'm so sure you're wrong about your memory, how can I be certain about my own? These might sound like small things when they apply to being grounded or cleaning a tub, but it represents a much larger issue about memory, about narrative, about the sources of both resentment and nostalgia. We're all the heroes of our own stories, which must include challenge and travail.

About becoming a father—I want to say to you, grab every moment you can with that little being while he or she is still small enough to fit in your arms, because that time passes so fast, and it never comes back. Obvious, yes—but oh, and oh, make sure you are there for as many of those moments as your life will allow. When your child's legs grow long enough to dangle over your arm, there's something lost. Other delights will present themselves to you after that, when the feet step one in front of the other, but there's something so rare in that smallness. It's the only time of their lives when you know that you can genuinely protect them, and they know it, too.

That sense of protection diminishes. I remember the very moment when you and I mutually knew that you'd discovered your life was something you had to handle yourself, that it was out of my hands to ensure anything but love. You were being wheeled away from me into the operating room when you had emergency stomach surgery, and I saw it in your eyes. I saw that you knew, in some essential way, the simple truth that we're in this life alone as well as with each other.

You're ready to become a parent. You're fully a man, a person of substance and dignity, one who knows himself. And I want to tell you that you're going to be one whopper of a father figure in your child's imagination. You can't help it. You're big and you're powerful and you have an air of natural, easy authority that's going to inspire respect and awe, and those qualities can be scary to a little person. (You scare *me* sometimes.) I know that you'll also be a playful father, a roll-on-the-floor-fooly-bear kind of papa, but please do know your power. You'll be gigantic in your child's eyes and heart. You'll be the stuff of mythic memory. Your child's stories about you as a parent, whatever else they contain, will begin with, "Well, *my* father . . ."

Love,
Mom

✱

Summer 1995. Sequoia Blue Sky George is six years old. Her mother, Mary Ellen Sullivan, is a potter and a weaver, as well as a student at Penn State. Bernie George is a police officer working toward his degree at Penn State— in psychology, ironically. Two weeks ago Bernie and Mary Ellen celebrated their almost fourteen years together, and occasionally apart, by marrying each other at my cliff-front cottage on Lake Erie. (They believe in long engagements? They just wanted to be sure?) For their invitations, a passage from Leslie Marmon Silko's "Lullaby":

We are together always.
There was never a time
when this
was not so.

Over a hundred friends and relatives assembled on the shore to witness their exchange of vows. Many people in these pages were present: Richard, Michael, Pat, Mac and his wife Elizabeth, Krissy and Ayron and Nancy, Bernie's father, my mother, Sue and Jim. Bernie wore his traditional Seneca ribbon shirt. An hour before the ceremony we ritually smudged the cottage windows and doorways, the path to the beach, the very rocks themselves with burning sage to purify their wedding place. The weather report was threatening—90 percent chance of torrential rains all day, continuous storm watches. Two miles to the east and west, it rained all day. Half a mile to the south, it rained all day. Yet after a momentary sprinkling well before the ceremony, it did not rain on us, despite our willingness to greet the rain as another kind of blessing. Over my children that day, the sky presided serene. The breeze fluttered Bernie's ribbons and Mary Ellen's scarf, the peaceful waves licked the beach stones.

"We invite you here because our sense of spirituality and the growth of our love is connected to this place. It has helped to give us a feeling of timelessness and peace and a sense of connectedness to all of life." They stood on their favorite rock, Sequoia between them, resplendent with love that has already endured years of hardships and delights. They gave each other rings and gave one to their daughter: "Sequoia, with this ring, you are embraced by our circle."

I held the copy of Joy Harjo's book that she had inscribed for Sequoia and quoted "Remember":

> Remember the earth whose skin you are:
> red earth, black earth, yellow earth, white earth
> brown earth, we are earth.

Bernie had asked Richard Lehnert to address the celebrants because, as he wrote Richard, "you have had a lasting impact on the way I think" and "you unknowingly provided me with direction and a sense of compassion in my childhood." From within this long knowing Richard spoke: "Weddings are joyful affairs, but most also have an undercurrent of apprehension, of fear of the unknown. . . . This one is different. . . . Bernie and Mary Ellen have paid for this day in the hard coins of pain, patience, and sacrifice; in the harder coins of the loneliness of separation and the sharper loneliness of being alone together. Neither of them has to put their faith in the 'hope' that the other is the right partner for them. They know that, in all ways except the legal one, they have already been married for years." Because they chose this family place on the brink of a natural American wonder, Lake Erie, as the site for declaring their continuous commitment to each other and to the land, I made a commitment to them: "I thank you for bringing into the world my granddaughter Sequoia, who carries on all of us in her eyes and her hands and her soul. I thank you for choosing this place, and in return I make you this vow: that this rock of Eden is yours; the place you have married will not leave the family; I will leave it to you, and I ask that you leave it to Sequoia, and she to her children, and they to theirs, until it falls into this great lake." Mac ended the ceremony with an Apache song:

> Now you will feel no rain,
>   for each of you will be a shelter to the other.
> Now you will feel no cold,
>   for each of you will be warm to the other.
> Now there is no loneliness for you,
>   now there is no more loneliness.

✳

The price of our special dispensation was soon exacted. A week later, this place that had granted us such grace gave us a reminder that it is not tamed, not controlled, not possessed by us. Mary Ellen was watching a storm on the lake from the cottage, accompanied by Sequoia and two other small children, when she was plunged into a darkened hell: the funnel cloud we were hearing about over the radio in Erie crossed over the lake and whipped itself into a tornado on our shore. Mary Ellen and the children took shelter under the tables while seven trees uprooted, furniture and canoes flew around the grounds, roof tiles peeled off, and picture windows billowed as if they would burst. Wind and rain belted through the cottage. When it was over, little was left untouched.

I drove there with Michael, on the way to drag the bottom of a pond with grappling hooks to find Dave and Donna's old dog who had disappeared, and stood in amazement, contemplating the devastation. Beginning the day with a tornado and ending it with a dead dog does not seem unusual to me. The life I have documented in these pages has not become calm just because I am trying to view it with calm detachment. The chaos of debris, contractors, and rebuilding will continue for months. But because no one was hurt, and the stone walls of the cottage held, I am grateful. I am coming to understand that I must find my internal equanimity in the very midst of chaos, as must almost everyone.

In the marriage ceremony, we had honored the winds with the words of two Native American writers. Joy Harjo: "Remember the wind. Remember her voice. She knows the / origin of this universe." Leslie Marmon Silko: "The winds are your brothers. / They sing to you." Through their song—male and female, brother and sister—I have received another windy lesson from the powerful natural forces, who keep buffeting me with their grace.

DIANA HUME GEORGE is a professor of English and women's studies at Pennsylvania State University at Erie, the Behrend College, where she has coordinated the women's and gender studies program and co-directed the creative writing program. Her critical studies include *Sexton: Selected Criticism, Oedipus Anne: The Poetry of Anne Sexton,* and *Blake and Freud.* She is also the co-editor (with Diane Wood Middlebrook) of *Selected Poems of Anne Sexton.* Her poetry books include *Koyaanisqatsi* and *The Resurrection of the Body.*